Shakila Reddy

Teenage Sexual Identity Constructions Within the Context of HIV/AIDS

An orientation to researching young adults'
sexual identity constructions within the
context of HIV/AIDS

LAP LAMBERT Academic Publishing

Impressum/Imprint (nur für Deutschland/ only for Germany)
Bibliografische Information der Deutschen Nationalbibliothek: Die Deutsche Nationalbibliothek
verzeichnet diese Publikation in der Deutschen Nationalbibliografie; detaillierte bibliografische
Daten sind im Internet über http://dnb.d-nb.de abrufbar.
 Alle in diesem Buch genannten Marken und Produktnamen unterliegen warenzeichen-, marken-
oder patentrechtlichem Schutz bzw. sind Warenzeichen oder eingetragene Warenzeichen der
jeweiligen Inhaber. Die Wiedergabe von Marken, Produktnamen, Gebrauchsnamen,
Handelsnamen, Warenbezeichnungen u.s.w. in diesem Werk berechtigt auch ohne besondere
Kennzeichnung nicht zu der Annahme, dass solche Namen im Sinne der Warenzeichen- und
Markenschutzgesetzgebung als frei zu betrachten wären und daher von jedermann benutzt
werden dürften.

Coverbild: www.ingimage.com

Verlag: LAP LAMBERT Academic Publishing AG & Co. KG
Dudweiler Landstr. 99, 66123 Saarbrücken, Deutschland
Telefon +49 681 3720-310, Telefax +49 681 3720-3109
Email: info@lap-publishing.com

Herstellung in Deutschland:
Schaltungsdienst Lange o.H.G., Berlin
Books on Demand GmbH, Norderstedt
Reha GmbH, Saarbrücken
Amazon Distribution GmbH, Leipzig
ISBN: 978-3-8383-4934-3

Imprint (only for USA, GB)
Bibliographic information published by the Deutsche Nationalbibliothek: The Deutsche
Nationalbibliothek lists this publication in the Deutsche Nationalbibliografie; detailed
bibliographic data are available in the Internet at http://dnb.d-nb.de.
 Any brand names and product names mentioned in this book are subject to trademark, brand
or patent protection and are trademarks or registered trademarks of their respective holders.
The use of brand names, product names, common names, trade names, product descriptions
etc. even without a particular marking in this works is in no way to be construed to mean that
such names may be regarded as unrestricted in respect of trademark and brand protection
legislation and could thus be used by anyone.

Cover image: www.ingimage.com

Publisher: LAP LAMBERT Academic Publishing AG & Co. KG
Dudweiler Landstr. 99, 66123 Saarbrücken, Germany
Phone +49 681 3720-310, Fax +49 681 3720-3109
Email: info@lap-publishing.com

Printed in the U.S.A.
Printed in the U.K. by (see last page)
ISBN: 978-3-8383-4934-3

LIST OF TABLES

LIST OF FIGURES

TABLE OF CONTENTS

AN ORIENTATION TO RESEARCHING YOUNG ADULTS'

SEXUAL IDENTITIES WITHIN THE CONTEXT OF

HIV/AIDS

CHAPTER TWO..15

UNDERSTANDING THE CONTEXT: HIV/AIDS AND

EDUCATION IN SOUTH AFRICA

CHAPTER FOUR **59**

ACCESSING YOUNG ADULTS' SEXUAL IDENTITIES:

APPROACH AND STRATEGY

CHAPTER ONE

AN ORIENTATION TO RESEARCHING YOUNG ADULTS' SEXUAL IDENTITIES WITHIN THE CONTEXTOF HIV/AIDS

1.1. Introduction

AIDS has been understood in different ways in western culture, from "a metaphor for morality, for human fragility and vulnerability", in Susan Sontag's words, to "a plague wreaked by a vengeful God", according to 'the un-Christian religious right', to AIDS activist, Cindy Patton's view "the battle-ground of moral courage" (Lather and Smithies 1997).

It is now three decades since the virus known as HIV has been around and the early responses to the HIV/AIDS crisis has been largely biomedical, focussing on preventing the spread of the disease. HIV/AIDS is no longer just a disease. It has grown into a *pandemic*, which is an entirely different though clearly linked phenomenon. According to Coombe (2002) the pandemic is a complex set of related problems which together constitute a phenomenon that needs understanding in very broad geographical, demographical, environmental, psychological, cultural, economic and social terms.

1

HIV/AIDS is a disease beset with contradictions: for one, it is a disease, which is not a disease, and for another, it is the greatest killer pandemic in modern history and is due to a virus that is not particularly contagious (See section 3.2 for HIV transmission). The routes to contagion are clearly defined, and herein lies the potential to understand its determinants and work toward its reversal. Coombe (2000:11) points out that sexuality is only one of the many elements in South Africa's social mix which determine the thrust and spread of HIV/AIDS, but it is one with which all educators must grapple, and the principle one to which the education system must respond. For any effective educational response to the HIV/AIDS pandemic, it is necessary to understand the construction of sexuality, risk, and relationships.

HIV/AIDS discourses have not only been successful in making people aware of HIV as a disease entity but have also opened up new ways of talking and thinking about sex and sexuality (Harrison 2000). From Foucault's work, I interpret discourses as that which both govern the way people act, think and feel and in turn are constructed by people through language in talk and action. Within this understanding of discourse the interrelationship between language, subjectivity, social organisation and power is emphasised. The term "discourse" as it has been used in cultural studies and the social sciences brings into close association ideas of knowledge, power and identity (Epstein and Johnson 1998).

The HIV/AIDS pandemic has forced HIV prevention campaigns to respond to the reality of a socially diverse population and to address sexuality as public issue in ways unimaginable in previous decades. In South Africa, as well as elsewhere, the pandemic has been the site of continuing struggles over questions of gender, sexuality, race and sexual differences. The language and practices related to these issues have increasing become more transparent in an effort to achieve normative heterosexual identity[1]. My interest is to understand secondary school learners' sexual identity constructions, which includes how they understand, manage, explore, and represent their sexual selves.

---

[1] The heterosexist nature of schools has been questioned by theorists such as Epstein (1996) and Mac an Ghaill (1996).

It is generally accepted that in most societies, youth sexuality has very limited social acceptance. Epstein and Johnson (1998) point out that talking about sexuality and schooling in the same breath can be seen as disturbing in many societies. They suggest that this may be partly because schooling stands on the "public" side of public/private divisions, while sexuality is definitely on the "private" side. They argue that as places of everyday-life activity as well as public or state institutions, schools are sites where sexual and other identities are developed, practiced and actively produced. This study does not focus primarily on the ways in which schools produce sexual identities, but on how learners manage and explore their sexual identities within this HIV/AIDS environment. I recognise that schools are not the only sites for the production of sexual or other social relations; neither is everything that happens in schools the result of schooling alone. However it is within the context of a school that my work with secondary school learners is located.

There is no denying the proliferation of HIV/AIDS messages in the media. Governmental and non-governmental organisations have taken up the cause with much vigour (perhaps not soon enough, as discussed in Chapter Two). I show later that the HIV/AIDS campaigns have had some success in raising the basic knowledge levels of young people. I assume this context in this study, and I explore the ways in which young people understand their own developing notions of sexual identities within the context of HIV/AIDS. Which sexual identities are privileged and which are marginalised or rendered *–Other*[2]*?* I explore the ways in which young people appropriate, re-work or reject dominant or hegemonic[3] versions of sexual identities and the ways in which HIV/AIDS impacts on their sexual decision-making. Sexual behaviour is both a communicative and symbolic form, both reflective and reflexive, subject to interpretation that differs by individual, and created interactively between sexual partners (Lear 1996).

In this first Chapter, I outline the rationale for this study on young adults' notions of their developing sexual identities within the context of HIV/AIDS. I start with a brief review of the theories from mainstream *Psychology* and *Sociology* that had been used

---

[2] See Butler (1990, 1993)
[3] Dominant or hegemonic ideas are those which, for most people, seem to be common sense, almost uncontestable.

to explain and predict risk behaviour and behaviour-change, and explain my interest in employing *Identity* as a conceptual lens in this study. I briefly describe the methodology and methods used in this study. I then discuss the significance of the knowledge produced in the process of this study.

1.2. Rationale for the Study

There is no doubt that for a disease not known to exist until the last three decades, AIDS (acquired immune deficiency syndrome) has rapidly grown into pandemic proportions. While our understanding of virology, immunology and epidemiology of AIDS has rapidly increased in a relatively short time, no present cure is known. It is a commonly held opinion that communication is central to the efforts to stem the spread of HIV (human immunodeficiency virus) and the efforts to prevent transmission must be expanded. This requires a commitment to understanding and intervening in human behaviour. HIV intervention strategies targeting sexual behaviour change must be based on a thorough understanding of the structural influences and interpersonal dynamics shaping sexual practices, instead on a narrow focus on medical and biological aspects of infection and disease.

1.2. 1. Why secondary school learners?

The rate of newly acquired infections in sub-Saharan Africa is highest among 15-24 year olds (UNAIDS: 1998). Varga (1999) points out that South Africa is typical in this respect. She adds that the epidemic is no doubt fuelled by the country's youthful age structure: 21 per cent (8.8 million) are between the ages of 15 and 19 years, with a further 10 per cent (4 million) aged between 20 and 24 (Central Statistical Services: 1998, quoted in Varga: 1999). The suggestion is that young people do not fully understand the impact of AIDS. The long latency period means that there are few school learners with full-blown AIDS. Secondary school learners are at a stage in their lives when they face many counteracting influences, including the desire for social acceptance, social pressure, situational constraints, fear of rejection and personal embarrassment. Weiss et al. (2000: 233) motivate for the need to focus our attention on adolescents:

> " *As they enter a world of new social relationships, they are challenged with reconciling cultural and familial norms of behaviour with emerging sexual feelings and desires*"

Weiss et al. (2000) assert that because young people are in the early stages of developing attitudes, communication patterns and behaviour related to sex and relationships, intervening at this point can have a profound effect on slowing the course of the HIV/AIDS epidemic. They further point out that this window of opportunity is being recognised worldwide, as demonstrated by the attention paid to young people during the 1994 United Nations International Conference on Population and Development held in Cairo, by the 1995 UN Fourth World Conference on Women in Beijing, and by the 1998 and 1999 World AIDS Campaigns co-ordinated by UNAIDS. This research contributes to the growing body of data that support the allocation of resources and programs aimed at young adults.

1.2.2. HIV/AIDS knowledge and sexual practices

A South African researcher, Haldenwang (1993), optimistically asserted, "In the absence of a cure or vaccine for the disease, education is the most important strategy in limiting the spread of HIV/AIDS". He shared this hope with most people that the way to change peoples' practices for the better, is to increase their awareness of HIV/AIDS. Shell and Zeitlin (2000) point out that there is no evidence that this will automatically happen in South Africa. There are numerous attempts from various sources such as schools, churches, homes, clinics and the media to raise the awareness about the causes and the consequences of HIV/AIDS. The World Health Organization (WHO) and The Joint United Nations Programme on HIV/AIDS (UNAIDS) had estimated that during 1999, 5.6 million people in South Africa became infected and this is equivalent to 1500 new infections per day. It is evident from these staggering statistics that new infections continue unabated, indicating a limited impact of the educational initiatives on un-safe sexual practices. Given the apparent limitations of the current knowledge-based intervention programmes, it is clear that broader understandings are necessary to complement these. There are obviously other factors at work that override the perception of risk that is intended to be created by improved knowledge about HIV/AIDS.

1.2.3. *HIV/AIDS and Risk Behaviour*

Explanations of the incidence and transmission of HIV/AIDS have revealed the gaps in the understanding of how human behaviour is motivated and how it can be changed[4]. Traditionally, mainstream psychological theories to explain behaviour and behavioural change with respect to HIV/AIDS, have suggested that behaviours are essentially caused by beliefs (Terry et al. 1993). Developments on this idea led to behaviour being explained in terms of efficacy beliefs (Bandura 1992). These models are discussed in detail in section 3.4. From an educational point of view, this is a pessimistic way of looking at risk behaviour, since beliefs are rather fixed and resistant to change (Reddy 1999). Another problem with these models is that they tend to describe individuals in deficit terms. Mainstream psychological models are limited because they tend to focus on the individual and do not easily accommodate sociocultural variables such as gender, race/ethnicity, sexuality, culture or class.

Social science approaches, on the other hand, suggest that social conditions, such as the lack of adequate health care facilities, racial and ethnic discrimination, unemployment, lack of public monies to promote AIDS prevention, contribute to the social context in which AIDS transmission is prone to occur (Auerbach et al. 1994). This approach implies that better knowledge of the structures of social life that affect the transmission and prevention of HIV is required and that interventions for prevention of AIDS needs to be implemented at the level of the social structures of society. This is a highly deterministic view of behaviour and does not take into account the individual (agency).

Current theoretical developments attempt to bring together ideas from psychology and social sciences. In the context of this inquiry, one of the ways of doing this is to understand and explain behaviour in terms of "identity". *Identity* is a more fluid concept and has the possibility of bringing together structure and agency in trying to understand the complex issues related to sexual practices.

---

[4] See section 3.3. for a discussion on the links between HIV/AIDS knowledge and sexual behaviour

1.3. Theoretical Framework

One of the ways to understand the choices young adults make in sexual situations is to employ the theoretical lens of *identity* and processes of identification and identity construction. "Identity" is a word, which is ubiquitous in both academic and political contexts. Its strength is that it captures the possibilities of unravelling the complexities between "structure" and "agency". Sociologists typically theorise identity as the bridge linking the individual to society (Carpenter 2001). A detailed discussion of Identity and Gender/sexual identity is presented in section 3.6. I find Judith Butler's (1990) theory of "performativity" which is in part inspired by Foucault's speech act theories, to be useful in my understanding of the relationships and interconnectedness between sexual identity and sexual behaviour. Butler (1990) argues that sex (male, female) is seen to cause gender (masculine, feminine), which is seen to cause desire (towards the opposite gender), and this is seen as a continuum. Her approach is to challenge the supposed links between these, so that gender and desire are flexible, free floating and not "caused" by other stable factors. According to Butler (1990: 25):

> *There is no gender identity behind the expressions of gender; ...identity is performatively constituted by the very 'expressions' that are said to be its results.*

This implies that gender is a performance; it is what you do at particular times, rather than a universal who you are. Judith Butler (1993) argues that gender is systematically spoken through a 'heterosexual matrix' in which heterosexuality is presupposed in the expression of 'real' forms of masculinity and femininity.

Within this framework, we might begin to rethink gender/sexual identities as performances. As performances, they have the possibility of reconfiguration. In the context of HIV/AIDS, this practice to refigure gender and sexuality can open up a path of understanding sexual choices and sexual practices that have been neglected.

1.4. Aims

Patti Lather (2001) cites Habermas (1972), who constructs the definition of worthwhile knowledge as understanding around three cognitive interests:

> ➢ Prediction and control,

7

- ➤ Understanding and interpretation,
- ➤ Emancipation and freedom and

Patti Lather (2001) adds another

- ➤ Deconstruction

The knowledge produced in this study is intended to advance the latter three of the research interests mentioned above. The broad aim of this study to explore some of the complexities of the processes and mechanisms through which young people construct, experience and define their sexual identities and sexual practices within the context of HIV/AIDS.

Given that the nature of schools and indeed South African society on the whole have changed dramatically over the past two decades, *understanding* is an important aim in this study. It is clear that "quick-fix" solutions are inadequate to address the HIV/AIDS crisis. A deeper understanding of sexual behaviour and its determinants is required in order to be better informed towards embracing a more holistic approach to HIV/AIDS education. An important aim of this study is to understand the interrelatedness of HIV/AIDS knowledge, the construction of young adults' sexual identities and their sexual practices.

I have attempted to operationalise an *emancipatory* research method, as advocated by feminist theorists such as Lather (1986), which emphasises collaboration, reciprocity and reflexivity. One of the ways in which I do this is by giving high status to the knowledge, understandings and feelings of the participants by privileging their voices throughout the study. Examining learner perspectives can provide new insights into the specific dynamics of sexual identities.

In this study, in exploring young adults' sexual identity constructions, I aim for a theoretical shift away from sex-role socialisation to a *deconstruction* of sex/gender identities- a shift away from simple concepts of power to the complexity of the politics of difference (Epstein and Johnson 1998). The feminist position extends itself to understand power relations, and within the context of this study, I attempt to include an understanding of age relations, while keeping gender relations as an important focus.

1.5. Critical question

The following critical question is addressed in this study:

How do young adults construct their sexual identities within the context of HIV/AIDS?

In responding to this critical question, the two fundamental propositions that guide this study are:

➢ Identity constructions are dynamic and profoundly shaped by other social factors, and

➢ In order to plan any effective response to the HIV/AIDS pandemic, understanding the constructions of sexuality and sexual identity are crucial.

1.6. Methodology and Methods

The study is largely qualitative in nature, although I did complement the qualitative data with some quantitative data. As I mentioned above, I have attempted to operationalise an emancipatory research method, which emphasises collaboration, reciprocity and reflexivity. Towards this end, I focussed almost exclusively on the voices of the participants and allowing them, to a certain extent, to determine the research agenda.

1.6.1. Participants

The study participants were male and female learners in a selected co-educational secondary school in KwaZulu Natal, South Africa. This school is situated in a suburban working class area. A shifting sample consisting of mix of African and Indian learners, aged between 15-19 years participated in the study.

1.6.2. Generation of data

I used a variety of methods to generate data about young adults' notions of their developing sexual identities within the context of HIV/AIDS. The use of multiple methods in feminist research, work to enhance understanding, both by adding layers of information and by using one type of data to refine another (Reinhartz 1992). The following methods were used to produce data in this study (these are discussed fully in Chapter Four)

> - Elements of PLA (Participatory Learning action)
> - Scenario writing
> - Questionnaires
> - Focus-group interviews
> - Individual interviews
> - Research diary

I employed a gendered approach in the production of data, working with groups of girls; groups of boys; boys and girls together as well as individual girls and boys.

1.7. Significance of the study

This research is intended to add to the growing body of understandings about young adults' sexual practices with a view to planning strategies to address and reverse the effects of the HIV/AIDS pandemic. It is hoped that the knowledge produced as a result of this research provides a stimulus for educators, researchers and programme developers working in the field of HIV/AIDS education and prevention.

The findings from this study are intended to advance knowledge and understandings about why the present AIDS education initiatives fail to bring about the desirable changes in sexual practices. Designing educational strategies as if learners are objectified entities is not likely to effect desirable changes in sexual practices. This study will provide deeper insights into socio-cultural and interpersonal factors which impact on young adults' sexual behaviour choices by providing an understanding of how young adults' developing sexual identities inform their practices, and vice versa, with a view to suggest ways in which education can connect with identity to influence sexual behaviour.

This study utilises theories of *identity* that emphasises fragility, contradictions and ambiguity in the multiple processes of identity construction. Identity is not a fixed characteristic, but changes in different spatial, temporal and social contexts (Coole 1995). Furthermore gender identity is constructed in interaction[5]. It is very likely that the participants' identities had to some degree been shaped during the course of my research. The methodology raised questions to heighten the awareness of the participant's sexual practices, which shapes and is shaped by their sexual identity. The process of interviewing and group discussions was not just about gathering information, but about speaking identities into being, about confronting and reworking limiting sexual identities, and appropriating those that contribute to their sexual safety. It has the potential to be of benefit to the participants in the research since the participatory methods employed in this study, has the potential to raise the awareness of the participants and to deepen their understandings of the causes and consequences of HIV/AIDS. Listening to the voices of young people is an important aim of this study and will alert those who work with young people to the significance of difference.

Working with individuals, single-sex groups as well as mixed-sex groups allowed me to explore sexual identity constructions of individuals in the different group settings. Together with the study participants, I explored the assumptions that the different groups had of each other, and what was expected of themselves in a relationship. The mixed-sex group interaction provided a platform for the participants to voice and challenge some of these assumptions.

1.8. Conclusion and Outline of chapters

In this chapter, I began with the rationale for the study, which is done by: a justification for the focus on secondary school learners, risk behaviour and sexual practices within the context of HIV/AIDS. In rethinking sexual identities, a theoretical framework is postured with a view to understanding young adults' sexual choices. The aims of this study and the critical question are presented. The chapter concludes by providing a methodological position located within feminist research, and the

---

[5] Conceptions of identity are explained in detail in Chapter Three.

significance of the study is forwarded, with a view to developing an argument for the ambiguities and contradictions in the multiple processes of identity construction.

This research report is organised in the following way:

CHAPTER TWO frames the context of this study. I outline the extent of HIV prevalence in South Africa and KwaZulu Natal, in comparison to the rest of the world. I then examine the past and current HIV/AIDS education strategies in South Africa. I discuss the social and political factors that have contributed to complicating the implementation of national AIDS plans over the last two decades. I then briefly describe the context of the school, *Boss Secondary*, which is the site of this research.

CHAPTER THREE presents a critical examination of the existing literature on HIV/AIDS prevention programmes in South Africa and internationally. In this literature synthesis I:

➢ Summarise some of the biological and medical aspects of HIV/AIDS;

➢ Explore the links between HIV/AIDS knowledge and sexual behaviour.

➢ Critically examine some of the theories that have been used to explain HIV risk behaviour

➢ Critically examine some of the South African research on adolescents and HIV/AIDS

➢ Develop *Identity* as a theoretical framework

➢ Explain the conceptions of the construct *Identity* and examine the literature that helps me explore the links between identity and behaviour.

CHAPTER FOUR discusses and provides a justification for the methodology and methods employed in this study. I begin by describing the broad methodological approach and a justification for the use of feminist research methodology. I critically examine the inclusion of learner voice as an emancipatory and empowering strategy. I then fully explain and describe in detail the ways in which data was generated and analysed for each of the instruments.

CHAPTER FIVE. This chapter presents and discusses the findings of this study that were generated using a variety of methods (as discussed in Chapter Four). Concentrating on the voices of the participants, I focus, here, on the social construction and expectations of teenage years as an identity dynamic and explore the performances of sexualities and how they are impacted upon by knowledge about HIV/AIDS. The chapter therefore represents the theoretical understanding of Identity which foregrounds the interrelatedness of:

> ➢ identity constructions and performances;
> ➢ conceptions of "self" and influences of "others";
> ➢ internal policing and policing by peers and adults and
> ➢ mutual shaping of sexual identity and the HIV/AIDS climate.

All these interrelated correlates are presented for the sake of emphasis and clarity in separate sections. They should not be understood as essentialising the young adults' sexual identity constructions within the context of HIV/AIDS.

CHAPTER SIX presents a synthesis of the findings of this study in dialogue together with the literature I have reviewed, the theoretical framework employed in this study as well as the research methodology. I have structured this chapter into different sections, which are in many ways linked, and I specifically discuss the themes in the context of the HIV/AIDS pandemic. The discussions in this chapter, focus on age relations, gender relations, the and power dynamics associated with each.

CHAPTER SEVEN. In this concluding chapter, I reflect on the processes and products of this study. This chapter is organised into three parts in the following way:

PART ONE

In Part One, I summarise some of the key theoretical, contextual and methodological insights that emerge from this study;

PART TWO

In Part Two, I discuss the interrelatedness of HIV/AIDS, sexual identity and sexual practices develop the thesis of *identity* as a negotiated *process* between often competing forces.

PART THREE

In Part Three, I discuss the pragmatic insights generated through this research in terms the implications of the findings for understanding young adults' sexual identities and its significance for effective HIV/AIDS education design and implementation (section 7.5.). Section 7.6. discusses the implications of this study for future research.

CHAPTER TWO

UNDERSTANDING THE CONTEXT: HIV/AIDS AND EDUCATION IN SOUTH AFRICA

2.1. Introduction

This study is carried out in a secondary school in KwaZulu Natal, South Africa. In this Chapter, I outline the extent of HIV prevalence in South Africa and KwaZulu Natal, in comparison to the rest of the world. I then examine the South African AIDS education strategies, and factors that have complicated implementation of national AIDS plans over the last two decades. I then briefly describe the school context (which is the site of this research)

2.2. HIV/AIDS in South Africa – The Statistics

In sub-Saharan Africa, more people die of AIDS-related illness than any other cause and South Africa has the highest absolute number of infections of any country in the world: 5 million (Lamptey et al. 2002). South Africa is one of the few countries with HIV seroprevalence[1] over 20% in the general population (National HIV survey 1998). The 1998 national survey revealed 22.8% seroprevalence, which is a 42% increase over the previous (1997) figure (National HIV Survey 1998). These statistics make

---

[1] The percentage of people who have been found to be HIV-positive

South Africa among the hardest hit countries in the world; with the fastest growing HIV/AIDS epidemic. Furthermore, some sites in KwaZulu Natal have recorded up to 40% seroprevalence (National HIV survey, 1998). Contrary to earlier understandings that AIDS was a homosexual disease, it has been found that as in most sub-Saharan African countries, the HIV epidemic in South Africa is primarily experienced and transmitted heterosexually (Varga 1999). Sixty percent of HIV infections occur through heterosexual contact. (UNAIDS 1998).

The HIV/AIDS pandemic in South Africa has been conspicuously gendered. Whiteside and Sunter (2000) estimate that women comprise approximately 56% of those infected with HIV, with the majority of these women being between the ages 15-34. In KwaZulu Natal it is estimated that among 15-19 year olds (which is the age range of the participants in the present study), 15.64% of Black African girls were likely to be HIV positive compared to 2,58% of Black African boys; 1.25% for White girls and 0.26% for White boys; and 1.29% for Indian girls and 0.26% of Indian boys (Morrell et al. 2001)

The figures showing HIV infection rates are, to say the least, alarming. It follows that the numbers of people affected, such as, partners, children, family members, friends, community members, workmates, employers, etc, are phenomenal. What makes the South African situation so different? Webb (1997) has suggested that the spread of HIV/AIDS virus has been almost unhindered in southern Africa, and it is reasonable to assume that governmental intervention in the region has had very little impact on the course of the epidemic. He offers two possible explanations for this: first, that the government's responses were too inadequate in formulation, extent and timing to have any impact on the spread of HIV; second, it can be argued that the complex nature of the epidemic required an institutional response beyond the means and resources of governments. Webb (1997) asserts that an analysis of the situation in South Africa and more widely southern Africa reveals that both of these explanations are equally applicable.

In addition to the ineffectual governmental responses being held responsible for the course of the epidemic, the social context of South Africa has been seen to be a contributing factor to the high rates of HIV infection in the country. Marais (2000) offers the following as reasons for the rapid spread of HIV/AIDS in South Africa:

➢ The legacy of apartheid and the migrant labour system

➢ The disruption of family and communal life

➢ High levels of poverty and income inequality

➢ Very high levels of other sexually transmitted diseases (STDs)

➢ The low status of women

➢ Social norms which accept and encourage high numbers of sexual partners, and

➢ Resistance to the use of condoms

Despite the high rates of HIV infection in South Africa, and the seriousness of its effect on all South Africans, South African society has approached the matter in a complex and contradictory manner. Marais (2000: 8) expressed concerns about what constitutes an effective preventative strategy in South Africa:

> *"Eluding South Africa still is an answer to these questions: What might be an effective response to a disease that is, in discursive terms, as complex as AIDS in a country as divided, as wracked by contradictions and stereotypes, and as filled with silences as ours? Exactly what interventions should practically constitute that response?"*

GLOBAL SUMMARY OF THE HIV/AIDS EPIDEMIC DECEMBER 2002		
Number of people living with HIV/AIDS Total		42 million
	Adults	38.6 million
	Women	*19.2 million*
	Children under 15 years	3.2 million
People newly infected with HIV in 2002 Total	5 million	5 million
	Adults	4.2 million
	Women	*2 million*
	Children under 15 years	800 000
AIDS deaths in 2002	Total	3.1 million
	Adults	2.5 million
	Women	*1.2 million*
	Children under 15 years	610 000

Figure 2.1. Global summary of the HIV/AIDS epidemic (UNAIDS/WHO 2002)

2.3. HIV/AIDS and South African Schools

There is no definite way of knowing the rate of HIV infection in schools, since available statistics generally emerge from tests of pregnant women in antenatal state clinics, or from tests conducted for insurance purposes. Morrell et al. (2001) used the data taken from the 2000 Metropolitan life study, which estimates infection rates by race and age, to give some sense of the "health" of the school population. They suggest that amongst 15-19 year olds, 15,64% of Black African females are likely to be HIV positive, compared to 2,58% of Black African males.

Coombe (2000) cites Buga et al. (1996) and concludes that adolescents are sexually active when they are young. In rural KwaZulu Natal, 76% of girls and 90% of boys are reported to be sexually active by the time they are 15 to 16. Boys start sexual intercourse before girls and have more partners and nearly twice as often have an STD history.

Furthermore, the rate of newly acquired infections in sub-Saharan Africa is highest among 15-24 year olds (UNAIDS: 1998). Varga (1999) points out that South Africa is typical in this respect. She adds that the epidemic is no doubt fuelled by the country's youthful age structure: 21 per cent (8.8 million) are between the ages of 15 and 19 years, with a further 10 per cent (4 million) aged between 20 and 24 (Central Statistical Services: 1998, quoted in Varga 1999). In a study by the National Progressive Primary Health Care Network (NPPHCN) in 1995, it was found that:

> ➤ Many young people receive conflicting messages about sex and sexuality;
> ➤ Non-penetrative sex is not considered to be proper sex;
> ➤ Widely believed myths reinforce negative attitudes about safer sex and contraceptive use, and
> ➤ Most adolescents make decisions about sex in the absence of accurate information, and access to support and services.

This information is crucial to the creation of both policy and programs for intervention strategies to contain and reverse the effects of the AIDS epidemic in South Africa. There is no doubt, from the statistics alone, that schools are definitely a high priority site for HIV/AIDS intervention programs.

Increasingly, school environments are coming to be viewed as risky environments instead of the safe havens we would hope for them to be. Morrell et al. (2001) contend that the high rates of violence against women, a proportion of whom are at school, would seem to suggest schools as a key site for interventions to address violence and HIV. Morrell et al. (2001) quote the study by Erica George (2001) of South African schools, which documents widespread sexual violence, both in schools and on the way to schools. They suggest that schools are not simply the safe places of rational learning portrayed in the literature on school-based interventions.

Shell and Zeitlin (2000: 2) express similar sentiments about school environments as Morrell et al. (2001). They point out that over one third of the South African population of 41 million, as measured by the consensus of 1996 are engaged in education, but argue:

> *"On the one hand, this is a good thing. Until there is a vaccine, education is the only antidote to HIV/AIDS. But, on the other hand, the education system, by concentrating the population of children together, is a source of infection".*

2.4. Introduction of HIV/AIDS Education in South African Schools

The introduction of AIDS education into state schools in South Africa has been a source of controversy. The highly fragmented nature of South African society and education system, and debates within the communities and education departments have been major stumbling blocks. Early State advertising campaigns proved controversial, the race of the people on the posters were questioned (they featured white characters with their faces coloured in). The posters with pictures of skeletons as bed partners were very confusing and they were seen as trying to "scare people". AIDS education has also been met with the resistance from groups that have resisted sex education, believing that it promotes adolescent sexual experimentation. Prior to 1994 schools were organised and controlled along racial lines, with each education department deciding separately about curriculum issues. A pilot AIDS program in the Transvaal Education Department (TED) in 1991 did not include teaching white children how to use condoms because parents would not permit it (Weekly Mail 1991).

In January 1991 a government committee on AIDS prevention publicly announced strong support for an AIDS education program (Cape Times 1991). A compulsory AIDS education program was due to start in all Black and White secondary schools in early 1992, and a government-sponsored AIDS education kit was released. This effort was unsuccessful and the education kit was subsequently withdrawn later in the year amidst controversy. The reason for the withdrawal was explained by the head of the Department of National Health and Population Development's AIDS unit, Natalie Stockton, as: " it had been too expensive and glossy. It was geared toward more developed communities and did not meet the needs of individual grassroots communities" (Race Relations Survey 1994: 143). Meanwhile, in a private sector initiative, a major insurance company and a publishing house arranged a package for Black children in 6th and 7th grades, consisting of books, teaching guides and training workshops for teachers. This was only implemented in some schools, with many educators reluctant to engage with issues of sex and sexuality.

It was not surprising that the early attempts at HIV/AIDS education had limited implementation. Educators were not equipped to deal with issues of sex and sexuality, as this required that issues that were considered to be private had to be addressed as public discourse. However, HIV/AIDS continued to be considered an emergency and the *Life Skills and HIV/AIDS Education* programme was introduced by the government in 1997. The Department of Education set up a group of life skills trainers throughout the country who developed a core curriculum for teacher training and for classroom use. Despite wide distribution of materials, this initiative had limited impact, partly because of its very prescriptive approach to dealing with HIV (Crewe 1997).

In spite of the early resistance and ongoing contradictions, many government and community programmes have been launched to combat the spread of HIV. In particular, the mass media has publicised HIV/AIDS through television programmes such as *Soul City*, a weekly drama series that covers a wide range of health issues, hence propagating basic information about the epidemic and its consequences. Radio has also been an important medium for HIV/AIDS education. More recently, *Lovelife*, a national youth sexual health initiative, has started a mass media campaign, using newspaper advertisements, billboards, radio and other mediums to address sexual health issues and the underlying causes of HIV/AIDS, including gender issues and sexual coercion.

Until late in 1999, the Department of Education has had no policy on HIV/AIDS. In August 1999, the Department's Corporate Plan, 2000-2004 identified action on HIV/AIDS as one of its five priorities. Three objectives related to HIV/AIDS were highlighted:

> ➢ Raising awareness about HIV/AIDS among educators and learners,
> ➢ Integrating HIV/AIDS into the curriculum, and
> ➢ Developing models for analysing the impact of HIV/AIDS on the education system (Coombe: 2000).

Coombe (2000) asserts that implementation of life skills curricula varies from province to province, but has generally been inefficient. Progress on teaching safe sex and creating a culture of care in schools has been slow. There is evidence (Human Science Research Council 2000, cited in Coombe 2000), that only 15 per cent of schools have a policy on HIV/AIDS.

In 2000, the new Minister of Education prioritised HIV/AIDS in his *Tirasano* plan of action. This was a move towards embracing a more holistic approach to AIDS and sexuality education. The objectives of the *Tirasano* plan include gender equity in schools, promoting conflict resolution, developing self esteem, building a democratic school culture and securing schools against violence (Harrison et al. 2000). Whether schools are equipped to engage in such complex whole school solutions remains to be seen.

HIV/AIDS education in and out of schools has been met with major stumbling blocks. In the next section I discuss some of the political issues that are seen to be hindering effective HIV/AIDS prevention strategies.

2.5.The Politics of HIV/AIDS Education in South Africa

"It is cruel irony of South African history that the ending of apartheid should coincide with the beginning of the AIDS epidemic" (Van der Vliet 1994). During this period of transition in the country, AIDS runs the risk of being highly politicised or alternatively ignored while leaders concentrate their energies on transition itself. The colossal triumph of the local political process and the coincidental appearance of an already stigmatised and deadly virus have together led the country into a complex set of denials of the post-apartheid reality (Shell and Zeitlin 2000). The South African government has targeted poverty as the nation's most urgent problem, but as Shell and Zeitlin (2000), caution, AIDS will bury South Africa before poverty can be alleviated in any significant way.

Controversy over AIDS education continued into the new democratic administration. The development of an AIDS education play *Sarafina 2* cost the government R14m (Mail and Guardian, 9-14 March 1996). The success of the play was overshadowed by the media attention, which focused on the enormous cost of production, which represented one fifth of the annual AIDS budget. The history and origins of HIV and its link to AIDS has been another major source of controversy. Many experts complained about the South African president, Thabo Mbeki giving voice to dissident scientists who were questioning the link between HIV and AIDS. Many working in the field of HIV/AIDS prevention, claim that this has harmed South Africa's awareness campaign (Ramsay 2001).

There is growing support for the theory that the shocking increase in the incidence of young infant rape, in South Africa, is related to a myth that sexual intercourse with a very young infant will enable the perpetrator to rid himself of HIV or other sexually transmitted diseases. This myth is thought to have originated in Central Africa and has moved south along with the infection (McGreal 2001). Pithcher and Bowley (2002: 275) contend that the indulgence with the dissident view has contributed to the spread of the "young virgin myth".

> *The naïve and dishonest view that there is no proven, causal link between HIV and AIDS will perpetuate crimes of this nature. The failure of the political leadership to frankly acknowledge the causes, effects, and treatment of HIV/AIDS has been the fertile ground for bizarre and dangerous myths to take*

> *root and flourish. The central government should openly debunk the 'young-virgin myth'.*

The following cartoon shows that President Mbeki has distanced himself from the dissident view, much to the relief of most South Africans.

Source: Daily News, April 2002

2.6. The study site: Boss Secondary School

This study on young adults' sexual identity and sexual practices within the climate of HIV/AIDS was conducted in a co-educational secondary school in KwaZulu Natal, South Africa. The school, Boss Secondary[2], is situated in the peri-urban high-density area close to Durban, a large port city. The low cost homes in the surrounding area had been built, in the apartheid days, for the Indian community. Indian and African working class families now own these homes. Boss Secondary School caters for grades 8-12 and draws learners from the formal housing surrounding the school as well from the informal housing close by (see *Appendix 4* for photographs of houses surrounding the school). The majority of the learners walked to and from school and some used public transport. The racial breakdown of the learner population for 2002 is as follows:

---

[2] Boss Secondary is a pseudonym and it was negotiated with the school management team.

RACE	NO. OF BOYS	NO. OF GIRLS
African	276	309
Indian	226	263
Coloured	15	9
Total	517	580

Table 2.1. Racial breakdown of the learner population of Boss Secondary School

I focused on grade 11 and grade 12 learners and they were between the ages of 15 and 20. There were 3 grade 11 classes, and 3 grade 12 classes in the school, the total number of learners in grades 11 and 12, being 155 and 101 respectively.

Boss Secondary is a state school that is relatively well resourced compared to former African township schools in Durban. However, compared to former White schools, their staff: student ratios are high, school textbooks and stationery are in short supply and although the school has sport fields, sport equipment is not adequate. There are 14 male and 15 female teachers and they are all qualified educators. HIV/AIDS education featured in the life skills program in grades eight and nine. There is also a full time guidance counsellor who teaches one guidance lesson in every eight-day cycle and is also available for individual consultations. The guidance counsellor pointed out in an interview that she mainly counselled learners that were referred to her by the educators or their parents, with respect to behavioural problems. It was not common practice for learners to request for assistance (see *Appendix 4* for more information about Boss Secondary School, and for photographs of the school and surrounding areas).

2.6.1. Learners' sexual activity

Both girls and boys displayed much interest in relationships with the "opposite sex". Most of the girls talked about other girls and boys having sex; they seldom mentioned their own sexual activeness, in face-to-face interactions. Girls unwillingness to talk freely about being sexually active is not surprising, given that virginity is valued in girls and sexual activity is reserved for after marriage (see section 7. 4). Most of the boys, on the other hand, willingly talked about their sexual activeness, sometimes boastfully. Many boys also admitted lying about their sexual activeness because experience and multiple partners are considered desirable in boys. These factors made it difficult to separate the acts from the facts, during discussions and interviews. The anonymous questionnaire that was administered to 72 participants provided an opportunity for them to privately disclose their sexual activeness and the responses are represented in the table below.

| | | | Sexually active? | |
			yes	no
Sex	male	Row %	52.6	47.4
	female	Row %	11.5	88.5

Table 2.2. Male and female responses to whether they are sexually active

The above table shows that 52,6% of the boys, and 11,5% of the girls responded that they are sexually active.

2.7. Conclusion

In this chapter, I have discussed the extent of HIV prevalence in South Africa and KwaZulu Natal. I then presented a brief overview of the South African AIDS education strategies, and factors that have complicated implementation of national AIDS plans over the last two decades. A description of the school context (which is the site of this research) was also presented. In the following chapter, I critically analyse the existing literature in this field of study and discuss the use of *Identity* as a theoretical framework for this study on young adults' sexual identity constructions within the context of HIV/AIDS.

CHAPTER THREE

HIV/AIDS AND IDENTITY: EXTENDING THE BOUNDARIES OF EXISTING FRAMEWORKS

3.1. Introduction

In the last chapter I looked at the South African situation with regard to the seriousness of the HIV/AIDS situation and the national educational responses to address this pandemic. In this chapter I critically examine the existing literature of relevance to the present study. This review will enable me to:

➤ Understand some of the biological and medical aspects of HIV/AIDS;

➤ Explore the links between HIV/AIDS knowledge and sexual behaviour;

➤ Critically examine some of the theories that have been used to explain HIV risk behaviour;

➤ Critically examine some of the South African research on adolescents and HIV/AIDS;

➤ Develop a theoretical framework and;

➤ Explain the conceptions of the construct *Identity* and examine the literature that helps me explore the links between identity and behaviour.

3.2. HIV and AIDS

The Acquired Immune Deficiency Syndrome (AIDS) and the Human Immunodeficiency Virus (HIV) that causes AIDS are epidemic worldwide. It is important to differentiate the biological roots of the disease from the roots of the epidemic. The virus, human immunodeficiency virus is the etiological agent associated with the disease, while the epidemic is driven by behaviour. According to Schoub (1994:17) AIDS has four cardinal features, which together make it a formidable disease. Firstly, it is infectious and transmittable from person to person. Secondly, once infected it follows a course to disease and eventually to death, in most cases. Thirdly, all persons infected with HIV apparently remain infectious and fourthly, the reservoir of infection is constantly and progressively expanding. What is more alarming is that seropositive individuals can remain asymptomatic for many years and during this time unwittingly infect others.

HIV is known to infect mainly two systems of the body, the immune system and the central nervous system, and the disease manifestations are principally consequent to damage on these two systems. Transmission of the virus depends to a large extent on individuals engaging in risk behaviours that expose them to the virus. There are three principal ways in which HIV may be transmitted. These are: unprotected vaginal or anal sexual intercourse; direct exposure of bodily fluid to semen, organs, blood, or blood products (mainly involving reuse of, or accidental injury with, inadequately sterilized needles or syringes or blood transfusion); from a mother to her unborn child. While the pattern varies geographically, the majority of infections worldwide have been found to be via sexual intercourse (Terry et al. 1993). It has been estimated that 70% of global infections by early 1991 had been via vaginal intercourse (WHO 1992).

Developing effective AIDS education strategies require a deeper understanding about how people think about the risks of AIDS and their practices regarding those risks. AIDS education has largely been through instruction in strategies for reducing that risk. In the next section, I examine the literature on the relationship between knowledge about HIV/AIDS and sexual practices.

3.3. HIV/AIDS knowledge and sexual practices

In theory, increased knowledge lead people to recognise that new behaviours can meet a personal need, to decide to take action and, eventually, to adopt new practices (Mi Kim et al. 2001). It is reasonable to assume that knowledge about HIV and AIDS would be the most powerful weapon to combat and reverse the pandemic. However, several researchers have shown that higher levels of knowledge about HIV and AIDS are substantially unrelated to sexual practices (Abbott 1988; Fawole et. al. 1999; Flischer et al. 1999; Turtle et al. 1989). Furthermore, several researchers such as Bennell, Hyde and Swainson (2002), Diclemente et al. (1990) have shown that even when adolescents' knowledge about HIV is high, it is not generally translated into safer sex practices.

Similarly, several South African studies have demonstrated adequate to high levels of HIV knowledge (Naidoo et al. 1991; Richter 1996; Varga and Makubalo 1996). A further significant finding in the above studies points to increasing self-perceived risk for HIV/AIDS among South African youth. It has been suggested that the reasons for the potentially positive effect of increased self-perceived risks not being realised, are feelings of fatalism[8] and helplessness (Naidoo et al. 1991; Richter 1996; Varga and Makubalo 1996). Akande (2001) agrees that youth are fairly well informed about HIV/AIDS. He asserts that perhaps the most fundamental change over the past two decades in the area of prevention is that African youth in most communities have become much more knowledgeable about HIV and AIDS, about behaviours that confer risk and about risk reduction steps.

Clearly, the HIV/AIDS knowledge levels of youth have been well documented. These studies have mainly been surveys which provide a critical descriptive foundation for understanding adolescent sexual behaviour and sexuality. However, the investigation and research has proceeded no further than to acknowledge the disjuncture between HIV/AIDS and sexual practices. The research does not explore why the seemingly adequate knowledge about AIDS and the risks involved fail to lead to significant changes in sexual practices. Furthermore, it reveals little about the sociocultural and interpersonal factors, which determine youth sexual behaviour, or about AIDS-related sexual negotiation. According to Harrison et al. (2000), the impact of many prevention programmes are limited because of the emphasis on knowledge and prevention without imparting skills needed to achieve these ends and they therefore ignore the underlying causes of the HIV/AIDS epidemic and do not address fundamental issues that confront people when making decisions about sexual activity.

Increasing awareness and specific knowledge about HIV transmission should however, not be underestimated. Ingham (1995), in his study of AIDS knowledge, awareness and attitudes across different countries and different age groups, found that while knowledge about the actual routes of HIV transmission (sexual, mother-to-baby, sharing injecting needles) was high among young people, accuracy levels regarding the possibility of HIV transmission through casual routes (shared utensils, mosquitoes and shaking hands) were very poor. This is clearly an area that needs attention. Ingham (1995), notes that the impact of such misinformation is potentially very dangerous, in that it can increase general levels of anxiety, leading to possible sense of helplessness (which may inhibit any change at all) and likely discrimination against people known or thought to be HIV positive.

Misinformation and myths about HIV transmission and cure has already proved to have alarming effects. One of the dangerous myths is linked to the belief in a "virgin cure" for venereal disease. This myth is thought to have originated in Central Africa and has moved south along with the infection (McGreal 2001). Adults, who fear that their peers might be infected with HIV, turn to children who are presumed to be free of HIV. The Crime Information Management Centre of the South African Police Force recorded 221072 sexual offences in 1999 against persons aged less than 17 years (quoted in Pitcher and Bowley 2002). Some desperate men living with HIV have come to believe that sex with a virgin will actually cure them and this has led to the increase in very young infants being raped. Media reports of the brutal rape of nine month old baby *Tshepang* in *Uppington* in South Africa in 2001 has shocked the local and international community.

---

[8] Fatalism refers to the attitude that you have to accept and submit to what happens, regarding it as inevitable and helplessness refers to being incapable of action.

Based on the findings from previous studies on youth HIV/AIDS knowledge in South Africa and elsewhere, the present study will assume that South African secondary school learners are adequately knowledgeable about HIV/AIDS issues. Knowledge about HIV and AIDS is certainly a vital first step in the protection against the virus. It appears from the studies above that knowledge is a necessary, but not sufficient condition for appropriate action. Given the apparent limitations of knowledge-based interventions, it is important to understand why people engage in practices that put them at risk of exposure to infection and why they do not engage in practices that reduce that risk.

In the following section I discuss some of the theories from psychology and social sciences that have been used to explain risk behaviour in relation to HIV transmission.

3.4. HIV and Youth Risk Behaviour

Epidemiology has had the task of identifying the determinants and distribution of HIV and AIDS. It has done this by defining, categorising and monitoring "risk factors", "risk groups" and "risk behaviours".

3.4.1. Psychological Theories of Behaviour Change

Theoretical models, mainly from psychology have been used either to predict risk behaviour or predict behaviour change, and to a limited extent, maintenance of positive behaviour changes. Early attempts to identify determinants of HIV risk behaviour included the Health Belief Model (Becker 1974) and the Theory of Reasoned Action (Ajzen and Fishbein 1977).

The Health Belief Model was specifically developed in the context of health education and public participation in screening programs as an endeavour to explore decisions about volitional behaviours that affect health status. This model suggests that individuals make rational decisions to perform behaviours that reduce health risks. Several authors have found this model to be of limited use for HIV prevention in the context of sexual behaviour. Several authors have commented on the problems of the application of models based on value-expectancy theories of decision-making, or rational volitional control to sexual behaviour (Brown et al. 1991; Kirsch and Joseph 1989; Rosenthal et al. 1992, Quoted in Terry et al. 1993).

Similar to the Health Belief Model, the Theory of Reasoned Action is based on the general idea that people make decisions to perform behaviours. The application of these models is based on the assumption that when making behavioural decisions, people consider the information available to them and make decisions to perform behaviours. Both the Health Belief Model and the Theory of Reasoned Action assume that in the final analysis, behaviours are caused by beliefs (Terry et al. 1993). In the context of HIV risk, it implies that an individual will have an intention to use condoms if he/she has a belief that condom-use prevents HIV transmission. The recommendation is that intervention strategies should revolve around identifying beliefs that lead to risky or risk-reducing behaviours, and designing interventions to change the former or encourage and maintain the latter (Terry et al. 1993).

Bandura (1992) has applied the Social Cognitive Theory, which was initially used to help people overcome phobias, to HIV risk behaviour. Central to this theory is the idea that translating health knowledge into self-protective action against HIV infection requires social and self-regulatory skills and a sense of personal power to exercise control over sexual situation. Bandura (1992) sees the major challenge not in teaching people safer sex guidelines, which is easily achievable, but equipping them with the skills to put those guidelines consistently into practice in the face of counteracting influences. According to Bandura (1992), to be most effective, health communication should instil in people the belief that they have the capacity to alter their health habits and should instruct them on how to do it. Self-efficacy reflects a person's belief about whether they think they can perform a given activity. Bandura (1992), noting the discrepancy between peoples' HIV knowledge and behaviour, suggests that when people lack a sense of self-efficacy, they do not manage situations effectively, even though they know what to do and possess the skills. This theory is a development on the Health Belief Model and the Theory of Reasoned Action in that self-efficacy beliefs include outcome efficacy. For example, if a person has a belief that condom-use will prevent HIV transmission, then he/she must have the belief that he/she can successfully negotiate the use of a condom during a sexual encounter.

The Self-Efficacy Theory differs from the Theory of Reasoned Action, in that while the latter deals with situations in which people have volitional control over their behaviour, the former attempts to predict behaviours when volitional control over the behaviours is questionable. Explanations for HIV risk behaviour using the Self-Efficacy Theory are not useful ways of thinking about behaviour change in terms of HIV/AIDS. Social Cognitive Learning Theory constructs people as being in deficit - you either have the right beliefs, or you do not.

It appears from the discussion above that these psychological models to explain behaviours relating to HIV and AIDS are limited in general ways. Firstly, much mainstream psychology has a compartmentalised, individualised perspective, which explains behaviour as a rational choice based on individual concerns alone. This focus on individuals does not easily accommodate contextual and sociocultural variables such as gender, sexuality, race/ethnicity, culture and class. For example, gender roles and cultural values and norms influence the behaviour of women and men and the nature of the relationship in which sexual activity occurs. Much work needs to be done to integrate the theories of gender and culture with models of behaviour change. Friedman (1993) argues along similar lines when he contends that mainstream psychological models that examine relational factors and cognitive processes that shape the isolated individuals' decision-making patterns, have obscured the social and relational factors involved in behaviour such as the role of peer pressure, emotions, cultural beliefs, and organizational structures of communities at risk. Secondly, mainstream psychological theories rely heavily on the notions of "belief" to understand and explain behaviour. This is problematic because beliefs are strongly held convictions, which are static and resistant to change (Reddy 1999). It is perfectly possible for someone to hold a belief without having any reason for it. Armstrong (1973: 9) explains the constant nature of beliefs by suggesting that "a satisfactory way of thinking about belief, which is implicit in Western philosophical thought, is as "a certain continuing state". He adds that these are *imprinted* or *stamped* in a certain way (emphasis from the original text). In the planning of intervention strategies to change risky sexual practices, thinking of behaviour being a consequence of beliefs, is not helpful since it leaves limited space for modification of behaviour.

3.4.2.Social Science Perspectives on Behaviour and Behaviour Change

Several social science researchers such as Friedman (1993) and Kayal (1993) contend that an overemphasis on behavioural change at the individual level has weakened the attempts to reduce the spread of HIV and is partly to blame for limited success of behavioural interventions. Social science perspectives argue that individual behaviour occurs in a complex social and cultural context, and analysis that removes that behaviour from its broader setting ignores essential determinants.

According to Auerbach et al. (1994) several levels of social arrangements can affect behaviours related to the transmission of HIV, ranging from couples to social networks to the community and to society as a whole, and that each level of analysis reveals different factors that shape behaviour, and demonstrates that individual behaviour cannot be accurately analysed apart from the social and cultural structures in which it is embedded. Earlier social science approaches suggest that, at the broadest level, social conditions, such as the lack of adequate health care facilities, racial and ethnic discrimination, unemployment, lack of public monies to promote AIDS prevention, contribute to the social context in which AIDS transmission is prone to occur (Auerbach et al. 1994). This implies that better knowledge of the structures of social life that affect the transmission and prevention of HIV is required and that interventions for prevention of AIDS needs to be implemented at the level of the social structures of society.

While these social science authors criticise the exclusive focus on individuals as appropriate strategy for AIDS prevention, their own position is devoid of any reference to the capacity of individuals to act as responsible agents and to react differently to a certain set of conditions. Focusing on structures in society alone, on the other hand, removes the responsibility from individuals for their behavioural choices. This approach can lead to a sense of helplessness and of irreversible fatalism.

A review of the literature on behaviour and behavioural change, presented in this report, reveals that theories from mainstream psychology, which focus on individuals alone, and earlier theories from sociology, which focus on the structures in society, are inadequate to explain youth sexual behaviour. Current theoretical developments attempt to bring together ideas from psychology and social sciences in understanding the complexities of the structure-verses-agency debate. It is argued that cross-disciplinary research in this regard will play an important role in improving the design and application of HIV preventive interventions.

Holland et al. (1991:128) argue that the assumption of many HIV-prevention campaigns that using condoms is a rational strategy that people can discuss and decide about prior to sexual intercourse, ignores the social constraints on behaviour. They maintain that condom-use involves a very complex process of negotiation. Consequent to examining condom-use in heterosexual encounters, they argue:

> ➢ The issue cannot be understood without taking account of the gendered power relations that construct and constrain choices and decisions, and
>
> ➢ that condom-use must be understood within the context of the contractions and tensions of heterosexual relationships.

Having looked at the limitations of understanding youth sexual behaviour exclusively in terms of individuals (agents) or society (structures) in the previous two sections, in section 3.6. I explore the use of *Identity* as a conceptual and analytical tool in the design of this study of secondary learners' sexual identities, and its relationship to their sexual practices. One way to understand the choices they make in sexual situations is to employ the theoretical lens of *identity* and processes of identification and identity construction. *Identity* is a more fluid concept, and has the potential to bring together structure and agency in order to understand and explain behaviour. Sociologists typically theorise *identity* as the bridge linking the individual to society (Carpenter 2001).

I continue the review of literature in this chapter by examining some of the recent research on gender and HIV/AIDS in Africa, and then go on to develop a theoretical framework for use in this study, and then examine some of the existing research that use a similar or related theoretical framework. I have used the term's "behaviour" and "practices" interchangeably in the last section since a large part of the literature comes from psychology, which uses the term "behaviour". I personally prefer the term "practices" because it would appear to be more contextually dependent and less globalising than behaviour.

34

3.5. Gender and AIDS in Africa

For all of the Sub-Saharan Africa, young women, aged 15-24, who were infected with HIV were twice as many as men (World Bank 1999). In 2001, an estimated 6-11% of young women aged 15-24 were living with HIV/AIDS, compared to 3-6% of young men (UNAIDS/WHO 2002). There are physiological and socio-cultural reasons why women are more at risk of contracting HIV than men. For example: the physiological reasons for increased risk of infection in women include their receptive biology during sexual intercourse and the storage of semen within the vagina; and the socio-cultural reasons include the low status of women in society, manifested in economic disparity and domination by men. Baylies (2000), focusing on gender and AIDS in Africa, asserts that gender relationships not only underlie women's vulnerability, but they also inhibit women's attempts to protect themselves. She adds that if interventions around AIDS are to be effective, they must address the factors which drive the epidemic and that such factors are deep-seated and intransigent, embedded in the very power relations which define male and female roles and positions, both in intimate relations and the wider society.

Within the context of the HIV/AIDS epidemic, safe sex as a set of knowledge is inevitably impacted by conceptions of gender/sexual identities. Erni (1998:18) contends that by exerting pressure on a system called "safe sex", we see that it includes the following components, many of which are distinctly marked by gender and sexual differences:

> ➢ generational differences and their implied sociopsychological states (e.g., recklessness, "wish for immortality", maturity, responsibility);
> ➢ individual and social definitions of what constitutes eroticism in sex;
> ➢ the degree of safe sex across relational zones (e.g., one night stands, open relationships, committed relationships);
> ➢ the shifts of degree of safe sex over time in those relationships;
> ➢ impact of alcoholic and narcotic influences (and the gender implications in the moment of sexual negotiation under those influences);
> ➢ locations of sex (and their implied seduction of "dare' implied by the locales);
> ➢ the impact of new treatment options to prolong lives on various populations (e.g., how do lesbian and gay men differ in their respective negotiation

35

between the benefit provided by the new protease inhibitor combination therapy and the meaning about the consequences of safe sex practices?);

➤ all of the human indignities of low self-motivation, confusion, impatience, and various psychological tendencies couched in the name of love, or in the name of jealousy, spite, disappointment;

➤ differences in all of the above across cultures, races, and classes (each imbued by their pressures of gender and sexual conformities).

Erni (1998) further points out that the above list should do more than complicate the picture of sex, more than point out the imperfections brought about by human frailties, but at whichever level of understanding- socially, psychologically, privately, ideologically- the practices of safe sex must be continued, and the dimensions in the above list must be incorporated into safe sex education.

A study focussing on the abuse of schoolgirls in Zimbabwe by Leach et al. (2000) found that masculine and feminine identities were powerful determinants of the behaviour of boys and men towards girls. This study found that females are seen as the property of males to serve and obey them. Boys are taught from an early age that male control and dominance over females is the norm, while girls are taught to be submissive and dependent on men, and to accept male aggression passively (Leach et al. 2000). A further significant finding in the above study was, given the prevailing power relationships; there was very limited evidence of abuse of males by females.

While the study by Leach et al. (2000) focused on females, a study by Bok (1997) focused on males and arrived at similar findings about male dominance over females in sexual relationships. Bok (1997) examined the way HIV/AIDS/STD education programmes can influence attitudes and behaviour of adolescents in Tanzania. He studied the ways masculinities are constructed within the gender relations and concluded that the concepts central to describing the different constructions of masculinity are *tabia* and *tamaa*. *Tabia* is explained as a combination of moral character and personality. It is partly inherited and partly learned and is influenced by the external environment and things such as alcohol and money. *Tamaa* is the core component of *tabia* and can be described as desire. AIDS is associated with a life of bad *tabia* and excessive *tamaa*.

The control and dominance of males over females is consistent with the findings of the National Progressive Primary Health Care Network (NPPHCN 1995) survey, which demonstrates that it is boys who determine when and how sex occurs, and that girls commonly experience rape, violence and assault, including within relationships. In addition, a study among pregnant adolescent women, by Wood and Jewkes (1988), revealed that violent and coercive male behaviour, combined with young women's limited understanding of their bodies and the mechanics of sexual intercourse, directly affect their capacity to protect themselves against sexually transmitted diseases (STD's), pregnancy and unwanted sexual intercourse.

The studies mentioned above represent much of the social research on sexual decision-making and negotiation, which focuses on either women or men. Available research on sexual decision-making and negotiation frequently considers the views and characteristics of one gender in isolation, not as a dynamic between two individuals. Research on sexual decision-making and negotiation in Africa mainly focuses on women. The male perspective remains a largely unknown element in the sexual equation. The result is an incomplete portrayal of a situation which is by definition dyadic in nature. Furthermore, focussing on girls only, or boys only, implies a false unity in the lives of girls and of boys. The present study will explore the dynamics between and among girls, between and among boys and between and among girls and boys. It is important to explore the context in which risk behaviour takes place, including the factors that contribute to unprotected sex, and how these factors are similar or different for young males and females. Such insights are critical for interventions that meet the gender-specific needs of young adults.

Varga (1997) investigated sexual decision-making and negotiation amongst youth in KwaZulu Natal, South Africa. She explored choices made by young men and women regarding sexual activity and the extent to which it is influenced by HIV/AIDS. Findings from this study reveal that communication between partners was poor and young women appeared powerless to enforce their preferences in sexual situations. Most female participants felt that they could not discuss AIDS-related issues with a male partner for fear of rejection or stigmatisation and fear of physical abuse or coercion. While the male participants frequently discussed disbelief in the existence of AIDS and the opinion that it is the female partner's responsibility to protect against

HIV infection. The dynamic within the relationship was routinely guided by the preferences of the male partners and was acknowledged and seemingly accepted, by majority of the male and female participants. The men were unanimous on the importance of achieving "*isoka*" as a means of social recognition and manhood ("*isoka*" is a Zulu term used to describe a man with many partners). Another significant finding in this study was that AIDS was not a significant factor in any aspect of decision-making.

In a subsequent paper, Varga (1999) reports that while obstacles to behaviour modification are considerable, there is still reason for the potential for positive behaviour change among Zulu youth in terms of HIV/AIDS prevention. She notes that there has been a change in attitudes and approaches to HIV, which provides the groundwork for behaviour modification. These changes include:

> ➢ HIV is increasingly part of the sexual discourse of youth, which at the very least suggests that perhaps the stigmas against HIV are starting to disappear;
> ➢ Youth are internalising HIV infection as significant and life threatening. There have been indicators of willingness to use condoms and embrace the positive value of practicing safe sex;
> ➢ Some young people seem to recognise the need to modify gender-specific behaviour patterns. In this respect, the apparently shifting value of "isoka" status is one example.

While Varga (1999: 31) suggests that a change has begun in youth's worldview of HIV, which is a significant component of starting to change behaviour, she raises some important questions. For example,

> "...*What else needs to be done to enable long-term behaviour modification, how soon the shifts observed here will translate into large-scale change, and if such change will take place soon enough to affect the HIV epidemic in South Africa*"?

Having examined some of the recent African studies on gender and HIV/AIDS in this section, I continue with the discussion of a theoretic framework that I alluded to in section 3.4.2.

3.6. Developing " Identity" as a theoretical framework

In order to understand the specifics of sexual identity, I needed to develop a more general account of how social identities are produced. I begin with a look at how *identity* is conceptualised in the literature and then look specifically at the theories of gender/sexual identity. I then examine some of the recent research exploring gender/sexual identities.

3.6.1.Conceptions of Identity

Stryker and Burke (2000: 284) assert that the language of "identity" is ubiquitous in contemporary social sciences, cutting across psychoanalysis, psychology, political science, sociology and history. They add that the common usage of the term *identity* belies the considerable variability in both its conceptual meanings and its theoretical roles and even when consideration is limited to sociology and social psychology, variation is still considerable.

Understandings of identity are complex and may be derived from different sources. A question often asked by those interested in understanding identity, is, "to what extent is the individual a creature of society?" The distinction between processual and structural conceptions of identity is evident in much psychological literature, which attempts to differentiate between personal identity and social identity. Tajfel (1982) distinguishes between personal identity (that part of the self-concept which is unique to the individual, a product of purposive action) and social identity (that part of the self-concept derived from group and category memberships). Tajfel (1982) defines social identity as the individual's knowledge that he/she belongs to certain groups together with some emotional and value significance to him/her of the group membership. Social identity can be constituted by identifications with many different groups. The identities we bring to the fore, e.g. black, white, male, female, straight, gay... are highly contingent. Breakwell (1992: 4) in her introduction to *Social Psychology of Identity and the Self Concept*, argues that this strict dichotomy of personal and social identity is spurious, resulting from modelling the structure of self-concept at one moment in time rather than examining the processes whereby it is generated.

Stryker and Burke (2000) compare and contrast the two parts of identity theory, where one emphasises the social structural forces of identity and the relations among identities, and the other focuses on internal, cognitive identity processes. They move towards integrating the two parts and suggest that they meet at behaviour that expresses identities, often in interaction with others.

3.6.2. Identity Dynamics

It is a commonly held view that *identity* is something fixed that people have within them that determines who they are. Foucault (1981) has rejected this view by suggesting that people do not have a fixed identity within themselves; *identity* is just a discourse- a way of talking about the self. According to Foucault (1981), *identity* is not a fixed attribute, but a shifting, temporary construction, which is communicated to others in your interactions with them.

Writers such as Breakwell (1992) and Coole (1995) agree that *identity* is not fixed, but is a characteristic of the individual that changes in each spatial, temporal and social context. Woodhard (1997) agrees that *identity* in the contemporary world derives from a multiplicity of sources: from nationality, ethnicity, social class, community and religion. He adds that such sources may produce different versions and might conflict with the construction of identity positions and lead to contradictory, fragmented identities. Furthermore, as Burke and Franzoi (1988) point out, people have multiple identities, not all of them invoked at any particular time or in any particular context. This means that as a person moves into a new situation, or redefines an old one, particular identities are selected from the repertoire of possible identities – or perhaps that new identities might be constructed and reconstructed?

Castells (1997) describes three forms of identity construction:
> ➢ Legitimising identities are introduced and sustained by the dominant institutions in society to secure control,
> ➢ Resistance identities are generated on the margins, in opposition, by the excluded and

> ➤ Project identities involve building new identities that refine subjectivities, and by so doing, seek transformation of the overall social structure.

This conceptual framework offers possibilities of compliance with dominant identities, resistance to these without necessarily seeking to transform them, or to new forms of identity that go beyond compliance and resistance to build new transformative forms of subjectivity. These analytical tools further emphasise that identity is not fixed, absolute or pre-given, "but rather a product of historically specific practices of social regulation" (Hall 1990: 4).

Grumet (1990: 282) concurs and extends the idea of the dynamism of identity to include history and desire:

> *"Identity construction is a dynamic process grounded in history, and desire, subjected to description and reflection and constantly presented and negotiated with other people"*

To understand how practices might be informed by *identity*, I find it is useful to consider interrelationships between the unique and private method of self-conceptualisation, and those which are associated with self-formation by public roles and group classifications. Gender/sexual identity forms a significant part of one's identity and in the next section; I examine the ways in which the literature develops these concepts.

3.6.3. Gender/ Sexual Identity

Feminine/masculine, male/female, women/men, girl/boy- terms of sexual and gender division like these permeate the way we think about ourselves and each other. Siann (1994) points out that on most occasions we find their use unproblematic and we employ them easily, but at other times, we may find this ease illusory. This introduces the idea that gender is not fixed in advance of social interaction, but is constructed in interaction.

Much has been written about the links between biological sex and gender. Foucault (1981), in *The History of Sexuality*, criticised the traditional understanding of sexuality as natural libido. He argued that desires are not controlling biological entities, but rather, that they are constituted in the course of specific social practices. He pointed out that new sexualities are constantly produced and hereby emphasised that the body is produced through power, and is therefore a cultural rather than a natural entity. Martin (1998) in *Feminism, Criticism and Foucault* notes that Foucault insists that our subjectivity, our identity, and our sexuality are intimately linked; they do not exist outside or prior to language and representation, but are actually brought into play by discursive and representational practices. According to Bok (1997), Foucault's work is based on the assumption that human sexuality is not comprehensible in purely biological terms and this way of thinking is crucial if you want to think about changing sexual practices through education programs. Most psychoanalytic theories see the self as being constituted at an early age and continuing into adult life, cutting across division race, class and ethnicity. Against this invariant notion of identity, Foucault's account of the self emphasises the variety of ways in which identities are constituted.

Judith Butler (1990) who is in part inspired by Foucault argues that sex (male, female) is seen to cause gender (masculine, feminine), which is seen to cause desire (towards the gender) and this is seen as a continuum. Her approach is to challenge the supposed links between these, so that gender and desire are flexible, free floating and not "caused" by other stable factors. According to Butler (1990: 25):

> *There is no gender identity behind the expressions of gender; ... identity is performatively constituted by the very 'expressions' that are said to be its results.*

Which means that gender is a performance; it is what you do at particular times, rather than a universal "who you are". Judith Butler (1993: 238) argues that gender is systematically spoken through a 'heterosexual matrix' in which heterosexuality is presupposed in the expression of 'real' forms of masculinity and femininity. She writes:

> *Although forms of sexuality do not unilaterally determine gender, a non-causal and non-reductive connection between sexuality and gender is nevertheless crucial to maintain. Precisely because homophobia often operates through the attribution of a damaged, failed or otherwise abject gender to homosexuals, that is, calling gay men "feminine" or calling lesbians "masculine", and because the homophobic terror over performing homosexual acts, where it exists, is often also a terror over losing proper gender (' no longer being a real or proper man' or ' no longer being a real or*

proper women'), it seems crucial to retain a theoretical apparatus that will account for how sexuality is regulated through the policing and shaming of gender.

Butler (1990) notes that feminists rejected the idea that biology is destiny, but then developed an account that asserted that "women" were a group with common characteristics and interests. Butler further argues that this reinforced a binary view of gender relations in which human beings are divided into two clear-cut groups, women and men, rather than opening up the possibilities for a person to form and choose their own individual identity. I find Butler's work particularly useful for her idea that gender is a performance and that gender is inevitably linked to what she refers to as the "heterosexual matrix", that is, the idea that gender is culturally understood through the notion of heterosexual attraction to those of the other sex. Butler (1993) favours "those historical and anthropological positions that understand gender as a relation among socially constituted subjects in specifiable contexts". This means that rather than being a fixed attribute in a person, gender should be seen as a fluid variable, which shifts and changes in different contexts and at different times.

In *Gender Trouble,* Butler (1990) effectively deconstructs heterosexuality and challenges the logic that maintains it as a dominant, obligatory, "compulsory" sexuality in contemporary societies. Her idea that gender performances are all imitation makes a valuable contribution, unseating the idea of fixed gendered identities grounded in nature, bodies or heterosexuality. Butler (1990) states that the foundationalist reasoning of identity politics tends to state that an identity must be in place in order for political interests to be elaborated and, subsequently, political action to be taken. She argues that there need not be a "doer behind the deed," but that the "doer" is variably in and through the deed. This is not a return to the existential theory of the self as constituted through its acts, for the existential theory maintains a prediscursive structure for both the self and its acts. It is the discursively variable construction of each in and through the other that has been of interest to Butler.

The above discussion suggests that our identities, gendered and otherwise, do not express some authentic inner "core" self but are the effect (rather than the cause) of our performances. This idea that identity is free-floating, not connected to an essence, but instead as a performance, is one of the key ideas in queer theory. Queer theory[9] is a set of ideas based around the idea that identities are not fixed and do not determine who we are. According to Gauntlet, it suggests that it is meaningless to talk in general about 'women' or any other group, as identities consist of so many elements, that to assume that people can be seen collectively on the bases of one shared characteristic is wrong and that it actually proposes that we deliberately challenge all notions of fixed identity in varied and non-predictable ways.

In attempting to understand how specifics of identity worked in schools, Epstein and Johnson (1998), used as a starting point, the self-production of individual and collective identities, processes which are often co-terminous. They assert that these are active processes on the part of those involved and that struggling to acquire a means to represent themselves to self and others is part of growing up. They recognise that this active work always occurs under socially given conditions, which include structures of power and social relations, institutional constraints and possibilities, but also the available cultural repertoires. They also suggest that both individual and collective identities are constructed through processes of self-narration and self-imaging, particularly the telling and retelling to self and others of versions of the past, present and future. Epstein and Johnson (1998) use Butler's (1990) idea of gender being a performance and suggest that identity is always "performed" in a sense that we produce ourselves through what we do/tell ourselves/think. Epstein and Johnson (1998: 116) explain the extent to which individuals as agents in the production of their identities are influenced by recognition from others:

> *Inner performance and narratives may well rehearse a public identity or may never be performed publicly at all- indeed may never be allowed. In other words identity solidifies through action in the word through action and collaboration with others. In order to acquire a sense of reality about who we are, our versions, however represented, must be recognised by others as well as by ourselves.*

In attempting to understand the connections between power and sexuality, I looked at the work of Jennifer Harding (1998): *Sex Acts: Practices of Femininity and Masculinity*, where she critically examines various aspects of contemporary discourse on sexuality. She concentrates on power and the construction of subjectivity at the

---

[9] See Gauntlet www.theory.org.uk resources: Queer Theory

level of discourse. Harding's (1998) theoretical analysis is based on Foucault's conceptualisation of power and discourse and explores how sexuality straddles public and private domains and the implications of this dual positioning. She contends that the private and public are interdependent; neither has meaning without the other. Furthermore, many meanings of sexuality are constituted in relation to changing definitions of public and private, and a shifting border between them. Transgressions of the border help to constitute categories of sexual experience and perform a normative function, because representations of private sex made public are accompanied by an indication of whether they should be tolerated.

Similar to other theorists (such as Butler 1990; Foucault 1981), Harding (1998) challenges the essentialist view that sexuality is a natural phenomenon comprised of fixed and inherent drives which determine gender/sexual identities. Early sexologists viewed male and female sexuality as fundamentally opposite: one aggressive and forceful and the other responsive and maternal, and early sex researchers helped to affirm 'male domination as biological necessity, portraying "the sex act", understood as heterosexual genital engagement, as its exemplary moment' (Segal 1994, cited in Harding 1998). Harding (1998) points out that the impartiality and objectivity claims by sexologists who have attempted to bring sexuality under the control of science, have been challenged by the assertions that these definitions are themselves political. Moreover, many of these categories used in sexology to describe sexual life have been shown not to be universal but highly localised.

> *If sex felt individual and private, individuality and privacy were ideas which also incorporated the roles, definitions, symbols and meanings of the worlds in which they were constructed: they were culturally and historically contingent. (Harding 1998: 16).*

I would like to return to Michel Foucault, who has had an immense influence on contemporary feminist scholarship on the themes of power, sexuality and the subject. On power, Foucault (1981) writes that people do not have power within them; rather power is a technique or action, which individuals can engage in. *Power* is not possessed, it is exercised. Foucault's ideas of power and discourse – in particular, the ideas, firstly that discourses are not super structures but practices that are lived, acted out and spoken by individuals and operate as fields of fluid and mobile relations which produce power/knowledge, and secondly, power is positive, productive and creative (Foucault 1981). The aspects of his work that are related primarily to the problematic of power have been used for feminist ends[10]. Foucault's (1980) reference to power as agonic, or agonistic[11], denotes his assertion that power circulates, is never fixed, and is a network of relationships among subjects who are in some minimal sense free to act and to resist. This is the concept of power developed in *Power/Knowledge: Selected Interviews and Other Writing*. His development of an agonistic model of power in which multiple interrelated power relations are viewed as inherently contested, as best expressed by his adage " where there is power, there is resistance."

Deveaux (1994) notes that Foucault's work on power and the notion that "where there is power, there is resistance", as well as assertion that individuals contest fixed identities and relations in ongoing and sometimes subtle ways, has been particularly helpful for feminists who want to show the diverse sources of women's subordination as well as to demonstrate that we engage in resistance in our everyday lives. She draws on Foucault's treatment of power in his *Power/Knowledge, History of Sexuality (vol. 1)* and " *The Subject and Power*", and shows how he challenges the assumption that power is located exclusively or even primarily in state apparatus or in prohibition. Deveaux (1994) point out that by demanding that we look at the productive character of power and to the existence of multiple power relations – rather than to a dualistic, top-down force, Foucault helps us move from a "state of subordination" explanation of gender relations, which emphasises domination and victimisation, to a more textured understanding of the role of power in women's lives. Understanding power in contemporary society as predominantly productive rather than repressive, Foucault (1981) argues that sexuality is brought under control by the power that is exercised through discursive strategies. Such an analysis of power challenges what Foucault calls the "repressive hypothesis" in relation to sex. The repressive hypothesis proposes that power is primarily exercised by means of prohibition and repression. Foucault (1981), in *The History of Sexuality* argues that sex has been kept a secret and there has been a struggle against secrecy and repression towards greater freedom and liberation, as we gradually rid ourselves of sexual constraints. Forbes (1996) notes

---

[10] See, for example, Judith Butler 1990,1993.
[11] Agonistic comes from the Greek, agon, or combat, and connotes both the exercise of power and struggle

that in elaborating a critique of this historical model, Foucault stresses that repression is not the only way, nor even the principle way in which power in modern society operates.

Bartky (1998) commends Foucault's work on disciplinary practice in modernity and the construction of docile bodies. However, she cautions that Foucault sees it as if the bodily experiences of men and women did not differ. She criticises Foucault for not acknowledging those disciplines that produce a modality of embodiment that is peculiarly feminine. Bartky (1988) asserts that femininity (unlike femaleness) is socially constructed by describing three kinds of practices that contribute to construction of femininity: exercise and diet regimes aimed at attaining an "ideal" body size and configuration; an attention to comportment and a range of "gestures, postures and movements"; and techniques that display the feminine body as an "ornamental surface", such as the use of make-up. The three areas combine to "produce a body which in gesture and appearance is recognisably feminine" and reinforce a "disciplinary project of bodily perfection". She questions whom the disciplinarian in all this is, and suggests that we need to consider the dual nature of feminine bodily discipline, encompassing its socially "imposed" and "voluntary" (or self-disciplining) characteristics. Bartky (1988) explains the voluntary, self-disciplining aspects of these techniques in two ways. Women internalise the feminine ideal so profoundly that they lack the critical distance necessary to contest it and are even fearful of the consequences of "non-compliance", and ideals of femininity are so powerful that to reject their supporting practices is to reject one's own identity.

Having looked at the theories of gender and sexuality in this section, I do not think that it is useful for me to pin my theoretical framework to one particular theorist, since they are in some ways linked, although I do lean on Judith Butler's "performativity" theory idea in that it is necessary to deconstruct heterosexuality and challenge the logic that which maintains it as a dominant, obligatory, "compulsory" sexuality. I also find Foucault's ideas of power and sexuality to be useful. Working within the framework of "identity", I see the potential to begin to rethink gender/sexual identities as performances. As performances, they have the possibility of reconfiguration. In the context of HIV/AIDS, this practice to refigure gender and sexuality can open up a path of understanding that has been neglected. In the next section I examine some of the recent research into gender/sexual identity.

3.7. Studies on Gender/Sexual identities

One of the key themes in gender identity studies concerns ways in which other differences such as race, class, age, sexuality, region, location, among others, shape and modify our conceptions of gender. Gendered identities include both masculinities and femininities (Ranson 2001) and my use of the plural here signifies that these are not static or mutually exclusive terms. Definitions and conceptions of masculinity and femininity differ from culture to culture and from time to time and also differ among men, among women and between men and women. To represent masculinities and femininities as both multiple and socially constructed is to assume that these refer to more than undifferentiated attributes of categories of individuals known as men and women. Ranson (2001) suggests that masculinities and femininities are produced as individuals interact with one another in local situations, which are powerfully influenced by broader social patterns of expectation and sanction. Kimmel (2000) asserts that gender must be seen as an ever-changing fluid semblance of meanings and behaviours.

Kimmel (2000: 6) further asserts that

> *Individual boys and girls become gendered- that is, we learn "appropriate" behaviours and traits that are associated with hegemonic masculinity and exaggerated femininity, and then we each, individually negotiate our own path in a way that feels right for us.*

However Kimmel (2000) adds that this is not done by ourselves, in gender-neutral institutions and arenas. Schools, families, workplaces and politics are gendered sites where dominant definitions are often reinforced and reproduced.

In the current climate of masculine backlash politics and the emergence of " what about the boys?" issues, as well as the awareness of male dominance and sexual violence, there have recently been a number of studies, which focus on constructions of masculinities (see, for example: Abrahamsen 2001; Mac an Ghaill 1994; Morrell

1998; Ranson 2001; Swain 2000; Szasz 1998). In the sexual arena, it is both masculinities and femininities that come into play. Blackmore et al. (1992) argue that emphasising the relational aspects of gender, by making both femininity and masculinity problematic, is an essential move in addressing gender reform. The suggestion is to move away from categorical theories that emphasise that gender/sexual relations are shaped by a single overarching factor and recognise that these relations are multidimensional and differently experienced and responded to within specific historical contexts and social locations (Mac an Ghaill 1996).

A study by Mac an Ghaill (1994) investigated the social construction and regulation of masculinities in a state secondary school in the UK. His primary concern was to explore the processes involved in the interplay between schooling, masculinities and sexualities. In order to understand this complex inter-relationship, he found it necessary to move beyond the traditional areas of concern regarding gender issues and to view schools as complex gendered and heterosexual arenas. He argues that the school microcultures of management, teachers and students are key infrastructural mechanisms through which masculinities and femininities are lived out. Mac an Ghaill (1994) maintains that masculinities are problematic, negotiated and contested within frameworks at the individual, organisational, cultural and societal levels.

According to Mac an Ghaill (1994), sexuality has been an unclear field of study in which complex theories are being developed that fail to connect with individual experiences. He suggests that one of the aspects of the complexity of researching and writing in this area is the question of elusiveness, fluidity and complex interconnectedness of sexualities in modern societies (Mac an Ghaill 1994).

Following a feminist tradition that questioned the "naturalness" of heterosexual sexual practices, this study seeks to explore the power relations, contradictions and confusions related to normative sexual practices. One such example is a paper by Holland et al. (2000), which explored young people's accounts of first sex. This paper draws on findings from two primarily qualitative studies of young people's sexual practices and understanding: the *Women, Risk and AIDS Project and the Men, Risk and AIDS Project*[12]. The main research method employed in this study was in-depth one-to-one interviews. The final samples were 148 young women (aged 16-21) in Manchester and London and young men in London.

Holland et al. (2000: 221)) assert:

> *Heterosexual sexual practice had mostly escaped the attention of social research, which historically focussed on those sexualities defined by the law and by medicine as marginal, problematic or perverse.*

They explored the way in which gender relations operate in heterosexual encounters, by using the example of young people's first sexual experiences. This paper suggests that men and women not only experience heterosexual intercourse differently, but that it is socially different. Negotiation of the rules of the heterosexual encounter is not just a matter for the woman and her sexual partner; reward and sanction are in the hands of the wider peer group, and exercised through social mechanisms such as sexual reputation. While for young men, first (hetero)sex is an empowering moment through which agency and identity are confirmed; for young women the first (hetero)sex experience is more complicated, and their ambivalent responses to it are primarily concerned with managing loss. This paper provides valuable insights into the asymmetry of desire, agency and control within (hetero)sex. Holland et al. (2000) contend that given this asymmetry, it is not surprising that young people's accounts of virginity are narratives of loss and gain. In young people's accounts of first sex, a man gains manhood through a woman's loss of virginity.

In a similar vein, Carpenter (2001) talks about "virginity loss" and investigated the ambiguity surrounding virginity loss as defined and interpreted by young people in the United States. Carpenter (2001) assets that definitions and interpretations of virginity loss serves as tools for constructing sexual identity at both the social and personal levels. She draws on in-depth case studies of 61 women and men of various sexual orientations, ages 18-35. The participants in this study defined virginity loss in physiological terms, with scarcely any mention of virtue or sin. There was agreement with the common belief that otherwise sexually inexperienced individuals would lose

---

[12] The Women, Risk and AIDS project (1988-90) was staffed by Holland J; Ramazanoglu C; Sharpe, S, and Thomson, R. The Men, Risk and AIDS Project (1991-1992) was staffed by Holland, J.; Ramazanoglu, C.; Rhodes, T.; Sharpe, S. and London.

their virginity the first time they engaged in coitus. However, there was considerable disagreement about which sexual activities can result in virginity loss. Carpenter (2001) also found a similar ambiguity pertaining to virginity loss and sex, because different people ascribe diverse meanings to all manner of sexual experiences. She contends that different definitions of virginity loss enables people to construct personal identity in different ways, allowing them to choose, within constraints, the point at which they move from virgin to nonvirgin identity. She asserts that recognising that definitions and interpretations of virginity loss vary, is an important step toward developing a thorough understanding of adolescent sexuality and that sex education programs that assume homogeneity in beliefs may fail to affect their audiences as intended.

Several researchers point to the salience of gender identities in relation to sexual behaviour. Redman (1996:170) writes:

> *I would want to suggest that it is all but impossible to envisage an effective form of sex of HIV education that does not also involve a commitment to addressing the subordination of women, gay men and particular forms of masculinity implicit within conventional gender and sexual relations.*

It is argued that HIV/AIDS education and sexuality education, more broadly defined, presents a particular challenge to dominant forms of masculinity, and that programmes need to address gender, power and heterosexuality if they are to have a positive impact on HIV-related discrimination and homophobia. An article by Harrison (2000) draws on findings from an evaluation of a pilot sexuality education programme conducted in two secondary schools in Australia, to examine gender differences and the production of difference. The participants in this study were aged between 14 and 15. Harrison (2000) uses two examples: gender, power and menstruation and homophobia to analyse the language and practices students engage in as part of the process of achieving (hetero)sexual identity. The schools were required to include teaching which interrogated gender, power relations and homophobia and this was seen as an attempt to incorporate the discourse of differences. She found that gender, power and menstruation, and heterosexism and homophobia have similar practices of exclusion at work in the process of achieving a normative heterosexual identity. Harrison (2000) asserts that many young men and women have considerable investment in continuing the privileges that normative heterosexuality brings, despite its discontents, and in this context the difficulty of deconstructing heterosexuality at the school level needs to be acknowledged. It was found in the Harrison (2000) study that although change was slow and incremental, there was some change in thinking after programs that explored HIV/AIDS in the context in which gender power relations were deconstructed. His study did not explore whether the changes in thinking led to any changes in practices.

Research into sexual identities has mainly looked at sexual identity as being synonymous with sexual orientation and has mainly focussed on those sexualities that are seen as marginal or anything other than hegemonic heterosexual sexual practices. This is clear in a paper by Gary Hollander (2000) that reviews definitions of sexual orientation, identity, and questioning youths. He concludes that questioning youths can be viewed in numerous ways, but may be seen as either at a stage of identity development when youths are either uncertain of their sexual identities or in the process of self-categorisation and navigating seemingly competing identities. He contends that because a significant number of youths are uncertain of their sexual identity, schools and communities can have an important role in assisting these youths in their development process through implementing programs that address their need for safe affiliation and support. In this paper, sexual identity is seen as being synonymous with sexual orientation.

I find the explanation of sexual identity as offered by Santrock (2001:356) useful:

> *The construction of a sense of sexual identity involves learning to manage sexual feelings, such as sexual arousal and attraction, developing new forms of intimacy and learning the skills to regulate sexual behaviour to avoid undesirable consequences.*

Santrock adds that developing sexual identity involves more than sexual behaviour, and that it includes interfaces with other developing identities.

My interest in studying notions of sexual identity of teenagers is because I think that there is a strong link between sexual identity and sexual practices (see section 4.3.2). However, a paper by Steward et al. (2000) challenges the assumption that identity informs behaviour. They draw on two independent yet conterminous Australian qualitative studies of sexual identities and practices to examine how young women and men's identities resist occupying stable, predictable and causal relationships to sexual practices. The first of these studies involved an interview sample of twenty 16-17 year old young women. The individual interviews employed a sexual history framework, which involved the interviewee telling her life story of sexual relationships and practice, and were used to locate the discussions of femininity, identity and sexual practice. The second project was a condom-use study of 60 Melbourne men aged between 18 and 35 years. Semi-structured interviews were employed and a sexual history framework was also used here. The interviews focused on a range of sexual events from first sexual experiences to recent protected and unprotected sexual encounters.

The data from the above two studies were used as a basis for discussion in their paper which challenges some of the dominant assumptions underpinning the nature of sexual identity. In this paper they focus upon three particular aspects of identity: assumption, imposition and expression. They examine the flux, fluidity and uncertainty within the human sexual agenda and caution about the misinformation, which uncritical assumptions about "gay", "straight" or various masculinities and femininities may deliver. They contend that in the discourses surrounding the identity-practice nexus, fluidity is marginalized. Sexual identities are often constructed in a causal relationship to particular sexual practices, and hence to levels of HIV/AIDS and sexually transmitted infection risk. This paper draws on two studies that focus on very different sample cohorts. Women and men are examined separately. The examination of female sexual identity focuses on dominant views of femininities and the ways in which the women in the study challenge these. They assert that in terms of health promotion, the implications of young women's contestation of traditional femininity-in this case a femininity that links sex and love- suggests that interventions based on these dominant discourses fail to engage those young women who may, through their multiple sexual encounters, be at risk of STI's including HIV. Their examination of male sexual identity focuses on gay/straight categories and the contestation within these categories. They assert that the importance of these data for sexual health promotion concerns the issue of target groups- where STI and HIV prevention has focused on target groups defined by sexuality such as "gay" and "straight". The contribution of this paper to the present study is that it illustrates the complexities between the relationships of sexual identities to sexual practices. One of the limitations of the above studies is that the authors see sexual identity as being synonymous with sexual orientation, and their argument is that gay/straight identity does not inform sexual behaviour. Furthermore, like various previous studies (e.g. Leach et al. 2000; Paulsen 1999), they consider the views and characteristics of one gender in isolation not as a dynamic between two individuals. The result is an incomplete portrayal of a situation, which is by definition dyadic in nature. Furthermore focussing on women only or men only implies a false unity in the lives of girls and of boys. The present study will explore sexual identity construction in a co-educational school setting, where I will focus on both girls and boys, in single-sex as well as mixed-sex groups.

The studies reviewed above indicate that any understanding of *identity* clearly is complex. Different dimensions of identity are invoked in different contextual situations, and this dynamic and shifting nature of identity makes it a challenging area for study.

3.8. Generational Identities

It is a cliché of traditional "youth" studies of different theoretical persuasions that the term refers to a stage of life, which is essentially transitional. Many psychological theories (see, for example, Erikson 1968; Paul and White 1990) suggest that the transition usually is to a relatively stable adult identity. Love, romance, sexual experimentation, and intense friendships have long been recognised as part of the adolescent experience (Paul and White 1990). Erikson (1968) viewed peer group and youthful romances as mechanisms in the service of identity development. In Eriksons'(1968) theory on psychosocial development, the young adult crisis over intimacy follows the adolescent crisis over identity. Erikson (1968) identifies autonomy, initiative, industry, identity and intimacy as sequential development concerns. Paul and White (1990) criticise this sequence and contend that identity and intimacy are both "development tasks" of the late adolescent transition, and that progress toward a mature identity and a mature intimacy takes place concurrently.

This transitional status together with dominant heterosexual morality and gendered power relations may serve to inhibit young people in their exploration of sexuality. Studies of generation as a dimension of identity are relatively rare. West (1999) argues that studies of youth sexuality have been approached almost exclusively using the lens of gender. She notes that while age or youth are often referred to in passing, there is little systematic examination of age or generation as a social dynamic. She examined the social constraints on young people's opportunities for talk and discussion about sex, with particular reference to their experiences of sex education and services in sexual health. She also sought to identify the social relations as well as normative constraints that inhibit young people's sexual expression. She interviewed 147 young people (89 women and 58 men) aged mainly between 14 and 21. West (1999) argues that previous studies have tended to examine the difficulties in negotiating sexual encounters within a gendered context only, although the basis for sexuality is usually openness, trust and respect. West (1999) found that young people, both men and women, experience a gap in all of these in their tentative explorations of sexuality, both with each other and in their dealings with adults.

Mac an Ghaill (1994) investigated the social construction and regulation of masculinities in a state secondary school in the UK. Although his primary concern was to explore the processes involved in the interplay between schooling, masculinities and sexualities, he significantly draws attention to the critical role of the school as a " site in their coming of age" and the need to focus on power relations within institutions. Epstein and Johnson (1998) also show that schools are a site where sexualities and sexual identities are constructed.

A study by Mirembe and Davies (2001), focusing on AIDS education in Uganda, found the school to be a site of extensive set of gendered practices which constituted risk in themselves in terms of sexual health. This research considered four linked forms of control in schools: hegemonic masculinity, gendered discipline patterns, sexual harassment and 'compulsory' heterosexuality. They found schooling's privileging of conformity, in terms of gender roles and expectations to be a key problem, and that mixed-sex schools are not necessarily safe places for either girls or boys in the current AIDS era. Mirembe and Davies (2001) conclude that by failing to challenge power imbalances and by promoting conformity within a particular gender regime, schooling reinforces the macro customs that place undue pressure on boys to exploit the power gap and on girls to accept a male leadership role.

The studies mentioned above focus on young adults in schools but do not specifically examine generation as an identity dynamic. The present study will look at age relations within gender relations and deconstruct the notion of generation as a fixed stage of development.

In this chapter, I presented a critical look at both conceptual and research issues. My review of the existing literature on HIV/AIDS knowledge and sexual practices and research into gender/sexual identities has revealed certain limitations in these studies. These limitations and their implications for the present study are discussed in the following section.

3.9. Implications of this Literature Review

a) Available South African research on sexual issues is limited in scope. Several researchers have conducted surveys on knowledge, attitude and practices (KAP) in relation to HIV/AIDS and have found that youth HIV/AIDS knowledge is adequate but this does not translate into safer sexual practices. These provide a critical descriptive foundation for understanding adolescent sexual behaviour and sexuality. However, many of the studies do not proceed further than the description, and reveal little about the reasons for the disjuncture between knowledge and practices. This study will attempt to provide deeper insights into socio-cultural and interpersonal factors which impact on youth sexual behaviour choices.

b) Theories from mainstream psychology, which have mainly been used to explain HIV risk behaviour, rely heavily on the notion of "beliefs". This is problematic because beliefs are static and resistant to change. Furthermore, mainstream psychological theories of behaviour focus on individuals, ignoring important aspects such as culture and society. Sociological theories on the other hand, explain behaviour in terms of the structures of society, ignoring the role of individual agency. On their own, each of these theories is inadequate to explain complex phenomena of risk behaviour and behaviour change. A useful way of bringing together theories of psychology and sociology is through the notion of "identity". The more fluid conception of identity formation allows me to understand the dynamic and contextual nature of sexual identities. This study utilises theories of identity that emphasise fragility, contradictions and ambiguity in multiple processes of identity formation, which might involve identification with hegemonic gender orders, counter identification and resistance, or disidentification and transformation.

c) Social research into sexual identities has mainly focussed on those sexualities that are seen as marginal or anything other than hegemonic heterosexual sexual practices. Following a feminist tradition that questioned the "naturalness" of heterosexual sexual practices, this study seeks to explore the power relations, contradictions and confusions related to normative sexual practices. Much of the gender research does not proceed beyond descriptive studies of male and female aggression within sexual relationships.

d) While *age* or generation have often been referred to in passing much of the research on young people, there has been limited systematic research into age as an aspect of identity. In this study on young adults' notions of their developing sexual identities, I will include an exploration of generation as an identity dynamic.

e) There is a tendency, in much of the research on gender relations, to focus on women as the marginalised and disempowered group. While focus on women is crucial for empowerment, it is necessary to understand the context in which men and women live. Available research on sexual decision-making and negotiation frequently considers the views and characteristics of one gender in isolation, not as a dynamic between two individuals. Research on sexual decision-making and negotiation in Africa mainly focuses on women. The male perspective remains a largely unknown element in the sexual equation. The result is an incomplete portrayal of a situation, which is by definition dyadic in nature. Furthermore focussing on girls only or boys only implies a false unity in the lives of girls and of boys. The gendered approach employed in this study will explore the dynamics between and among girls, between and among boys and between girls and boys.

3.10. Conclusion

In this chapter I have begun with a brief discussion of the biological and medical aspects of HIV/AIDS. I then examined the existing literature on the impact of HIV/AIDS knowledge on sexual behaviour, and critically discussed some of the dominant theories that have been used to explain HIV risk behaviour. I have developed *Identity* as a theoretical framework for this study and also looked at the African and international research on sexuality and sexual identities.

In the next chapter, I discuss my methodological considerations in the design of this study on young adults' sexual identities within the context of HIV/AIDS and describe in detail the methods and instruments employed in this research.

CHAPTER FOUR

ACCESSING YOUNG ADULTS' SEXUAL IDENTITIES: APPROACH AND STRATEGY

4.1. Introduction

Having examined the relevant literature on HIV/AIDS, sexuality and sexual behaviour, and developed *Identity* as a theoretical framework, in the previous chapter, this chapter provides a discussion and justification of the methodology and the methods employed in this study of young peoples' construction of their sexual identity within the context of HIV/AIDS.

I begin by discussing the broad methodological approach. This sensitive area of research begs many questions about research relations and methodological issues, such as how to access the invisible, especially if it includes issues that are considered private? These issues have been the focus of much feminist research methodology (Dunne 1996; Jayaratne and Steward 1991; Lather and Smithies 1997). My methodological considerations include the choice of a methodology that facilitates the spread of authority and allows for the participants, to a certain extent, to determine the agenda. Furthermore, the development of a trusting relationship between researcher and researched, and the goal of using social research to further the interest of the participants have been the avowed aim of many feminist research studies (Seale

1998). Feminist research methods are most appropriate in this study. This argument will be developed in section 4.2.1.

As advocated by feminist theorists such as Lather (1986), I have attempted to operationalise an emancipatory research method, which emphasises collaboration, reciprocity and reflexivity. This goal is in part achieved by privileging learner voices throughout the study. Giving voice has the potential of being empowering but does not automatically imply empowerment. This discussion is taken up later in this chapter (see section 4.2.2.).

I discuss issues of access, and detail the sampling procedure (section 4.4.). In this chapter, I also detail the various research methods employed in this study (section 4.5.) and explain the methods used to analyse the data that is produced (section 4.7.). Some of the benefits and limitations of the research approach and strategy are discussed at each stage of the generation of data.

4.2. General Approach

Within social science research, the choice of which aspects of the social world to research, the methods for collecting the data, and then the ways to interpret those data is informed by the broad theoretically informed framework within which the research is carried out, and it is these combined aspects which constitute methodology (Brunskell 1998). I have chosen to use a feminist research approach in this study of young adults' sexual identities within the discourse of HIV/AIDS. In the following section I discuss the rationale for a feminist approach.

4.2.1. Feminist research methodology

In justifying my choice for using a feminist research approach, I needed to examine what constitutes feminist research and how it is different from non-feminist research. Skeggs (1994a) summarises three areas to consider in relation to what constitutes feminist research:

> ➢ *Ontology*, this is, what is knowable?

➢ *Epistemology*, that is, how we know what we know and what is the relationship of the knower to the known

➢ *Methodology*, that is, how do we get to know?

According to Skeggs (1994a), the ways in which these different questions are answered or ignored in the research process will demonstrate the different theoretical positions held by the researchers. In differentiating feminist from non-feminist research, Skeggs (1994b: 77) asserts, "feminist research begins with the premise that the nature of reality in western society is unequal and hierarchical". It has been suggested that the preconceptions of feminist science would be:

> *One in which no rigid boundary separates the subject of knowledge (the knower) and the natural object of that knowledge; where the subject/object split is not used to legitimize the domination of nature; where nature itself is conceptualized as active rather than passive, a dynamic complex totality requiring human cooperation and understanding rather than a dead mechanism, requiring only manipulation and control. In such feminist imaginings, the scientist is not seen as an impersonal authority standing outside and above human nature and concerns, but simply a person whose thoughts and feelings, logical capacities, and intuitions are all relevant in the process of discovery. Such scientists would actively seek ways of negotiating the distances now established between thought and feeling, between knowledge and its uses, between objectivity and subjectivity, between expert and the nonexpert, and would seek to use knowledge as a tool of liberation rather than domination. (Fee 1986: 47 in Blaikie 1993)*

Feminist research typically challenges the legitimacy of research that does not empower oppressed and otherwise invisible groups. Usher (1996) addresses the emancipatory element of educational research – the research should be empowering to all participants. She sets out several principles of feminist research:

➢ The acknowledgement of the pervasive influence of gender as a category of analysis and organisation,

➢ The deconstruction of traditional commitments to truth, objectivity and neutrality,

➢ The adoption of an approach to knowledge creation, which recognises that all theories are perspectival,

➢ The utilisation of a multiplicity of research methods,

➢ The inter-disciplinary nature of feminist research,

➢ The involvement of the researcher and the people being researched and

➢ The deconstruction of the theory/practice relationship.

These principles of feminist research suggest elements that are appropriate to achieve the goals set out in my study of secondary school learners' sexual identities, within the context of HIV/AIDS (see the aims of the study, section 1.4.)

Figure 4.1. summarises some of the broad differences between the three approaches to the study of behaviour, as outlined by Cohen, Manion and Morrison (2001:35).

Normative	Interpretive	Critical
Society and the social system	The individual	Societies, groups and individuals
Medium/large scale research	Small scale research	Small-scale research
Impersonal, anonymous forces regulating behaviour	Human actions continuously recreating social life	Political, ideological factors, power and interest shaping behaviour
Model of natural sciences	Non-statistical	Ideology critique and action research
'Objectivity'	'Subjectivity'	Collectivity
Research conducted 'from the outside'	Personal involvement of the researcher	Participant researchers, researchers and facilitators
Generalizing from the specific	Interpreting the specific	Critiquing the specific
Explaining behaviour/seeking causes	Understanding actions/meanings rather than causes	Understanding, interrogating,
Assuming the taken-for-granted	Investigating the taken-for-granted	Critiquing the taken for granted
Macro-concepts: society, institutions, norms, positions, roles, expectations	Micro-concepts: individual perspective, personal constructs, negotiated meanings, definitions of situations	Macro- and micro-concepts: political and ideological interests, operations of power
Structuralists	Phenomenologists, symbolic interactionists, ethnomethodologists	Critical theorists, action researchers, practitioner researchers
Technical interest	Practical interest	Emancipatory interests

Figure 4.1.Differing approaches to the study of behaviour (Cohen, Manion and Morrison 2001: 35)

4.2.1.1. The Quantitative/qualitative debate in the Social Sciences

Many feminist researchers have argued for a replacement of quantitative, positivist, objective research with qualitative, interpretive, ethnographic reflective research (See Denzin 1989; Haig 1999; Mies 1993). Much of this debate has been around the claim that quantitative research techniques, involving the translation of an individual's experience into categories that have been preconceived by researchers, distort women's experiences and result in a silencing of women's own voices. Advocates of qualitative methods have argued that individual women's understandings, emotions, and actions in the world must be explored in those women's own terms (Jayaratne and Steward 1991).

One frequent source of interest in qualitative research stems from its potential to offer a more human, less mechanical relationship between the researcher and the researched. For example, Oakley (1981: 41) suggests that

> The goal of finding out more about people through interviewing is best achieved when the relationship of interviewer and interviewee is non-hierarchical and when the interviewer is prepared to invest his or her personal identity in the relationship.

Jayaratne and Steward (1991), contend that much of the feminist debate about qualitative and quantitative research has been sterile and based on a false polarisation. Furthermore, other feminist researchers have challenged this polarisation of qualitative and quantitative and advocate the use of multiple methods (such as Dunne 1996; Jayaratne 1993). Jayaratne (1993) contests the argument that quantitative methods are unsuitable for feminists because they neglect the emotions of the people under study. She argues that there is a need for feminist quantitative data and methodologies in order to counter sexist quantitative data in the social sciences. Dunne (1996) claims that the methodological position, as concerned with theory and analysis of the research process is of greater significance to interpretation than any particular method or data-gathering technique used in research. She argues that the combination of methods does not necessarily pose a problem; rather, they may be complementary if the strengths and limitations of each of the traditions are acknowledged. Dunne (1996) presents this argument through a discussion of the use of quantitative data (within a qualitative study) to inform equal opportunities work.

Although I did not initially intend using quantitative methods of data production and analysis, when the occasion presented itself, I administered a questionnaire (that I had developed for use in focus group discussions) to a convenience sample of 72 participants, and have subjected the data from those to statistical analysis. This quantitative analysis allowed for comparison and statistical aggregation of the data (Patton 1990). I then used a mix of quantitative and qualitative data. Qualitative methods of data production typically produce a wealth of information about a much smaller sample of people (Patton 1990).

Locating myself within the position of feminist research also means acknowledging my own position as an adult researcher, researching youth. The generational difference between the participants and myself makes it difficult for me to gain access into their world, a youth culture that I know very little about. In view of this, I chose to privilege the voices of the young adults (the secondary school learners) in my inquiry about the developing notions of their sexual identities and sexual practices within the climate of HIV/AIDS. However, this is not completely unproblematic and I discuss some of the implications of using learner voices, in the next section.

4.2.2. Learner Voice

In keeping with feminist research, I have given high status to the knowledge, understandings and feelings of the participants by privileging their voices throughout the study. "Voice" privileges experience over theory or training, as a basis of our understanding and rather than being sanctioned by others, its validity comes from who is speaking (Hadfield and Haw undated). Hadfield and Haw assert that a great deal of emphasis is placed on the gains for young people, when their voices are included because articulating their opinions is seen as an intrinsically worthwhile activity with outcomes that range from increased self-confidence, through developing specific skills to enhance attitudes about political and civil life.

According to Britzman (1990) (cited in Connelly and Clandinin 1990):

> *Voice is meaning that resides in the individual and enables that individual to participate in a community... the struggle for voice begins when a person attempts to communicate meaning to someone else. Finding the word, speaking for oneself and feeling heard is all part of this process.*

Examining learner perspectives can provide new insights into the specific dynamics of their understandings and experiences in relation to their sexual identities. Although "voice" is about issues of participation and empowerment, it is necessary to caution against claims that inclusion of "voice" necessarily leads to empowerment. The intention is to avoid the polar opposites of, on the one hand, ignoring or excluding the speech of young people and, on the other hand, treating its inclusion as unproblematically insightful and liberating.

My intention to privilege the voices of the participants was driven by an intention to involve them as co-researchers, as well as to represent their voices as clearly and accurately as possible. Linda Alcoff (1992:9) aptly outlines this position of representation:

> " In both the practice of speaking for as well as the practice of speaking about others I am engaging in the act of representing the other's needs, goals, situation, and in fact, who they are. I am representing them as such, or, in post-structuralist terms, I am participating in the construction of their subject positions".

Giving voice has the potential of being empowering but does not automatically imply empowerment. According to Fielding (2001) if we are to avoid the dangers of developing increasingly sophisticated ways of involving students that often unwittingly, end up betraying their interests, accommodating them to the status quo, and in a whole variety of ways reinforcing assumptions that are destructive of anything that could be considered remotely empowering, then we have to explore approaches that have different starting points and quite different dispositions and intentions.

Fielding (2001) argues for "dialogic encounter", in which there is a genuine partnership between the researcher and the researched. He suggests that the hope of dialogic encounters lie more in the act of dialogue itself than in the content of what is said. The very act of speaking within these kinds of contexts encourages an epistemic agency, a capacity to construct legitimate knowledge (Fielding 2001).

The kind of argument for the development of dialogic encounters between researcher and researched for which Alcoff (1992) begins to develop has been taken up by other researchers, such as, Yvonna Lincoln and Margaret LeCompte in Tierney's important collection *Naming Silenced Lives* (McLaughlin and Tierney 1993). This dialogic encounter is characterized in the following way:

> ➢ The development of dialogic research is educative for those being researched,
> ➢ It is similarly educative for those conducting the research,
> ➢ It is essentially a partnership and

> ➤ The kind of dialogic research which involves the genuine partnership of the researcher and the researched has the potential to change more than the aspect of the their lives which happen to be identified by a particular enquiry.

Lincoln (1993) claims that those who have in the past so often been mere objects of investigation, themselves become the agents of their own transformation: 'the silenced in becoming producers, analysts, and presenters of their own narratives, cease to become the agents of the stories which are produced and consumed about them, and the agents and instruments of their own change processes' (Lincoln 1993: 43). It is inevitable that both the participants and myself have been changed by participating in the study. The research design changed over time, with "mutual shaping and interaction" between myself and the participants taking place.

Including the voices of the participants can never be total. The voices of the participants are certainly filtered through me since it is my interpretations of their accounts that are presented in this research report. It is inevitable that during the process of data analysis, a great degree of data reduction occurs. One of the ways in which 'reduction' is evident in this study is in the choices I have made in the themes (I explain this fully in section 4.7.) that I have represented in this study. There are bound to be some themes that have been omitted. In the final representation of the findings, even if the intentions are not deceptive, the editorial power of the researcher remains. Fielding (1998) cites LeCompte (1993:12) who reminds us that the discourse selected may be powerful, truthful and authentic, "but it is, in fact, still a partial discourse.... (which) often leaves the researcher as *an absent presence*". Patti Lather (2001) shares this view and cautions that we need to be aware that "we neither assume transparent narrative nor override participant meaning frames". She refers to the "loss of innocence" of feminist methodology, acknowledging that we get a cut of peoples' lives in the name of data and then further reduction of the data occurs. Locating my research within feminist methodology, I concede that my interpretations and representations are inevitably not "innocent". However, I have attempted to interpret and represent the voices of the participants as clearly as possible, through a multiple method approach (see section 4.6).

In this section, I discussed the rationale for the use of learner voice as means of data generation for this study. I also discussed some of problems associated with the claim that giving voice is automatically empowering. It is my contention that empowerment is a very likely outcome of changed consciousness resulting from articulating and hearing others articulate. In the following section, I review some of the previous literature on identity and behaviour with a view to gaining some insight into the methods used to access identity. I also look at the findings on the relationship between identity and behaviour.

4.3. Studies of identity and behaviour

According to Stryker and Burke (2000), a clearer understanding is required of the ways in which identities produce behaviours –expressions of identity. Stryker and Burke (2000) argue that developing such an understanding requires measurement procedures applicable to both identities and behaviours. Burke and Reitzes (1981) attempted to test one formulation of the link between identity and behaviour, by using a semantic differential scale (which reflects their view of meaning as internal, bipolar responses to stimuli) to measure college students' identities and behaviours along the same dimension.

Burke and Reitzes (1981) based their study on theoretical conceptions of identity, advances in its measurement, and the assumption that identities motivate behaviours that have meanings which are consistent with the identity. Their hypothesis was that identities and behaviours are linked by a common underlying frame of reference. They further hypothesised that this common frame of reference lies in the meaning of the identity and the meaning of the performance. To test these hypotheses they attempted to determine the meanings of identities and the meanings of behaviours and to use these to predict the direction and strength of the effects of identity on behaviours. They obtained data from college students, which they used to identify and measure four dimensions of meaning pertaining to the college student identity, and to assess the impact of student identities on the two performance variables of educational plans and participation in social activities. Their findings strongly supported the hypothesized linking of identity and performance through common meanings. For example, students' self-view as sociable (one dimension of the student identity) did not predict college plans while students' self-views of academic responsibility (another dimension of student identity) was a strong predictor of college plans.

The complexity of identities makes it difficult to study. Burke and Franzoi (1988) note that identities typically have been studied using retrospective techniques, in which individuals report the characteristics of various identities that were invoked in past situations. Respondents are removed from the situations and persons that normally invoke these identities. Burke and Franzoi (1988) assert that understanding identities removed from the situation in which they occur runs counter to the main tenet of symbolic interactionism, namely, that behaviour can only be understood within a particular situational context. Their study demonstrated that experiential sampling methodology (ESM) could be used to test important hypotheses in identity theory. In undertaking an investigation of the relationship between situation and self, they used ESM to tap into identities of people in daily situations. They obtained random samples of the participant's thoughts and feelings in situations as they were occurring. Their overall findings suggest that there is a strong relationship between people's identities and the situations they are in. The earlier work of Burke and Reitzes (1981) established a link between the meaning of a person's identity and the meaning of his/her behaviour when acting in that identity. They concluded that the findings from the later study complete the picture and shows that all three components are closely related: identity, situation and behaviour.

Walker (2001) used a narrative approach to examine the construction of masculine and feminine identities by students in an engineering department in a university. This study utilized theories of identity that emphasise fragility, contradictions and ambiguity in multiple processes of identity formation, which might involve identification with the dominant gender order, counter identification and resistance, disidentification and transformation. The question she addressed in this study was: what contemporary identities and constructions of self, of belonging and not belonging, are shaped in and through an educational site and in particular, one where the relative absence of women is significant enough to destabilise taken-for-granted asymmetrical power relations? She conducted in-depth unstructured interviews in groups and found that the interaction among students in the group discussions generated rich data, while also working to diminish the effects of power and unfamiliarity of the researcher's relationship with them. Her findings from this study demonstrate that while gender relations and expectations have changed significantly for young professional women, they and their male peers still reinscribe dominant notions of femininity and masculinity.

A significant contribution of the above studies exploring identity and behaviour is the methodologies employed to access identity. The methods of data production used in the above studies relied chiefly on the voices of the participants. This gives the researchers access to the thoughts, feelings and perspectives of the participants, which might not be accessible through observational methods.

The literature I have reviewed clearly indicates that identities have a strong influence on behavioural choices. My goal in this study is to employ the theoretical lens of identity and processes of identification and identity construction in order to generate further understandings of whether and/or how young people create their identities from their experiences and how they understand those experiences and the choices they make.

4.4. Participants

The participants in the study comprised co-educational secondary school learners in a selected school in KwaZulu Natal, South Africa. I focused on 15-19 year old learners. The school is situated in a working class area and draws learners from the area around the school. It is a well-resourced school with qualified educators and a specialist guidance counsellor. A mix of Indian and African learners participated in the study. Pseudonyms were chosen to reflect the sex and race of the participants. I work within the dominant culture of heterosexual learners although I do create opportunities for other forms to emerge. Because of the culture of compulsory heterosexuality promoted by schools and the family, as well as the peer policing of heterosexuality, it was clearly not going to be possible to deliberately seek out lesbian/gay learners within the school.

4.4.1. Sampling

Convenience and multi-phase sampling strategies were employed in this study. The initial choice of the school was as a result of convenience sampling. The choice of Boss Secondary School[13] was based on proximity of the school to my home and my place of work, as well as the established relationship between the school and my work institution. I chose to work with the older learners in the school (grades 11 and 12) on the premise that it was more likely that there were many more in the older group who were sexually active and/or in relationships than the younger learners in the school, and also that they would be better able to talk about these issues. I base this assumption on research by Nahom et al. (2001), who showed that the percentage of teens reporting ever engaging in sexual activity increased across the grades. I had decided to work within school hours because more participants within the chosen age group would be accessible to participate in the study. This also meant that I had to be as least disruptive of the academic programme as possible and led to some scheduling difficulties. There were three grade 11 and three grade 12 classes in Boss Secondary School, and I worked with all three grade 11 classes and two grade 12 classes, as whole classes (this relates to my access criteria, which I discuss later). I also interacted with learners on several walk-about sessions in the playground, where I reached a much wider sample.

I started by working with whole classes and then used a purposive snowball sampling method for focus group discussions and individual interviews. Initial respondents were those learners who volunteered to talk to me within their friendship groups, which were all single sex, and single race groups. I then asked the participants of these groups to identify target groups in which I was interested, such as the "in-groups" and the "out-groups". I had to deliberately structure groups that mixed in terms of race and sex. Only one learner that I approached refused to participate in the study and I did not question this choice, since I had offered the option to participate or not. Snowball sampling offered several advantages vital to achieving my research aims. Since I was unable to work with the entire school population, recruiting study participants through the learners own perceptions of others, provided me with an opportunity to gain access to a diverse sample. The shortcomings of snowball

---

[13] Boss Secondary is a pseudonym, and was negotiated with the school management.

sampling include their non-random, nonrepresentative nature, which prevents me from directly generalising the findings to the broader population. However, a non-random sample may be sufficient to explore the range of the developing notions of sexual identities and sexual practices in the given context. Even though I attempted to identify a diverse range of participants, and to structure the groups as creatively as possible, I was struck by the frequency with which similar themes were raised with different participants, which indicated that I had possibly plateaued with my analysis themes.

4.4.2. Gaining access and consent

As in much social research it was necessary to obtain the consent and co-operation of the participants who are to assist in the production of the data as well as the institution in which the study was being carried out (the school). According to Cohen, Manion and Morrison (2001), the principle of informed consent arises from the subject's right to freedom and self-determination. They add that being free is a condition of living in a democracy, and when restrictions and limitations are placed on freedom they must be justified and consented to, even in the research proceedings. I gained access to the school through arranging a personal meeting with the school management, where I outlined the purpose of my research and a description of the methods that I was going to use. I had initially anticipated difficulties in gaining access to schools since I was researching a rather sensitive area, and was not sure how much detail of the study I should initially disclose. However, the school management had already had a good relationship with the university at which I worked, and had supported research projects before and were satisfied with the outcomes and feedback. It was not possible to inform the school officials or the participants of the exact details of the methods of data production that I was going to employ in the study because much of it was developed during the process of the study. However, I explained as fully as I could at that point, and did not deliberately withhold any information. I worked well within the guidelines for reasonably informed consent, as outlined in Figure 4.2.

1. A fair explanation of the procedures to be followed and their purposes.
2. A description of the attendant discomforts and risks reasonably to be expected.
3. A description of the benefits reasonably to be expected.
4. A disclosure of appropriate alternative procedures that might be advantageous to the participants.
5. An offer to answer any enquiries concerning the procedures.
6. An instruction that the person is free to withdraw consent and to discontinue participation in the project at any time without prejudice to the participant.

Figure 4.2. Guidelines for reasonably informed consent

Source: United States Department of Health, Education and Welfare, *Institutional Guide to DHEW Policy, 1971* cited in Cohen, Manion and Morrison (2001: 51)

I guaranteed the relevant officials at the school that all participants will remain anonymous, and that I would not disclose any information that would identify the school in which the study was carried out. I negotiated access to the learners, and the time frame of my study at the school site at the beginning of the study. I had to renegotiate time when my data production process took longer than I had initially anticipated. The school management agreed to allow me to work with grade 11 and grade 12 learners within the non-examination class periods during the school time and when teachers were absent. I offered my services to the school as a relief teacher, with the understanding that I was going to use these relief periods for generation of data for my study. However, having the responsibility of the whole class made it difficult for me to work with selected participants and groups and I had to enlist the assistance of a colleague (which I discuss later in this chapter). I also gained permission to work with the learners during school break-times. I had been visiting the school regularly from August 2001 to May 2002 and had become a familiar sight to both the educators and the learners. I made a concerted effort, in my manner of dress, my attitude and by keeping out of the staff room, to remain detached from the school management and educators. I considered that it was important that I was not seen to be part of the establishment. I think that this allowed the learners to feel more at ease to communicate with me, without concern that I would be discussing their personal matters with their educators.

4.5. Ethical dilemmas: Privacy and confidentiality

The very nature of this research was to take an issue that was traditionally considered private and make it public knowledge. However, due to the sensitive nature of the area, it was necessary to safeguard the privacy of the participants. I did this by guaranteeing complete anonymity of all participants and the institution in the written report. In completing the written submissions, no identifying marks- names, addresses or coding symbols were used. While this fulfilled the requirement of anonymity, and ensured non-traceability, it had the effect of making selection for further investigations difficult. I often came across something that I wanted to pursue and could not because I could not trace the respondent. The participants in the focus-group interviews and the individual interviews could not expect anonymity and in these instances, I promised confidentiality.

As I had spent a long time in the school, and had been seen as independent of the institution, I had developed a trusting relationship with the learners. They often came to me in groups or individually, during break-times to discuss personal and relationship problems. The questions that troubled me are "when is casual conversation part of the research and when is it not"? Learners were often willing to share stories about sexual practices of other learners. "When is this just gossip and when is it not"? I did, however consider everything I saw and heard in the field, as data.

4.6. Data Production Methods

I have used a variety of methods, which overlap in addressing my critical question in this study, which is:

> *How do young adults' construct their sexual identities within the context of HIV/AIDS?*

Reinhartz (1992) points out that the use of multiple methods in feminist research, work to enhance understanding both by adding layers of information and by using one type of data to validate or refine another. Multiple methods also facilitate triangulation, which is an important way to strengthen a study design. Denzin (1978: 28) asserts:

> No single method ever adequately solves the problem of rival causal factors... because each method reveals different aspects of empirical reality, multiple methods of observations must be employed. This is termed triangulation. I now offer as a final methodological rule the principle that multiple methods should be used in every investigation.

I worked alone most of the time and had the assistance of a male colleague whenever he was available. My colleague, Wiseman, was suitable because he was an African male of twenty-one years. The idea was that his participation in the study would help minimise possible gender, race and generational barriers. Unfortunately he was unable to participate to the extent envisaged and had to take up employment elsewhere during the early stages of the study. I am unable to make any comparisons in the participants' responses to Wiseman and myself. For most of the time, I had the responsibility of the whole class and had to structure much of my work in a way that involved all the learners. This was useful in the sense that I had a captive audience and 100% returns on all the instruments, but it did not allow for private small group and individual interviews. Interviews had to be organised outside class time because it was not possible to take a group out of the class and leave the rest of the learners unattended. Verbal consent was sought from all participants prior to each data production exercise.

4.6.1. Working with Single-sex and Mixed-sex groups

Working with groups is significant since schooling has been organised in a way that educates groups, rather than individuals. It is only recently that there have been greater attempts at learner-centred education (in South African schools) that focused on individual learner needs. Working with groups also provided valuable insights into the ways in which identities of young people interact in different group settings. Some problems with working with groups include understanding the complexities of sexual identity and group identity. While group sessions have the positive potential of reducing the power difference between the researcher and the participants by allowing for interaction between the participants, it is possible that groups of young people may be constrained to expressing views that will be acceptable to the others in the group. I attempted to get past stereotypes and restrictions that were likely to emerge as a result of perceived group pressures, by working with individuals as well.

Much of the HIV/AIDS and sexuality researchers focus on single sex groups (for example: Leach et al. 2000; Paulsen 1999; Steward et al. 2000). I recognise the sensitivity of the subject and the possible embarrassment to talk about issues that continue to be, to a large extent, taboo. I decided to work with single-sex as well as mixed-sex groups. I was interested in interaction between girls and boys, and wished to provide the opportunity for discussion and debate between them. Young boys and girls need to talk among themselves, with the opposite sex, and adults to discuss and debate social norms, values, and gender expectations (Weiss et al. 2000). Besides providing opportunities to talk, this could also help young adults, particularly females, develop communication and assertiveness skills to resist physical and psychological pressure to have unwanted sex (Weiss et al. 2000). While I must emphasis that this research was not primarily action-focussed, increased confidence and assertiveness amongst the girls became evident in the focus group discussions, as the research progressed. In this study the mixed-sex group interviews were the longest in duration, with much spontaneous conversation, which provided the richest data. The single sex interviews provided groups of boys and girls with the opportunity to talk about shared experiences as a collective, or differing views about the "other" group (girls or boys respectively). The mixed-sex groups, on the other hand allowed for gender stereotypes, expectations and assumptions to be confronted and challenged. It also provided the opportunity for sharing and learning from each other. The sharing was apparent in the focus group discussions, since once they were started, the participants did not need prompting. The discussion developed a life of its own. The opportunities for learning from each other were there and very likely, but I did not formally assess for learning.

The following data production methods were employed in this study:
a) Elements of Participatory Learning Action (PLA)[14]
b) Scenario writing

---

[14] This approach has also been referred to as Participatory Reflection and Action (PRA) and Participatory Rural Appraisal.

c) Questionnaires

d) Focus group interviews

e) Individual interviews

f) Research diary

a) Elements of PLA (Participatory Learning Action)

PLA has been broadly defined as a growing family of approaches and methods to enable local people to share and analyse their knowledge of life and conditions, to plan and to act (Kaim et al. 1997). This method has increasingly been used in sexual health research in developed and developing countries. Cornwall and Jewkes (1995) assert that whilst conventional health research tends to generate 'knowledge for understanding', most participatory research focuses on 'knowledge for action'. The key element of participatory research lies not in the methods but in the attitudes of the researchers, which in turn determine how, by and for whom the research is conceptualised and conducted. The guiding principles of effective PLA are: good facilitation and communication skills, listening, asking open-ended questions, not prejudicing responses and relaying biases, actively working to reduce the social distance created by status and encouraging and enabling participants to express themselves. Building on these foundations, visualisation methods offer a means by which people can become involved in representing their own realities in their own terms.

PLA is usually used by teams of researchers to help participants carry out their own analysis and appraise their own situation. While I once again acknowledge that my study is not primarily action-focussed, change in behaviour as a result of heightened awareness about risk and sexual practices, is a possibility. Although I do not formally assess this in the course of this study, some positive change was evident in the ways in which learners discussed and debated controversial issues and stereotypes as the data generation progressed.

In this study, I did not use PLA as a method; instead I adapted some of the tools used in PLA to generate data in a participatory way. In particular I used mind-maps, and listing and ranking. Alongside these PLA tools, I used focus-group discussions and in-depth interviews.

I was aware, while planning my research, of my own identity as a female researcher, and its possible influences on the production of data, especially with boys, and looked at what the literature showed about these issues. Previous research indicated that girls were uneasy about discussing sensitive issues with males, but boys did not mind the presence of a female (Kaim et al. 1997). West (1999) found that both female and male respondents indicated a preference to talk to a woman rather than a man about sexuality issues. Being a female researcher, these findings were comforting, but I still chose to work with a male colleague, whenever possible, during the data production stages of the research to reduce the possible impact of the gender of the researcher. My identity as a female researcher is likely to have had an effect on the composition of my sample, which was largely opportunistic. Since much of the participation in the study was voluntary (when I worked with whole classes, there was only one learner who refused to participate in the study), and there were overall more girls who participated than boys, it is likely that girls were more comfortable to speak with me.

It was not easy to get to issues of sexual identity, since it is not an easily understood concept, and not something that could be asked about directly, or even less, observed. I was not only seeking access to the invisible, but also the very private, and often confused and ambivalent. I decided that I would have to infer notions of sexual identity from participants' inputs about themselves, their construction of ideal partners, their relationships with partners and other information that they were willing to share with me.

Mind maps

The mind map exercise was designed to generate data about ideal types and actual types of girls and boys as perceived by different groupings of learners (see table below). I structured the mind mapping exercise by asking the learners to discuss their ideas and reach consensus within the groups. They then had to draw and explain these representations. The drawings served to identify physical attributes and outward appearances, including dress, and the explanations included personal attributes such as personality. I worked with the whole class and for the drawing exercises, in groups of 6-8. The average size is 40. Participants were asked to organise themselves into groups in the following way:

2 X girls groups (6 each)

2X boys groups (6 each)

2X Mixed groups (4 girls + 4 boys)

In this activity, a consensus view is sought, and it was very early in the study when I discovered that working with groups was much more complicated than social science researchers made it out to be. The learners in this study were not accustomed to working in groups. I noticed that the task of producing the drawing became the most important focus and that the best artist in the group was selected to produce a good picture. In this case, as in many more, my own identity as a researcher and an educator came to the fore and I intervened and discussed some principles of group-work. The learners were encouraged to actively involve all members of the group in a discussion before consensus was reached. In many cases there were considerable differences in their ideas of ideal types of girls and boys. I roamed between groups to get a sense of the discussion (about which I made notes), and was particularly interested in any tension within the mixed-sex groups. The instructions to the different groupings are represented in the table below.

		Boys only	Girls only	Mixed group 1	Mixed group 2
An ideal girl	With girls	X	X	X	
	With boys	X	X		X
An ideal boy	With girls	X	X		X
	With boys	X	X	X	

Table 4.1. Summary of instructions for the mind map activity

Listing and Ranking

I worked with a grade 12 class and asked them to organize themselves into groups 5-6. The instruction was to form a list of attributes they would like to find in an ideal partner and then rank the list in order of importance. The participants had no problems with producing a list since it was easy to build a list by writing down the suggestions from individual members of the group. However, when it came to ranking the list, there was considerable disagreement. I decided then that this was not a suitable exercise to do with a group and consensus was not easy. The participants were happy to work on their individual lists. This was valuable in that it was a reminder that while interaction between participants was important, it was just as important to focus on subjective interpretations and experiences. It was also a reminder that educational programs and interventions that was aimed at groups and did not take into account difference, was not likely to meet the needs of individuals.

I worked with a second grade 12 class and asked them to write a list of characteristics that identified them. This was an individual task, which had to be completed during the lesson. Participants were asked to draw up a list that answered the question " Who am I"? (See appendix 1) The learners were surprised that they found this so difficult to do and we agreed that this was too complicated to rank.

b) Scenario writing

Participants were required to work individually and write a short description of a scenario involving a relationship. These provided insights into their awareness of the different kinds of sexual situations and the possible outcomes.

I suggested the following themes, which I selected, based on the literature on young adults' sexual practices within the context of HIV/AIDS:
- ➤ Young girl with a wealthy older man who buys her presents/gives her money,
- ➤ Sexually inexperienced boy discussing girls with his sexually experienced male friends,
- ➤ A girl and boy drinking alcohol on a date and
- ➤ A girl who is finally getting attention from a boy she has fancied for a long time
- ➤ A shy boy getting attention from a popular girl
- ➤ A boy pressurising his girlfriend to have sex
- ➤ Any other kind of relationship

This activity was carried out with a captive group of grade 11 learners. There were 15 boys and 20 girls in the class. By the end of the lesson, many had not completed the task and promised to hand in their written submissions the following day. This activity yielded poor returns, since only 5 boys and 10 girls were prepared to submit their writing and most popular topic (by girls and boys) was, *A boy pressuring his girlfriend to have sex*. I selected some of these written scenarios to stimulate discussion in the focus groups. It was useful to use the descriptions of the learners since it represented the language with which they were familiar.

c) *Questionnaires*
I had not initially intended using questionnaires in this study, which was designed to be a qualitative piece. I had the privilege of discussing my research plan with Patti Lather (who's ideas of feminist research influences my work) in November 2001, while she was at the University of Durban Westville. I mentioned my difficulties with designing instruments to access young peoples' sexual identities and she suggested that I use a short questionnaire in focus groups to stimulate discussion. The suggestion was that this would draw attention directly to the issues that I was interested in discussing and that it was a combination of distance and close methods.

I developed a one-page questionnaire with 5 open and 5 closed questions. The intention was to use a combination of distance and closeness in the process of data generation. Closed ended questions on their own are not very useful since they assume a priori knowledge of the possible range of understandings that people bring to issues such as sex, virginity, homosexuality, etc. Neither the girls nor the boys spoke openly about their own sexual practices and the anonymous questionnaire provided the opportunity to ask direct questions about their own sexual practices. The open-ended questions enabled me to understand and capture points of view of the respondents without predetermining those points of view through prior selection of questionnaire categories. The interviews that were used together with the questionnaires further provided participants with the opportunity, often lacking in traditional surveys, to explain understandings and experiences that elude simple classification.

The questionnaire was not designed in a way to facilitate coding for statistical analysis. I was fortunate to be at Boss Secondary School on a day that the grade 12 learners were rehearsing for their school "prom". I had access to all the grade 12 learners (72) that were not rehearsing on that day and decided to administer the questionnaire in the library, which was a spacious hall, where learners could sit and write privately. The questionnaires had to be completed in my presence and asked questions about:

- ➢ Some biographical details,
- ➢ Whether they were in a relationship,
- ➢ Whether having sex was part of the relationship,
- ➢ Whether they knew of other girls/boys who were sexually active,
- ➢ Whether knowledge about HIV/AIDS influenced their choices in any way and
- ➢ Why young adults engage in unsafe sexual practices

The questionnaires generated quantitative data that will be used for comparisons with the results of the data generated by the other methods.

d) Focus-group interviews

The focus group implies a degree of participation in the phase of data collection. The participants interact with each other rather than the researcher. Focus groups are contrived settings, bringing together a specifically chosen population to discuss a particular theme or topic where the interaction with the group leads to data and outcomes (Cohen, Manion & Morrison 2000). According to Morgan (1988), their contrived nature is both their strength and their weakness: they are unnatural settings and yet they are focused on a particular issue, and therefore will yield insights that might not otherwise have been available in a straightforward interview; they are economic on time, producing a large amount of data in a short period of time, but they tend to produce less data than the same number of individual interviews. This method is being used increasingly in HIV and AIDS research in Africa and bears directly on the way in which sexuality and norms of sexual relations, as well as being privately exercised, is also the subject of public knowledge (Baylies and Bujra 1995). According to Baylies and Bujra (1995), focus group interviews has particular merit in linking the generation of research "data" with collective consciousness raising and holds the potential for linking both to the generation of strategies of protection.

I conducted 9 focus-group interviews (3 boys groups; 3 girls groups and 3 mixed sex groups). Each group consisted of 4-6 participants each. The initial three groups were opportunistic and to a certain extent, self selected. I then recruited other participants through these participants.

I selected some of the scenarios that were written by other learners to stimulate discussion in the focus group. This was a useful approach since it took the attention away from the participants' own sexual practices and focused on an arbitrary situation. The participants interacted actively with each other, with very little input from me. Some of the questions for discussion were about understanding the scenario and possible reasons for particular behaviours, and also to identify possible strategies for protective behaviour. It was very interesting to note the ways in which they tested their ideas against each other, and it seemed obvious to me that opportunities to talk about issues concerning sexuality and relationships were rare. I had been unduly concerned that it would be difficult to get young adults to talk about issues that are usually considered private. Their eagerness to talk within the focus group came as a surprise. Many learners also sought me out during school breaks and came to me in pairs or individually, to ask for advice on relationship problems, or to offer stories of other girls/boys in the school.

The second method that I used to stimulate focus-group discussion was a short questionnaire at the beginning of the discussion. This approach is discussed in the section on questionnaires above. The short questionnaire was intended to draw attention directly to the issues that I was interested in and asked questions about participants own sexual practices as well as what they knew about others. The participants were required to fill in the one-page questionnaire without discussing it with others. They were not required to provide their names. When I observed that they were not keen to have other learners look at their responses and either turned the page over or tried to cover their responses with their hands, I collected the questionnaires and kept them aside during the course of the discussion. I started the discussion with questions about other young adults and then got to more personal questions and information after participants chose to offer personal accounts.

Since the focus group discussions were largely determined by the participants, I did not ask the same questions in each group interview. This makes the analysis of the interview data tricky, and although there were some common themes that emerged in the different interviews, some new themes emerged, and I attempted, where possible, to pursue them in the subsequent interviews. This was a form of snowballing of themes (one theme led to another) and was useful but I was not sure that it was possible to get to an exhaustive list. I selected the most frequently occurring themes for discussion in this research report.

e) Individual interviews

Individual interviews provided insights into aspects of agency at work in the construction and enactment of sexual identities. Issues of sexual identity and sexual practices are often considered private and may not be easily accessed in the presence of peers. The individual interviews were conducted toward the end of my fieldwork, by which time I had been visiting the school for almost year. It was easier to recruit participants for the individual interviews, than I had anticipated. I asked around and identified the most popular boy and the most popular girl in the school and selected two other "more reserved" boys and girls. There were 6 "formal" individual interviews. However, the individual interviews were not easy and did not last for a long time. Compared to the group interviews, which were more conversational, the individual interviews turned out to be more formal than I had intended them to be and participants answered in short sentences and seldom offered more than a straightforward answer to my questions

All interviews were audio recorded, with the consent of the participants. I did not take detailed notes during the interviews, which facilitated a more informal, conversational manner. I did, however, make brief notes on non-verbal responses and also formulated new questions while the interview was in progress. All interviews were fully transcribed (see appendices 6-10 for sample interviews).

f) Research diary

My research diary is an important data source. I wrote detailed descriptive notes from the beginning of my fieldwork. Based on my assumption that everything that I observed and experienced in the field was data, I made notes on the scene, whenever that was possible or alternatively, did so as soon as I left the field. My field notes comprised my observations and recording of interaction between the participants during planned activities, as well as during periods of informal and unplanned activity. I spent a lot of time on the playgrounds, observing and having informal discussions with the learners. This provided me with the opportunity to talk to the participants, outside the planned activities, about how they were experiencing their participation in the study. I had many informal conversations with pairs or groups of learners in the playground. Although the learners mainly initiated these conversations, I used these opportunities to ask questions and probe issues that had arisen in the more formal interviews. I did not take notes during these conversations, since that would have had an impact on the interaction. I tried to record the conversation as accurately as possible as soon as I returned from the field.

The research diary was also used to record my own feelings, reactions to the experience and any preliminary interpretation categories that came to mind. The field notes are an important data source and recorded information about where the observation took place, who was present, what was the physical setting like, what kinds of social interactions occurred?

A summary of the different method used to generate data in this study is represented in table 4.2.

Summary of Data sets

Method		No. of girls	No. of boys	Mixed-sex groups	Total nos.
Elements of PLA	Mind-map of an ideal girl	2 x 6	2 x 6	2 x (4girls+4boys)	40
	Mind-map of an ideal boy	2 x 6	2 x 6	2 x (4girls+4boys)	40
	Matrix ranking of an ideal partner	20 x	9 x		29
	Matrix ranking of problems	3 x 6	3 x 6		36
Scenario writing		10 x	5 x		15
Focus group discussions		3 x (4-6)	3 x (4-6)	3 x (4-6)	36-54
Individual interviews		3 x	3 x		9
Questionnaire		53 x	19 x		72

Table 4.2. Summary of data production methods

4.7. Ensuring Research Rigour

"Rigour" is not a word that am comfortable in using. I feel entrapped in some of this language as I attempt to reconceptualise what these young adults in the study are saying, and know that I am going into a language that is "scientific". I use "rigour" because the language of research is limited in this respect. I have demonstrated, throughout this chapter, continual reflection and reflectivity and in addition to this, triangulation gives me the confidence that I am representing the data as clearly as possible.

To ensure research "rigour", I used three different methods of triangulation:

➢ Multiple methods triangulation
➢ Multiple sources triangulation
➢ Analytical triangulation

Multiple methods triangulation:

I used multiple methods to generate data in this study. Multiple methods facilitate triangulation, which is an important way to strengthen a study design. The quantitative data generated through the questionnaires provided a useful opportunity to compare with the data generated through the qualitative methods. Also, using different qualitative methods to answer the same research questions allowed for comparison and crosschecking the consistency of information derived at different times and by different means within qualitative methods (Patton 1990). This allowed me to compare observational data with written responses and interview data, and to compare what participants say within a group and privately (see section 6.7).

Multiple sources triangulation:

Although the voices of the learners were main source of data in this study, I interviewed the guidance teacher about the nature of sexuality education in Boss Secondary School, and whether and the kinds of concerns the learners brought to her relating to HIV/AIDS and sexuality. This provided me with the opportunity to triangulate the data generated, to a certain extent, by using more than one source.

I also used different learners to check out my preliminary interpretations of the data. I had promised confidentiality to the school and the participants in the study. Since I had not asked for any identifying markers (such as names) in all of the written submissions as well as the interviews, I could not do validation checks with specific individuals and groups. In order to check whether the interpretations that I was making were valid, I took these to other groups of learners and asked whether they agreed with the assumptions and interpretations. In this way, I negotiated the themes that I had selected for analysis of the data (see section 4.6). This method of triangulating data sources proved to be valuable. The participants were very interested in what there colleagues were saying and when they did not agree with my interpretations, it led to interesting discussions about alternative interpretations.

Analytical triangulation:

I used the assistance of a colleague, who is an experienced researcher, and who is familiar with my research, to do a form of analytical triangulation. I gave her a list of the themes that I had decided upon and unmarked transcripts of the focus group discussions (FGDs) and interviews and asked her to read through the transcripts and "label" different responses in the margins (according to the chosen themes). There was much agreement on the classification between my colleague and myself, and we discussed the differences in opinion. A similar process was followed with the coding and classification of the responses to the open-ended questions in the questionnaire. There were some important insights that emerged from the different ways in which two people look at the same set of data

4.8. Methods of data analysis

Although data analysis was continuous throughout the fieldwork, when it formally ended, it was time to consolidate the final analysis. Having generated masses of data using multiple methods, I faced the task of making sense of all of this. The challenge was, how to reduce the volume of data without losing its essence, identify significant themes, and communicate these findings in a written document? I started with a descriptive report of the findings as a response to the critical question to be addressed in this study, namely:

> *How do young adults construct their sexual identities within the context of HIV/AIDS?*

The approach I used to analyse and interpret data, falls within the "hypothesis generating" side of the continuum (see figure 4.3. below). My collaborative-grounded analysis method included inputs from the participants, research colleagues, and myself in co-constructing the data. In this way I focused on the limits of my own interpretations and conceptualisations. I used a combination of a grounded analysis approach (data are not coded in terms of predetermined categories, but from themes that emerge from the data) and two parallel processes of negotiation: one in collaboration with my peers and the other in collaboration with the research participants. I had decided on tentative themes, which I discussed, with my research colleagues and, in separate instances, with research participants. Ambiguous and doubtful themes were negotiated.

The grounded approach helped me to focus on the meaning of the participants. Through involving both the participants and a research colleague in the construction of themes (categories), to interpret and analyse the data, I not only strengthened the analysis themes, but also saw the value of knowledge building in teams.

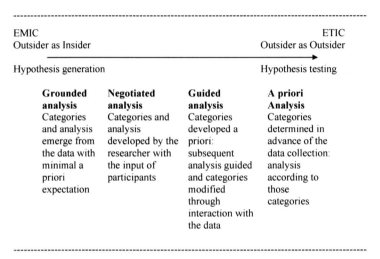

Figure 4.3. Data Analysis and Interpretation (Freeman: 1986: 372, adapted by Samuel 2002)

I began by reading and rereading all the different sets of data to look for prevailing themes that I could use to classify the data. The fluid conception of identity formation and social relations presents particular problems for formation of fixed categories, which have the potential to reify and essentialise social categories. The different data sets produced some common themes, and some that were unique to that particular method. I then organised all the different data sets and the analysis themes in a grid in order to understand how different data sets contributed to the selected themes. I read all the interview transcripts several times before I started making comments in the margins and sometimes attached pieces of paper with paper clips.

I selected emergent themes from frequently voiced understandings and experiences as well as those that were exceptional, the often-overlooked voices from the margin. These developed into the themes within which I eventually grouped the responses. I then began with cross-case analysis (Patton 1990). Patton (1990: 376) explains cross-case analysis as grouping together answers from different people to common questions or analysing different perspectives on central issues. In this case, I grouped responses according to some themes that emerged from the discussions and interviews. Many of these themes are those that emerged from previous data collection methods and some are new ones that came through in-depth discussion.

To analyse the questionnaire responses, I used a computer software program, SPSS (Statistical Program for the Social Sciences). Since I had not initially planned on using the questionnaire as a survey, but to stimulate discussion in small groups, the questionnaire was not constructed in a way that facilitated coding of the responses. It was easy enough to assign code numbers to the closed ended questions (for example, 1:male; 2:female); the open-ended questions required that I develop a coding frame. I did this by reading through a random sample of 10 per cent of the responses (for each of the five questions) and generating a tally of the range of responses as a preliminary to coding classification. I was aware of the dangers of reducing rich data from open-ended questions to a single category. This information was to be used generate frequencies of different responses, and to complement data generated from other methods employed in this study. Having assigned a code to each response on the questionnaires, I processed the data using the SPSS package. This provided useful information about frequencies of responses in terms of the other variables.

4.9. Representation of data

The participants clearly valued the opportunity that the research process opened up for them to talk amongst themselves about issues that are usually silenced. I also got a sense that they valued the opportunity to speak to me, since they often voiced concern about the lack of open communication about sexuality across the generations. I would assume that it was the non-judgmental stance that I had adopted in my interaction with the participants, as well as my deliberate attempt to disassociate with the adults with authority over them (their parents and educators) that allowed them to trust my intentions. It was clear that such opportunities for interactions with adults were rare.

As I have discussed before, I represent the data in terms of the themes that emerged from the data (see section 4.7). I draw on the data produced through the different methods that contribute to the different themes. The main methods of data generation were the focus group discussions and the individual interviews.

I tossed around with the question of how to represent the participants of the study. Although I use the term "adolescent" when I refer to literature mainly from psychology, I do not find this to be an appropriate term, as it has connotations of a fixed developmental stage with a fixed set of characteristics. The participants are secondary school learners, but calling them "learners" would imply that they were part of some intervention program, which was not the case. I thought about "youth", but this term has been masculinised in much of the literature. "Young people" seemed too vague, and furthermore, as a thirty-something researcher myself, I like to think of myself as a "young person". The participants were aged 15-19, which made them "teenagers", but this was not an accurate description since it is a grouping that includes 13 and 14 year olds as well. "Young adults" seem to be a more appropriate representation, as it does not have implications of the innocence of childhood, and acknowledges some maturity. The participants however refer to themselves as "girls" and "boys", and since my methodological stance is to celebrate their voices, I represent much the data in terms of "girls" and "boys".

4.10. Conclusion

In this chapter I began with a discussion of the broad methodological approach used in this study, including some conceptual issues related to the methodology that guides this research. I then detailed the sampling procedure and discuss the various research methods used to generate data in this inquiry and describe the methods of data analysis. In the following chapter, I present the findings and a discussion thereof.

As I stated in this chapter, I categorised the data into some common themes that emerged from the data (see Section 4.7.). These themes were in many ways linked and could not be viewed as strict categories. Therefore, where it is appropriate they will be discussed as linked themes in the next chapter.

CHAPTER FIVE

YOUNG ADULTS' SEXUAL IDENTITY CONSTRUCTIONS WITHIN THE CONTEXT OF HIV/AIDS: FINDINGS AND DISCUSSION

5.1.Introduction

In the previous chapter, I discussed the methodological considerations of the study and the different methods employed to generate data in this exploration of young adults' sexual identities within the context of HIV/AIDS. In this chapter, I extract the data generated through the various methods and tools simultaneously to launch a multifaceted discussion of participant's accounts of their sexual identity constructions within the context of HIV/AIDS.

As can be expected, striking differences between male and female responses did emerge, but some significant similarities were evident as well. Because of the largely opportunistic nature of the fieldwork, I did not work with the equal numbers of girls and boys, as I would have liked to. There were overall more girls than boys who participated in the study. I discussed reasons for such a sample in section 4.6.

Throughout the study, I have privileged the voices of the participants, and represent the findings in a way that reflects this methodological stance, by presenting much of participants' own articulations. I have already discussed the use of a gendered approach in the generation of data, focusing on girls (g); boys (b); and boys and girls (bg) together (see Chapter Four). Wherever possible, I will present and discuss the data within these groupings. This is neither to essentialise nor reify categories of boys and girls, as I look at the similarities as well as the differences within and between these groupings.

As I stated in the previous chapter, I categorised the data into some common themes that emerged from the data. The subheadings in this chapter are organised in terms of these themes. The findings from this study are represented and discussed in one unified chapter, which reflects the interconnectedness between the themes. The chapter therefore represents the theoretical understanding of *Identity* which foregrounds the interrelatedness of:

- ➢ identity constructions and performances,
- ➢ conceptions of "self" and influences of "others",
- ➢ internal policing and policing by peers and adults and
- ➢ mutual shaping of sexual identity and the HIV/AIDS climate.

All these interrelated correlates are presented for the sake of emphasis and clarity in separate sections. They should not be understood as essentialising the young adults' sexual identity constructions within the context of HIV/AIDS.

The first emerging theme from the data involves *Explanations for coupling* (section 5.2.). Forming relationships seem to constitute an important part of young adult's life and is often the place where young adults negotiate their sexual lives in an atmosphere of diverse understandings, which include personal, social and physical dimensions. The theme relating to *Nature and "jumping" hormones* (section 5.3.) follows and this section, and examines the understandings of the participants based on their biological development during their teenage years. The next theme that relates to self and peers, is *Body and beauty* (section 5.4.). In this section, I discuss the participants' understandings based on physical attractiveness: of self, and others. The theme, *Virginity, abstinence and marriage* (section 5.6) looks at the gendered differences in the context of the participants' present sexual relations and projected future sexual practices. The next theme, *The peer gaze* (section 5.7.), examines the ways in which the boundaries are policed by peers in constructions of sexual identity.

Heterosexuality and homophobic performances (section 5.8.), looks at the dominance of heterosexuality as a norm within which participants' sexual identity is negotiated. This is followed by *Disciplining of pleasure* (section 5.9.), which examines the ways in which the HIV/AIDS climate has impacted on young adults' sexual experiences. The final theme is *Intergenerational dynamics* (section 5.10.), which examines the generational tensions between the participants and adults (mainly parents and teachers).

5.2. Explanations for coupling

Love, romance, sexual experimentation and intense friendships have long been recognised as part of the adolescent experience (Paul and White 1990), and these have been taken-for-granted aspects of teenage life. I was interested in finding out why young adults felt that it was important to be part of a relationship. One of the open-ended questions in the questionnaire asked about the reasons young adults have girlfriends/boyfriends. For most of the participants, romantic relationships are understood as an important part of their social world. Their responses were grouped into categories and are represented in Table 5.1.

			relationships			
			peer pressure	phase of life	companio nship	sex
Sex	male	Row %	26.3	21.1	5.3	47.4
	female	Row %	28.8	36.5	28.8	5.8

Table 5.1. Questionnaire responses to, "Why do young people have girlfriends/boyfriends?"

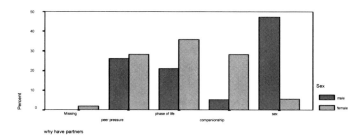

Figure 5.1. Graphical representation of the responses of boys and girls to question, " Why do young people have girlfriends/boyfriends?"

5.2.1. Girls: explanations for coupling

Of the 72 respondents on the questionnaire, 28.8% of the girls mentioned *companionship* as the reason that girls have relationships with boys, in comparison to 5.3% of the boys (see table 5.1.). The need to form relationships was seen as imperative at this stage in their lives. The motivation for increased interest in sexuality and gendered relationships stems from both cultural expectations and sexual maturation (Newman and Newman 1991). It is apparent that this need is understood in personal terms as well as in terms of the expectations of the peer group. Peer group influences are discussed in section 5.7.

Finding "Mr. Right" is one of the most important experiences that girls cite as giving meaning and significance to their lives. This idea came up often in the girls' focus group discussions as well as their individual interviews. For example:

> *By having a boyfriend you are able to confide in them. We are not insecure anymore and there is someone who cares. You then feel good about yourself. Having a boyfriend is a disadvantage because it affects school. But it is very difficult to avoid. (g #34)*[15]

The above respondent suggests the compelling nature of the need to be in a relationship. She also suggests that having someone who cares for you increases your

---

[15] This notation refers to a questionnaire response by a girl.

94

own self worth. Samet and Kelly (1987), in their investigation of the relationship of dating to self-esteem and sex role identity among adolescents, found that romantic involvement is associated with social competence and positive self-esteem.

Many of the girls equate not having a boyfriend to being *alone.* Having a boyfriend is seen to be so natural that being without a boyfriend is being with no one, and being alone is unnatural (Currie 1999, quoted in van Roosmalen 2000).

> *To explore and experiment. They probably also think it's "cool". They don't like to be alone. It scares them. It is "in" to be in a relationship. (g #4)*

> *Teenagers usually go through a hormonal crisis with confused emotions. They feel lonely, distant, isolated so they need a partner. I think girls are in love with the term love, and therefore rush into relationships at this age. (g #3)*

The above participant (g#3) introduces many complex ideas. She writes about 'hormones' (biological determinants) and the need to combat loneliness, as well as signals the confused reasons for relationship formation. The question addressed young adults in general, and did not ask about the individual participants, so the responses ranged from references to, young adults in general, to girls only (or boys only), to individuals, but seldom about themselves.

One girl even suggests that you are *incomplete* without a boyfriend. For example, responding to the question about why girls have boyfriends:

> *There is a stage that comes to life where young people feel like they are incomplete without someone to rely on. (g #64)*

Girls often mentioned the need to talk about and understand feelings and according to West (1999), feelings are seldom talked about in sex education. Overwhelmingly, the girls and boys talked of each other as "opposites" and displayed some curiosity about the other and a desire to get to know "the other". The following responses also demonstrate their understanding that relationships are natural during these years.

> *Teenagers like me out there feel they need love and attention from someone of the opposite sex and someone to talk to and someone who understands them and although a friend could fit this criteria, having a boyfriend makes me feel special and of course it is natural at our age. (g #19)*

> *Most youngsters want to know what it is like to be in a relationship. Many*
> *express that coupling provides an opportunity to discuss their personal*
> *problems and also for pleasures. They like to communicate with the opposite*
> *sex (g #17).*

It is unclear what "pleasures" g#17 refers to, it is likely it is sexual pleasures, but could also be social, personal pleasures.

In the self identity data (see appendix 14), 17 of the 20 girls identified themselves in terms of relationships (with boys), for example " *enjoy the company of the opposite sex*" and "*faithful partner*". This shows the value placed on relationships with "the opposite sex".

Girls mainly constructed ideal relationships in terms of *love* and *trust* and *companionship*. This construction of dominant forms of femininity by girls comes up frequently in the data. I discuss the implications of this construction for sexual safety in section 5.5.

It was evident in much of the girls responses that having a boyfriend was necessary to fulfil a "need", and this "need" was qualified in terms of sharing feelings, communicating and improving their self worth. This was markedly different from many of the boys' ideas of the need for relationships at this age, as they saw coupling as a means to gain access to sex (see section 5.2.2).

> *To be loved and feel wanted. To have someone you can confide in and trust.*
> *To experience what it's like to be loved by the opposite sex (g#20)*

> *I think they need someone to share their emotion and also to get attention from*
> *and to please themselves (g #33)*

In their constructions of ideal partners (see appendix 13), girls referred to desirable personality traits that they would like in a partner. *Honesty* and *trust* was seen to be the most valued trait in an ideal partner (13 of the 20 girls ranked *honesty* and *trust* toward the top of their ranked lists of desirable traits in an ideal partner). In the self-identity exercise (see appendix 14), 14 out of the 20 girls identified themselves as being faithful and honest within a relationship. The terms, "honesty', "trust" and "faithful" referred to being true to a relationship by not being part of another relationship at the same time. It is evident then that *honesty* and *trust* are seen by girls to be one of the most important basis for romantic relationships. They position themselves in these terms and expect it from their partners. However, they admitted that they were prepared to settle for much less. In the focus group interviews, girls often mentioned that their boyfriends did not treat them with the kind of respect and affection that they would like, but they were prepared to overlook the unhappiness some relationships with boyfriends brought them. It seems that being in a relationship was all-important, more important than exercising their agency within the interactions with boyfriends.

During my informal conversations with girls, they frequently communicated some inner conflict in their realisation that they often did not make any personal demands and often submitted to the boys' demands within the relationship, for fear of losing the boyfriend. The girls mainly coupled with older boys in the school or sometimes with boys outside the school. They were aware that boys, in their school, often gossiped to other boys and spread stories about what went on in the relationship, but felt powerless to act against this. This suggests that girls believed that boys were accustomed to revealing, or even fabricating the details of the romantic relationships. There was also awareness among the girls that not all boys were the same, that there were differences between boys and their interaction with girls.

I used a scenario written by another participant, which described an incident of a boy who pressured his girlfriend to have sex (see figure 5.2.) to stimulate discussion in focus group with girls. For example:

Topic: A boy pressurising his girlfriend to have sex

A boy said to a girl, "my girlfriend, I want to say something to you today. I know that you are going to say 'no', but I love you. You are my girlfriend. You are my only girlfriend, sweetheart. Darling, please for only today I want to show you how much I love you and how much I care about you. Please sweet come and lets kiss. Please girl, I feel like we can have sex". The girl says "no". "Why not? Please sweet I love you. See girl, there is nothing that can happen because I love you. Lets have sex." The boy romance the girl until the girl becomes very on. The boy said " I cant do it, honey". The girl said, " but...what but, because you love me and I love you". After the girl said "yes" they have sex. The boy feels very nice. The girl feels the same thing, terrible.

Figure 5.2. Scenario written by a girl. This was used to stimulate discussion in a focus group

There is evidence that girls struggle to be feminine (which includes depending on boys for affirmation, being submissive and displaying that they were sexually unknowing) and yet resist the cultural impositions of femininity. The following extract shows some of the inner conflict experienced by girls in their attempt to form and to maintain a relationship (these ideas are discussed further in section 5.5. in this chapter)

Thami (g):	*yes, it does happen. Boys think that if they tell you that they love you then you will have to do anything to please him.*
Zubi (g):	*Some girls are scared that if they refuse him then they will get dumped.*
Ayesha (g):	*Some boys are only interested in one thing.*
Thami (g)	*Not all boys, Mam*[16]. *Some boys, not all know how to treat a girl.*
Shakila (r)	*How do girls like to be treated?*
Thami (g):	*To be made special. To accept me for what I am.*
Zubi (g):	*To be faithful to you, not to dump you for someone else as soon as you say you don't want to go further than kissing.*
Shlo (g):	*Some girls like rough boys. These boys act like gangsters and the other boys are scared of them.*

Thami's response to the way in which girls like to be treated, reflects some of the ways in which young women attempt to challenge notions of traditional heterosexual femininity (which, in this case is to be "accept me for what I am") and at the same time, leave them in place ("made to be special" by boys). These types of contradictions between intention and expectation are discussed further in Chapter Six.

5.2.2. Boys: explanations for coupling

For many of the boys, having a partner is often associated with access to sexual pleasure. 47.4% of the boys mentioned having sex as the reason for having a partner, compared to 5.8% of the girls (see table 5.1). An example of a boy's response is:

They feel lonely and they get horny and they want to get it on (b #46)

In their ranked matrices of an ideal partner, both of the boys groups and 10 out of 13 (see *Appendix 13*) of the individual boys mentioned the willingness to have, and the

---

[16] This was the way they addressed their teachers, so it seems that despite my efforts to remain detached from the school, the participants saw me as an educator.

ability to enjoy sex as being important in a partner. Here, there seems to be an acceptance of female desire. However, it is only as a means to enhance male pleasure. These were evident in expressions such as: "must be horny", "must enjoy sex" and "must be highly sexed".

In the self-identity data (see *Appendix 14*), 5 of the 9 boys identified themselves in terms of their relationships with girls, for example, "love women". In the same exercise, only 1 out of the 9 boys identified himself as being honest and faithful within a relationship, in comparison with 14 out of the 20 girls who did so (see section 5.2.1).

Like the girls, most boys referred to girls as the "opposite sex". This setting up of each other in opposition to themselves, is what facilitated their understanding that they have different and separate needs and expectations of each other. The following is an example of such a view:

> *What I believe is that life can be really hectic at times so you need someone you can share your life with, someone of your opposite sex. Definitely you won't think the same and that way you are able to learn about the other species and face life's dilemmas with them. And of course natural people fall in love. (b#57)*

This boy goes further than "opposites" and sees girls as being of a different "species" from boys. His understanding of girls being and thinking differently from boys, is what makes a relationship between them possible.

In the following excerpt from an individual interview, Sibusiso shows some understanding about the coercive nature of male sexual behaviour and its effect on women. This kind of awareness and sensitivity was not a feature of boys' group discussions.

Sibusiso (b):   *A boy who pressurises his girl to have sex is not a patient person. He wants to rush the relationship just to have sex and if the girl says "no", then the relationship will end. So to let the relationship carry on she will have to say, "yes" although she does not want or not ready to have sex.*
Shakila: *What about (girls) having boyfriends for companionship?*

Sibusiso (b)   O.K. some, and there are some boys who are caring and patient.

In the focus group discussions (both boys' groups and mixed-sex groups), boys were silent about issues of feelings and love; instead they talked about sex, and put on a sexually knowing performance. Boys felt that they expected to, and were expected to know about sexual matters. However in the individual interviews, boys displayed a lot more sensitivity towards relationships and towards girls. In individual interviews, two of the boys mentioned that boys teased other boys who were in love and suggested that they were weakened and no longer in-charge. Showing feelings towards a girl meant that they ran the risk of being dependent on the girl, hurt, dismissed or rejected. It seems that in the presence of their peers, boys felt the need to talk in a sexually explicit way, distanced from issues of love and romance, but away from their peers, they demonstrated some characteristics usually associated with girls (such as hurt and heartache). This implies that the boundaries between masculinities and femininities, for these boys are not always clear, that they often become hazy. This is important to note, especially if we see the need the reconstitute notions of masculinities and femininities that inhibit positive change towards gender equity.

5.2.3. Girls and boys: explanations for coupling

The mixed groups provided the opportunity for discussion and sharing about the expectations from the "other" and the assumptions about the "other". Part of the focus-group discussion schedule was designed to probe the participants' ideas about expectations within and from a relationship, by partners as well as themselves. Sexual activity was viewed by many of the boys as a route to physical pleasure, while girls largely viewed sexual activity as an expression of intimacy. Some of the girls talked about sex as a sacred part of marriage and these views are discussed further in section 5.6.

The ways in which they generally discussed relationship matters made it clear that the majority of the participants continued to accept and perform traditional masculine and feminine identities. However, there were some signs of these notions being challenged, by girls as well as by boys. Below is a citation from a discussion within a mixed-sex group.

Smanga (b):	*... now at this stage he promise he'll be with you everyday. Let's say he*
	starts cheating on you, that gives you the right to cheat on him as well.
Simphiwe (g):	*I wouldn't cheat on him.*
Smanga (b):	*What will you do?*
Simphiwe (g):	*I'll just sit at home and wait for him...*
Smanga (b):	*Wait for him to come back?*
Simphiwe (g):	*Yes*
Gugu (g):	*Ha, ha, ha* (exaggerated laughter)

In the above snippet Smanga's "this stage" refers to the initial stages of a relationship. He postures the idea of gender equality within relationships, that girls should have the same demands for fidelity in a relationship that boys have, and challenges Simphiwe's submissive stance. The two girls differ in their ideas of ideal relationships. Gugu does not agree with Simphiwe's idea of remaining patient and pure in a relationship, no matter what your boyfriend does. Simphiwe clearly acts out aspects of dominant heterosexual femininity, while the boys and the other girl in the group show signs of resisting them.

Many of the girls expressed the opinion that girls and boys had different expectations within a relationship: boys expect sex, girls expect companionship and love, or in some cases, money. There is evidence for this in the different responses from girls and boys above. A commonly held view by girls was:

> *Having a relationship is not about sex; it's about love and care. Many girls are fooled by the boys because the only thing they want is sex. (g #34)*

For many girls there is no distinction between *love* and *sex*. Conforming to dominant notions of femininity, sex was "love-making". Many boys, on the other hand, saw the link between *sex* and *love* as being weak, at least in the way they spoke about it in group settings.

The issue of initiating sex in a relationship was one which surfaced repeatedly in the focus-group discussions. Many of the girls see sex as something that they can give to

101

a boy. The views frequently expressed suggested that boys are usually the agents and girls the objects, and that boys assume power, girls often relinquish it. It came as no surprise in their accounts of sexual initiation that there was overwhelming agreement by both girls and boys that it is (and should be) boys who initiate sexual activity. Moreover, many girls and boys agreed that it was not "normal", but it was now more acceptable for girls to initiate a sexual relationship. A typical response to who initiates sexual activity in a relationship was:

Thabisile (g): I think it's boys, that's how it has to be.

Girls were strongly policed by boys who found it easier to prescribe what girls should not do rather than what girls should do. The sex/gender boundary maintenance was expressed, as "girls should not behave like boys". Some of the girls and boys displayed an awareness that girls sometimes initiate relationships and sexual activity, but there was disagreement about the appropriateness of such practices.

Shakila: *Do girls come after boys?*
Colin (b):   *Yes Mam. Some girls are like boys. They just come up to you and ask you out.*
Shakila: *How do you feel about such girls?*
Alan (b):   *It's cool. They have equal rights. They always say that they are equal to*
                    us. Then they must prove it.
Colin (b):   *I don't really feel comfortable with that. I think that I like a girl, then I must go up to her. I don't like a girl who has been with every boy in the school.*

Even though Alan concedes that it is acceptable for girls to initiate a relationship, he follows this with suggestion of scepticism of equality between girls and boys. Colin is quite clear that it is the boys' prerogative to initiate relationships, and girls who do so are taking on a masculine performance. This construction of male and female sexuality possibly reflects the inequalities of the broader social patterns, but there seems to be an 'equal rights' approach to sex being postured.

In the following excerpt from a mixed-sex group discussion, both the girls and the boys agree that boys are more interested in sex than girls are. This was a commonly held view, although there was some indication (mainly from girls) that this was not always the case. There is some evidence that girls are actively constructing themselves as desiring beings.

Simmi (g):	*Do you think teenagers go out with each other because they want to have sex?*
Rita (g):	*O.K. majority, but not all.*
Vukani (b):	*Especially boys.*
Rita (g):	*Exactly. The males, especially the males.*
Raj (b):	*All I want to say is that if you'll are having sex; you'll must use a condom.*
Vukani (b):	*You must condomise, ya.*

Both Raj and Vukani display that they are sexually knowing and Vukani uses the slogan (condomise) from many of the HIV/AIDS education campaigns, showing awareness of safe sex discourses. It is also likely that this display was due to my presence as an adult researcher.

5.3. Nature and "jumping" hormones

On the item about the reasons for having partners during these years of their lives, in the questionnaire, 21.1% of the boys and 36.5% (see table 5.1) of the girls mentioned that this was natural and expected during these years of life.

5.3.1. Girls: understandings of hormones as a driving force

Many girls see their teenage years as a transitional phase, between childhood and adulthood. They understand this as a phase where it is only natural that they experiment with relationships with the "opposite sex". The following are examples of responses to the open-ended question in the questionnaire about why girls have relationships.

> *It is at this age that people become attracted to the opposite sex and seek companionship. The fact of being alone scares some females, as they will be thought as "off the shelf" later on. Therefore they long to be in a relationship at an earlier stage. (g #7)*

> *It is a stage in our lives when we are attracted to the opposite sex (g #5)*

103

> *Teenagers usually go through a hormonal crisis with confused emotions (g 3#)*

> *I think that they're at an age of so-called "maturity". They want to experience things. They don't want to be called "children" anymore. They want to fit in with the adult click. (g #30)*

Girls often talked about *sex* in the context of romantic relationships and love, and the need to be and feel loved. None of the girls mentioned their hormones being a driving force toward sexual activity.

> *To experience the different personalities of each other and to have experience in the sex field. It's important to be loved by the opposite sex, when life gets you down. Relationship may mature a couple. (g #28)*

> *For love, sex. They feel the need to be loved by someone. Experience sexual pleasure. Emotional feeling is intense for each other and they want to get to know more about the other sex. (g #10).*

5.3.2. Boys: understandings of hormones as a driving force

These years of their lives is understood by majority of the boys as being hormonal and experimental. For example, an individual response:

> *Because as we get bigger we have certain needs such as sex, so by having a girlfriend we can obtain these needs. (b #45)*

In a group of boys, similar ideas were expressed:

> *Themba (b):*   *The moment you reach 13, 14, 15, your hormones start*
> *Lucky (b):*   *Jumping*
> *Themba (b):*   *Then you wont be able to wait for the age of 27 to get married.*
> *Lucky (b):*   *He is talking on behalf of boys. (Mixed-sex interview 1)*

The following boy talks about sex as being an essential activity that marks the success of this phase of life. This understanding of biology as destiny, and of sex been a compulsory activity for boys at this stage of life, has the potential to lead to coercive behaviour being seen as a right. This is discussed further in section 5.8.

> *I think it's about experiencing life and to feel loved and knowing about sex because other teens speak about sex and if you haven't experienced it you feel the grief of making sure that you go through it (b #54)*

> *They feel lonely and they get horny and they want to get it on (b #46)*

Many of the boys see their teenage years as being transitory and preparation for their later adult lives and I was surprised at the frequency at which the boys mentioned future marriage plans. For example, responses to the question "why do young people have relationships?"

> *It's part of nature. We all need someone to share our joys and sorrows with, that's why we love and fall in love. At this age, it is our journey for our wedding. (b #59)*

> *To experiment in sexual activities. So when you are married you are experienced enough to satisfy and pleasure her well enough. (b # 48)*

> *So they will get to know each other better for the future stage- when they get married. (b #53)*

The above responses were typical of boys' ideas expressed in the questionnaire as well as in individual and group discussions. This is a further indication of teenage years being separated from adulthood, to which teenagers had to aspire.

The following boy is the only one who mentioned love and sex together, and even then, he talks about them as being independent of each other.

> *Boys have girlfriends to gain experience about love. Or just to have sex. (b #56)*

5.3.3. Girls and boys: understandings of hormones as a driving force

It was not only boys who thought that sexual experimental was natural at this stage of their lives. In a mixed-sex discussion, Andile introduces the idea that girls also experience desire. This is important because girls' sexual desire is seldom talked about. She also mentions that having sex was an essential aspect of one's life.

Andile (g):	*What if you want to have sex?*
Precious (g):	*Why should you want to have sex?*
Andile (g):	*To satisfy you needs. And it's good for your health.*
Lucky (b):	*Then you masturbate.*
Precious (g):	*Why should you masturbate?*
Andile(g):	*Because you are not having enough sex.*
Precious (g):	*I'm not masturbating and I am not having sex.*
Andile (g):	*Ya. Still early days dear, still early days.*
Precious (g):	*I am 16 and going to be turning 17.*
Themba (b):	*Maybe you do but you won't say it...*
Precious (g):	*Why should I do it?*
Andile (g):	*Because you will have sex sooner or later. Ya, we are supposed to do it.*
Precious (g):	*But I am different.*
Themba (b):	*You like mentally different! O.K. Priest?*

This was the first time that the issue of masturbation was raised by the participants. The fact that this was raised spontaneously in a mixed-sex setting surprised me. I became aware that these young people were very knowledgeable about sexual issues and had the vocabulary in which to express their knowledge. My initial embarrassment was a sharp reminder of the kinds of awkwardness adult sex educators are likely to face in dealing with traditionally taboo topics in a direct way. Masturbation has been conceptualised here as having a function of replacing (hetero)sexual activity. The participants in the above conversation (the boys and one of the girls) position sexual activity as a definite need at this age.

Precious was clearly seen to be different from other girls, by the girls and the boys in this group as well as by herself. This difference was explained by Andile to be a passing phase ("still early days"), while she assumes greater maturity. Themba mockingly points out that she is exceptional or odd ("priest").

I asked about what was an appropriate age to begin a sexual relationship and here again Precious expresses her differences with the rest of the group. Both the boys suggest a younger age than the two girls:

Precious (g):	*At least 21. all I can do now is have crushes and flings. I am not capable of that (a sexual relationship) at the moment. I am too young.*
Themba (b):	*Now is the right time.*
Lucky (b):	*Ya, 16.*
Andile (g):	*Mam, you can have a sexual relationship anytime you feel ready.*

106

Shakila:	*How old....?*
Lucky (b):	*O.K. 14.*
Precious (b):	*14! No ways. You can't even be responsible.*
Themba (b):	*16 is legal.*
Precious (b):	*16 is too young.*
Andile (g):	*Ya. When you are 18 you get involved in a sexual relationship.*

From the excerpt above, it is clear that there was much variation in the ideas of the appropriate age to begin sexual activity. The legal age[17] of consent to sexual intercourse was not clear, and it was not an important deciding factor in sexual negotiations.

In a mixed group interview, the boys explained their need to have sex at an early age as a means to ensuring sexual fidelity within later marriage. The girls in this group did not agree with this explanation that boys' early sexual experience was to ensure that they would make better husbands later on.

Themba (b):	*When you are 15, 16, 17, you just keep yourself cool. You don't go after girls. You say you are waiting to be married. You will find it a problem* *when you are married because it is a matter of must for a person 15, 16, to have sex. So when they get married they won't cheat on their wives.*
Precious (g):	*I disagree. It's not a matter of must.*
Lucky (b):	*That's what guys believe.*

In the above citation, Lucky typically agrees with the boys in the group about the compelling need for early sexual experiences for boys. During the course of the same discussion (below), he begins to challenge boys' understanding of power within relationships and then submits to the commonly male view, that boys are unable to control themselves in a sexual situation. This view that uncontrollable urges were a natural male reaction was accepted by girls as well.

Shakila	*If a girl says "no", what do you do?*
Lucky (b)	*One thing for sure, I won't be forceful.*
Themba (b)	*There are two different kinds of "no". There's a 'no" with a smile in it and there's a strong "no".*

---

[17] The legal age of consent for sexual intercourse, in South Africa is currently 18. This is presently under review.

Lucky (b)	*"no" is "no" anytime*
Shakila:	*How can you tell when "no" is not really "no"?*
Themba (b)	*They (girls) say "no" for their pride…*
Precious (g)	*When you say "no", the guy needs to back off.*
Themba (b)	*They say "no' too late. There are times when you haven't got to stop, you got to carry on.*
Lucky (b)	*Can I say something? Sometimes girls say "no" just for the sake of their pride. They can't say "yes".*
Shakila:	*So how do you know which times they mean it and which times they are not meaning it?*
Lucky (b)	*It's up to myself, I can't really say.*

From the above citation, it is apparent that subtle forms of coercion may not be interpreted, by boys or girls, as coercion at all. For some boys, resistance from girls is seen as a form of sexual play, only because she cannot say, "yes" too quickly. The girls in this group challenge that assumption.

5.4. Body and beauty

As it can be expected, girls and boys placed immense value on physical attractiveness- their own as well as potential partners'. According to Sears (1992) in the average American high school, the hidden curriculum teaches teenagers that in order to be popular, one has to be attractive, physically fit and able bodied, heterosexual, conform to gender-role expectations, and dress according to school norms. The same can be said for the hidden curriculum in South African secondary schools.

The table below summarises the responses of the different groupings (girls only, boys only, girls and boys, individual girls and individual boys) on desirable characteristics in an ideal partner.

Girls-only group	Boys-only group	Mixed-sex Groups		Individual girls	Individual boys
		Ideal girl	Ideal boy		
Good looks are important	Good looks are important	Good looks	Good looks	Good looks was second on the list	Good looks on the top of most lists
An athletic body is attractive	Mention of nice lips, nice size breasts, smooth legs, nice "butt"	Mention of long eyelashes, nice eyes, cute nose, long fingers.	Mention of muscles, nice chest, nice "bum", chest, nice hair	Mention of tall, big chest, nice hair, nice "butt", cute smile, "six-pack[18]"	Mention of shorter than them
Mention of kissable lips, perfect "butt", nice chest, muscular arms and legs	Sexy body	Mention of soft lips, nice size breasts, nice thighs, flat stomach			Good legs, nice "bum", big "tits", Sexy body
A sexy voice		Athletic body			

**Table 5.2. Summary of data from the mind-maps and matrix ranking exercise on what
constitutes an ideal partner.**

5.4.1. Girls: ideas on body and beauty

In their mind maps of ideal partners, it was unanimous in girl groups that good looks
are important. There was also special mention of an athletic body, and this was clearly
represented in their drawings (see *Appendix 11* for examples).

Girls also depicted attractive girls, with well-shaped bodies being preferred by boys.
The boys' representations of ideal partners were highly erotic and conformed to
stereotypically sexualised versions of girls (see *Appendix 11* for examples).

In the self-identity exercise (see *Appendix 14*), 5 of the 20 girls identified themselves
as being "good looking" or " beautiful". This construction of beauty is clearly in
terms of the male gaze. In their lists of problems faced by girls, all of the groups
mentioned physical appearance as being a significant concern, such as, "pimples" and
"facial hair".

---

[18] "six-pack" refers to a muscular abdomen with defined muscles

In my interview with the school guidance counsellor, I gathered that one of the sources of struggles over sexual identities in Boss Secondary School was the transgressing of proper school uniform and wearing of make-up by girls. This, together with my informal discussions with the learners in the playground led me to believe that that both learners and teachers see both dress and make-up as being overtly sexual. The wearing of make-up was therefore in conflict with the culture of the school, which prohibited overt display of sexuality. Nonetheless, I noticed a substantial number of girls wearing some form of make-up. I spotted girls having mirrors stuck to the inside of their desk-lids and occasionally touching-up lip-gloss or eyeliner, especially when they changed classes, or before they went outside during breaks.

There is a compulsory school uniform for girls and boys, in this school it was apparent that the girls individualise and customise their school uniforms as far as is possible within the school regulations. This is probably done mainly with an eye to fashion, but it can also be interpreted as being overtly provocative. While the wearing of trousers under the school dress was initially a cultural practice of the Muslim girls in school, it has currently become a common practice by the majority of the girls in school. Girls often wear very short dresses over trousers, and belts loosely around their hips. Some girls have their dress buttons daringly unbuttoned so that their cleavages are exposed. It was clear that many of the girls projected themselves as objects of male desire.

The wearing of make-up was also connected with issues of ethnic and religious identity. A Muslim girl, for instance is not expected to wear make-up or flaunt sexuality in the way she dresses or displays body language such as a style of walking and there is evidence of girls policing each other.

> *As a Muslim, Sumaya should be more respectful and not dress and walk like a
> cheap girl (a Muslim girl on dress)*

Learner judgement on their peers appears to be varied. Some girls were very sharp in their judgements about other girls. It presents an interesting example of how feminine heterosexuality may be split between the cultural versions of purity (a "good Muslim girl" should not display her sexuality) and the westernised version (girls should look overtly sexy to be desirable to boys). I did not systematically explore the influences of religion on sexual identity constructions, and only raise it as and when it comes through the accounts of the participants.

5.4.2. Boys: ideas on body and beauty

Boys' mind maps of an ideal partner revealed that an overtly sexy looking girl was favoured (see *Appendix 11* for examples). They also understood that girls preferred good looking and muscular boys. Boys' drawn representations of ideal girls were highly eroticised, and their written explanations were sexually explicit, through mention of girls' breasts, legs, and specific parts of the body.

In the self-identity exercise, none of the 9 boys identified themselves as being physically attractive, in comparison to 5 of the 20 girls. However, all of the boys' groups cited physical appearances that they associated with teen years as being a problem, such as "pimples", "lack of facial hair" and "shaving rash".

The strategy to individualise school uniform seems more resounding for girls than boys. The accounts of the guidance counsellor suggested that she either did not think that boys attempted much to individualise their school uniform, or she did not see the manner of dress to be an issue for boys. I observed that boys styled and gelled their hair into spikes but there was not much variation, since most boys wore their hair in a similar style, being very short around the back and sides and an upright flat top. It did not seem like make-up was worn by boys (except hair gel) and when I asked about this in my informal discussions with them, they thought that the very idea of boys wearing make-up was absurd. They obviously did not consider hair-gel to be make-up since make-up was only associated with girls attempts to beautify themselves.

5.4.3. Girls and boys: ideas on body and beauty

In the mixed-sex groups, during the mind-map exercise, I encouraged the participants to discuss and debate their ideas of an ideal girl and an ideal boy and represent their consensus view. Although there was much discussion, it was clear that both boys and girls agreed that physical attractiveness was significant in a partner. There were specific references to particular body parts, such as, "nice bum", 'nice chest", "nice muscles", "nice fingers", for an ideal boy, and "nice eyes", "long eyelashes", "nice size breasts", "nice legs", for an ideal girl. While athletic images were favoured in boys, eroticised images were favoured for girls.

In general, there was ample evidence to show that teenagers overtly sustain dominant notions of heterosexuality through the need to achieve stereotypical norms of physical attractiveness and wearing fashionable clothing. The findings from this study suggest that girls were more closely linked to and defined by their bodies (by themselves as well as by the boys) than boys were. Girls' dress changes from childhood to adulthood while boys dress remains relatively unchanged, as they grow older. It is evident that girls are much more looked at and prepare themselves to be looked at more than boys.

5.5. Ideal relationships – To love and trust?

The participants' accounts of ideal relationships were conspicuously gendered. Girls often saw love and trust as integral components of ideal relationships, which in itself sanitised sexual activity. Boys, on the other hand, remained largely silent about issues of love and trust.

5.5.1. Girls: constructions of ideal relationships

Girls often perceived unprotected sex to be insurance for benefits such as emotional intimacy and trust. Unprotected sex is often seen as a way of proving your love for the other and ensuring a continued relationship. For example:

To impress their partners... To gain security (g#18)

It is thought that having unprotected sex is having complete trust in your partner. Men sometimes feel it is better to have sex without a condom because it is tedious having to put on a condom or a femidom (g#7)

The following girl introduces many complex ideas about girls' experiences within relationships:

> *Because they feel insecure in their relationship when their mate gives them an ultimatum. Unprotected sex could also happen if there is low self-esteem or abuse in the relationship. (g#28)*

She makes reference to insecurity and low self-esteem of girls being result of coercion and abuse in a relationship.

The desire to love and be loved is one on the principle reasons given by girls for beginning a sexual relationship, and engaging in unsafe sexual practices, and they go to great lengths to prove their love.

Welile (g)   *He says you don't love him if you don't sleep with him.*

Girls also recognised that boys often used promises of love in order to gain access to sex. In the following citation, the girls display awareness that there are differences among girls and among boys.

Thami (g)   *Boys think that if they tell you they love you then you will have to do anything to please him.*
Zubi (g)   *And some girls are scared that if they refuse him then they will get dumped.*
Ayesha (g)   *Some boys are only interested in one thing.*
Thami (g)   *Not all boys, Mam. Some boys, not all, know how to treat a girl.*

My informal discussions with the girls revealed that where young women are influenced by feminism (by their mothers or their female teachers) there is a greater awareness of themselves as agents in resisting conventional femininity. These young women resisted the suggestion that their role was to be of service to boys.

Often love and trust are seen as protection against HIV/AIDS. This construction of ideal relationships is seen to reduce sexual risk. For example:

113

> *I thought about it and said to myself that I want to save myself (sexually for the right guy). HIV/AIDS is quite serious, but only if you have an understanding partner, then HIV/AIDS is not going to affect out relationship. (g#8)*

> *It (HIV/AIDS knowledge) teaches us that having sex is something serious. If you have sex you must be sure and be able to love and trust the person it happens with. (g#20)*

However, girls do demonstrate some recognition of the contradictions between safe sex choices and sexual practices based on pleasing partners and keeping a relationship.

> *It is all about self-respect, and what one think is good then, yeh- go for it. Unprotected sex is from within. I think they want to satisfy their partners by disrespecting themselves. (g#65)*

> *They feel that they love and trust each other, so whether they put on a condom or not, it doesn't really matter so long as they are having sex. (g#37)*

Pregnancy was often seen to be a bigger or as big a problem as HIV/AIDS.

> *They feel that if they have unprotected sex they will love one another more and they will share a better bond between them and they will have a better understanding in their relationship. Young people don't understand that unprotected sex is dangerous and they could stand a chance of falling pregnant. (g#40)*

There is some evidence of girls taking the lead in organising their own lives, and consequently exerting more power within relationships. Some girls suggested that they are not always passive victims and were able to decide on the terms of a relationship.

Thami (g)   *There's a lot you can do with your boyfriend. It does not mean that you have to sleep with him to prove your love for him... Trust is the most important thing in a relationship*

Thabilsile (g) *No (to sex on a date), I told them that if you love me, you love me; you don't love my private part*

114

Some girls also expressed concern about the negative connotations of introducing condom use into a relationship, since it not only suggested distrust in the sexual partner, but also suggested that they (girls) have been involved with other partners.

5.5.2. Boys: constructions of ideal relationships

Boys were very silent on issues of love and mainly talked about love as being something that girls were interested in.

> *They want "flesh to flesh" so that they can feel what their partners feel for them. (b#62)*

Some boys displayed resentment at girlfriends expecting them to spend much time with them, since being associated with one girl was not good for their masculine reputation.

Shakila	*Do you have girlfriends?*
Alan (b)	*Yes, girlfriends. We can't be tied to one girl and she wants to be with you twenty four, seven (24 hours a day, 7 days a week) you can't be with the guys and...*
Shane (b)	*Sometimes girls like to show other girls that they like own you and stuff. You have to be with her and hang around at lunchtime and after school.*

Boys' individual inputs were different from their performances within boys' group discussion. In private, some boys mentioned that love was important, but that it was not a good idea to declare your love for someone. Having their declaration of love rejected was a concern. This admission of "weakness" was not a feature of group discussions. Their performances in group situations showed that boys' relationships should be about "sex", and not "love", but in private they expressed a fear of rejection. These dissonant public and private performances are discussed in section 6.7.

5.5.3. Girls and boys: constructions of ideal relationships

In the mixed sex settings, some girls continued to talk about love and trust, and notions of ideal relationships which made sexual relationships safe. This idea was challenged by other girls, while boys remained silent about the possibilities of being affected by "love". Instead they were concerned with projecting masculine characteristics.

Mduso(b)	*Yes, you must practice.*
Simphiwe (g)	*Why do you need practice? It's (sex) something within you. You should know how to do it without any practice.*
Smanga (b)	*Let's say you never had sex then you would be with your wife who has done it then that will be a problem when she has to teach you.*
Mduso (b)	*That's very embarrassing.*
Simphiwe (g)	*No, it isn't.*
Mduso (b)	*It is, it is.*
Simphiwe (b)	*You shouldn't be embarrassed if you love someone, you should be able to do anything with them.*

Once again the boys are very clear that it is boys who should take charge of sexual activity and should therefore be experienced and knowledgeable about it, and if the woman partner was more knowledgeable about sex, it would be a problem. Simphiwe challenges this idea, but her main counterargument is that "love" is a solution to any problem in a relationship.

5.6. Virginity, abstinence and marriage

The table (Table 5.3.) below shows that the majority of the girls and a significant number of the boys indicated that they were not sexually active at that particular time. The question asked if they were having sex as part of a relationship, so is possible that these statistics do not represent virginity.

			Sexually active?	
			yes	no
Sex	male	Row %	52.6	47.4
	female	Row %	11.5	88.5

Table 5.3. Male and female responses to whether they are sexually active

116

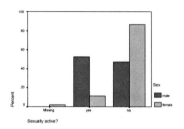

Figure 5.3. Graphical representation of male and female responses to whether they are sexually active

In the same questionnaire, with the same sample, I asked an open-ended question: "How does knowing about HIV/AIDS affect the choices you make in a relationship?" I grouped the responses into categories, and the table below represents male and female responses to this question. 28% of the girls and 0% of the boys mentioned sexual abstinence as a behavioural response to HIV/AIDS knowledge.

			Influence of AIDS knowledge							
			use condoms	abstain	no difference	faithful	faithful+condoms	checkout partner	is aware	spoil relationship/pleasure
Sex	male	Row %	27.8		11.1		5.6	16.7	22.2	16.7
	female	Row %	10.0	28.0	2.0	8.0	12.0	10.0	22.0	8.0

Table 5.4. Male and female responses to the influence of HIV/AIDS knowledge on their sexual practices.

5.6.1. Girls: ideas on virginity, abstinence and marriage

Many cultures place a high value on maintaining girls' virginity until marriage. In this study, the term virginity was usually associated with sexually uninitiated girls. In the anonymous questionnaire, the majority of the girls (88.5%) claimed that they were not sexually active (see table 5.2). To many of the girls, virginity was a valuable gift to be treasured and protected until marriage, and this links virgin identity with traditional feminine identity. 28% of the girls (see table 5.3) indicated that their response to HIV/AIDS knowledge was to abstain from sexual intercourse.

In a girls' focus group there was general agreement that girls' virginity is intimately linked to respect; both self-respect as well as respect from a future marriage partner.

Thami (g)	*There's a lot you can do with your boyfriend. It does not mean you have to sleep with him to prove your love for him.*
Zubi (g)	*Yes, I think he will have more respect for you if you are a virgin.*
Thami (g)	*It is important to keep your self-respect until you are married. Besides you don't know if he is only after one thing and says he loves you and all that but after you sleep with him, he might dump you for someone else.*
Shakila (To Zubi)	*Are you afraid that your boyfriend may leave you for someone else?*
Zubi (g)	*Mam, if he really loves me, he will wait until I am ready. If he can't wait then I don't care if he leaves me. It is more important to save myself until after I am married.*

In the above excerpt, Zubi displays intention to resist being coerced into a sexual relationship before marriage, even if it is at the expense of losing the relationship, but like for many of the girls, she sees marriage as the ultimate goal and finding "Mr. Right" as all-important. Girls also displayed distrust in boys' declaration of love and saw it as a means to gain access to sex. The reference to "one thing", meaning, "sex", was a common feature of girls' discussions about boys' intentions and expectations from relationships.

Young girls mentioned that they face great social pressure, especially within the family, to maintain an image of innocence and sexual ignorance, in spite of the true extent of their knowledge and sexual experience. While this was the case within the family, in the peer group, sexual experience was sometimes valued, and virginity was associated with lack of power against your parents and ignorance about sexual matters.

Most of the learners (both girls and boys) associated sex with vaginal penetration. There was some confusion about the meaning of virginity, as is evident in the following conversation:

Thando (g)	*Can you get AIDS if you are a virgin?*
Reshma (g)	*No, but if you are half a virgin.*
Shakila	*What is half a virgin?*
Reshma (g)	*I don't really know.*
Nisha (g)	*Hey once you sleep... you can never be a virgin again.*

This idea of "half a virgin" came up a few times in my discussions with girls, although none of the girls were able to explain exactly what that meant. I guessed that it referred to sexual activity without full vaginal penetration. Girls discourse on "loss" of virginity was very prominent, and first time sex was seen an irreversible loss of respect (self and of others).

Shakila   When is the right time to start a sexual relationship?
Precious (g) When you get married. No, you will have sex somehow but you don't just rush into things. When you rush into things you make huge mistakes without even realising it and then it's too late to go back and solve your mistakes.

Once again Precious constructs marriage as an important goal and a safe haven, and she carries this view throughout the discussion. Later she states:

Precious (g) It's (condoms) not hundred percent protection, that's why I am saying you should wait. You see if you are married and you fall pregnant, you can take care of your child with your husband. If you fall pregnant now it's only a problem to your parents and yourself.

This idea of marriage being a risk-free place, and a place of sexual safety for women does not go unchallenged among the girls.

Simphiwe (g) Now these are problems you have to go through when you just jump into bed. Now if you are married, you don't have to use...
Gugu (g)   Hey wena[19], if you are married or not married you have to use a condom.
Simphiwe (g) No, if you are married to someone you don't necessarily have to use a condom because you trust each other.
Gugu (g)   Aye[20], that's a problem.

While girls valued virginity for themselves, they often mentioned that they did not expect boys to be virgins. This relates to their understanding of sex as a biological need for boys, and that boys are driven by uncontrollable desires (discussed in section 5.4). Simmi suggests that it is preferable that the boy is sexually experienced. This expression of double standards is a common feature of both boys' and girls' responses.

Rita (g)   Guys can easily fool you and say that they will marry you. Every guy

---

[19] meaning: you

[20] meaning: yes

	wants a girl that has their virginity when they marry. I mean no guy wants a girl who has slept with every other guy. You know when they finally marry then he picks on her and stuff.
Shakila	*What about girls? Do want to marry a boy who is a virgin?*
Simmi (g)	*It is better if the guy is experienced and the girl is not?*
Rita (g)	*By experiencing he can pick up HIV and stuff.*
Simmi (g)	*Let's face it, right? Guys are generally non-virgins. You can't find one that's not.*
Rita (g)	*It's true.*
Simmi (g)	*If a guy likes you, right? He probably liked someone before you and slept with the person.*

The above citation demonstrates girls' acceptance of sexual double standards. Rita's confusion and contradiction is evidenced in her acknowledging that a sexually experienced boy carries the risk of HIV infection, and then conceding that it is not natural for boys to be sexually inexperienced. She also begins with a popularly held view by girls, that boys often promised marriage as a means to gain access to sex.

While most of the girls referred to other girls and boys in their responses to "why do young people engage in unsafe sexual practices?" (See figure 6.3), a few of the girls made reference to themselves and their own relationships. They indicated that were able to negotiate conditions within the relationship. For example:

> *I am in a relationship and when it comes to talking about sex, we talk about unprotected sex and we have decided that we should have a platonic relationship for now. Until we are married, then we could make choices about unprotected sex and a sexual relationship. (g#43)*

5.6.2. Boys: ideas on virginity, abstinence and marriage

More than half the number of boys (52.6%) who responded to the questionnaire claimed that they were sexually active (see table 5.2). It is possible that this is an exaggerated figure, as I have established during the interviews (especially group interviews), that boys often lie about their sexual experience. However, this was an anonymous questionnaire, so the need to lie about their experience should be reduced.

While for girls, virginity is associated with a physiological definition, for boys, virginity is associated with passivity and ignorance about sexual matters. None of the boys (questionnaire responses) mentioned abstinence as a practical response to HIV/AIDS knowledge (see table 5.3). This view was echoed in the boys' discussion groups:

Shakila	*Do you think that boys should wait to be married before they have sex?*
Shane, Colin and Anil (bs)	
	NO!
Alan (b)	*No, because then you won't know what to do and the girl will think that you are not experienced*

For many boys, virginity (not having had any sexual experience) was considered a stigma and they admitted lying about their virgin status to other boys and to girls.

5.6.3. Girls and boys: ideas on virginity, abstinence and marriage

It was interesting to note the gendered differences in the participants' ideas of abstinence. Traditional notions of virginity as a virtue in women and a negative trait in men (Carpenter 2001), is a view held by both girls and boys. Many of the girls stated that they would be "saving" themselves for marriage, while many of the boys stated that it was precisely because they would make better and faithful husbands, that it was necessary to be sexually experienced. To most girls, virginity was a "gift", to most boys; virginity was a "stigma".

In the following mixed-sex group discussion, Raj displays traditional versions of masculinity in his idea that the women he marries will have to be a virgin, even though he is willing to be sexually active with others at this stage. He also positions boys as being naturally dominant and superior ("we are the masters") to girls.

Simmi (g)	*(To boys in the group) Would you like girls to be virgins or non-virgins?*
Raj (b)	*I don't care, but as long as my wife is a virgin. If my wife is a virgin, I don't care about girls being a virgin. I'll do it with anyone.*
Simmi (g)	*So he just wants sexual pleasures?*
Raj (b)	*Exactly. True, true, true. Sex is true. Sex is fun. It's true what they say about a dog and his master.*
Shakila:	*What do they say?*
Raj (b)	*We are the masters and they are the dogs.*

(Girls protest loudly)

Anitha (g)   *They are pigs.*
Simmi (g)   *You are a dog.*

The majority of the girls held the view that marriage was a sanctuary, and that they could not fully trust their partners and feel safe in a relationship until they were married, and after that they did not have to be concerned. A few of girls challenged this idea and recognised that marriage alone was not a guarantee for sexual safety. For example:

Simphiwe (g)   *Now these are problems you go through when you just jump into bed. Now if you are married, you don't have to use ...*
Gugu (g)   *Hey wena, if you are married or not, you have to use a condom.*
Simphiwe (g)   *No, if you are married to someone you don't necessarily have to use a condom because you trust each other.*
Gugu (g)   *Aye, that's a problem.*
Simphiwe (g)   *If you know that your man was waiting for the right time ...*

A group of boys displayed similar awareness of marriage not being naturally sanitising in the following excerpt:

Vukani (b)   *You might get AIDS when you are married too.*
Chris (b)   *Ya, before you get married you must make the girl go for an AIDS test.*
Vukani (b)   *Before you get married you must wear a condom.*
Chris (g)   *Both of us must go for an AIDS test.*

5.7. The peer gaze: policing the boundaries

Much has been written about the power of peers in determining the sexual practices of young adults (for example Lear 1996, Holland et al 2000) and my data confirms that policing by peers is a significant source of concern for boys and girls.

5.7.1. Girls: experiences of peer-policing

The desire to fit in was significantly represented in both girls' and boys' responses to the reasons for having partners at this stage in their lives (26.3% boys and 28.8% girls).

Girls suggest that being with a boyfriend gives a girl status among her girlfriends. Finding a boyfriend is not just a matter of being in a relationship for the benefits the relationship has to offer, but also the affirmation of their attractiveness and desirability, and in many cases, is motivated by the desire to fit in among the peer group. According to van Roosemalen (2000), during adolescence, as girls begin to pull away from their parents, their search for peer group membership becomes all encompassing.

The following are typical responses by girls on the question of why girls have boyfriends:

> *Some people have boyfriends because they are attracted to each other, while others (or example in school) have boyfriends to blend into the crowd, because if you don't have a boyfriend, you are considered a nerd. (g#2)*

> *Most probably because they are at that age whereby they find themselves attracted to the opposite sex. Some on the other hand believe that they would not be seen as "normal" in the eyes of their friends. (g #29)*

It is evident from the responses above that having a boyfriend was important to fit into peer group expectations.

5.7.2. Boys: experiences of peer-policing

For boys, as with girls, policing by peers came from same sex as well as potential partners. Male peer policing constituted the infrastructure within which a range of social and sexual identities were negotiated and ritualistically projected.

> *...and knowing about sex because other teens speak about sex and if you haven't experienced it you feel the grief of making sure that you go through it (b #54)*

It was evident that policing by peers was a key feature of the learner microculture and provided a space within which masculine reputations were validated and amplified. In the following excerpt, the boys are clear about who should control the course of a

relationship and who has the right to start and end it. They admit lying to their friends
if things do not turn out this way.

Anil (b)	*Sometimes after they (boys) break up with a girl, they (boys) say stories about her.*
Shakila	*Do boys even lie?*
Anil (b)	*Ya, maybe. They can't say a girl gave him a duck. So they say they did this and that. And that they gave her a duck[21].*

Having a girlfriend also gave boys a certain status in school. Boys often talked of peer
influence as something that they were not themselves affected by, but as something
that affected other boys.

> *They want to become famous in the school and think they too hot in school (b*
> *# 49)*

> *Most of the time they influenced by their friends, especially boys influence*
> *other boys to have a girlfriend so he can have sex (b#51)*

Many of the boys admitted that boys often boasted about their sexual experiences. It
was important that the image they portrayed within the peer group conformed to
normative masculine heterosexuality, even if their practices did not. In the following
excerpt from a focus-group discussion with a group of 15-16 year old boys, they
admit to lying about their sexual status in order to conform to the peer group
expectations.

Shakila:	*Do you think boys of your age are sexually active?*
Makhosi (b):	*Ya, some of them are.*
Bheki (b):	*They talk about it.*
Shakila:	*Do they sometimes lie?*
Makhosi (b):	*Ya, sometimes.*
Sbu (b):	*Because other boys will laugh at them if they go with a girl and do nothing.*
Makhosi (b):	*Boys expect that if you have a girlfriend you must be sleeping with her, if you don't, they make fun of you.*

It was interesting, that when probed, boys admitted to lying about their sexual
activities and experiences. This is a further indication that complex issues such as

---

[21] Giving someone a duck, meant breaking off a relationship.

these cannot be adequately accessed using survey methods which form a major part of research into youth sexual practices and can be a gross misrepresentation of actual sexual practices.

5.7.3. Girls and boys: experiences of peer-policing

In the matrix ranking exercise where groups of girls and boys were asked about the most significant problems that they jointly experienced, every group had cited peer pressure toward the top of their lists. The groups of girls as well as the groups of boys specifically mentioned that the pressure to smoke, drink and take drugs, was a concern to them. These were seen as serious problems where peer pressure should be resisted. However, in terms of sexual behaviour and peer pressure relating to that, although there was mention of the need to fit-in, this was not seen as a problem, but an expected and normal state of things.

In a mixed group discussion, the girls acknowledged and understood the boys' need to lie about their sexual exploits.

Gugu (g):	*Mam, you know what they believe? Boys believe that they are stupid if they never have sex to this age.*
Shakila:	*(to the boys) Do you think other boys will laugh at you?*
Mduso (b):	*Ya, they do.*
Smanga (b):	*They do.*
Shakila:	*So do boys discuss what they do?*
Mduso (b):	*Ya, they do.*
Smanga (b):	*Ya, they do.*
Shakila:	*Do they even lie?*
Mduso (b):	*Ya, they do lie.*
Gugu (g):	*I think it's better off lying, than just doing it... they don't have to lie about a real person – just about a fantasy.*
Smanga (b):	*Most of the time when you talk to your friends at school and you lie, then your conscience will trouble you.*

In the above extract, it is interesting to note the way in which the boys are silenced when girls directly address and challenge masculine performances. Smanga demonstrates some conflict between what he thinks he should do and what he has to do to fit into the peer group. While this type of conflict often arose in mixed-sex group discussions, it was not a feature of boys only group discussion. This type of differences in the discourses of boys in their interaction within mixed-sex group discussions, and those within boys only groups is a further indication of the policing of sexualities that occurs within the peer group.

5.8. Heterosexuality and homophobic performances

Several researchers have argued that any examination of gender would be incomplete if it did not include 'issues of sexuality and homophobia' (see Boulden 1996; Epstein 1996). All of the learners in this study identified themselves as heterosexual and this is consistent with studies in Australia (see Harrison 2000) and in the United Kingdom (see Epstein and Johnson 1998) where the students overwhelmingly identified as heterosexual. I asked the participants whether they knew of same-sex relationships in their school, and their responses are represented in the figure below.

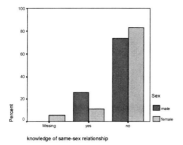

Figure 5.4. Graphical representation of male and female responses to knowledge about same sex relationships in school

5.8.1. Girls: responses to homosexuality

Discussion about homosexuality was difficult and there was much embarrassment around the issue. None of the participants identified themselves as being homosexual although some mentioned that they knew of others who were. Girls often reacted with silence or embarrassed giggles when asked about their knowledge about same-sex relationships.

Shakila   *Do you think there are same-sex relationships in your school?*

126

(Laughter)

Reshma (g)	*Yes*
Nisha (g)	*Yes*
Shakila	*Girls or boys?*
Nisha (g)	*Only girls*
Shakila	*How can you tell? Girls always hold hands.*
Reshma (g)	*The way they walk around other people.*
Nisha (g)	*Some of them come to you and ask you out.*
Reshma (g)	*Yes*
Shakila	*Has that happened to you?*
Nisha (g)	*No. To other girls I know.*

Generally, girls did not display hostility in the way they spoke about homosexuality, but they often chose to avoid the topic. They mentioned that boys not only policed each other in terms of homo/heterosexuality, but also attached labels to girls who did not perform traditional feminine identities. It was necessary be part of a heterosexual relationship, which was "natural" so that you were not labelled as being gay. For example in an interview with a girl:

Shakila	*Do you feel pressured to have a boyfriend?*
Reena (g)	*Yes Mam. These boys, when they know that you don't have a boyfriend and if you say "no" when the ask you out, they say you are gay and spread rumours*

Overall, the girls displayed an acceptance of homosexuality, but thought that it people should be discreet about it. This suggests that they, to a certain extent, rendered homosexuality as "other".

Sandy (g)	*It does not bother me, as long as they stay away from me.*

Harrison (2000) points out that the category "woman" in general is constructed in terms of tolerance and reciprocity in relationships, and although it creates problems for them in heterosexual relationships, may make them more tolerant of "Others".

5.8.2. Boys: responses to homosexuality

There were distinct differences in the ways in which boys talked about homosexuality, compared to the girls. There were widespread homophobic attitudes among boys, especially when the discussion was with other boys. In focus groups, boys tended to use derogatory terms to refer to homosexuality.

Stated as a problem by a boys' group: *"fags- they make us sick"*

Given the widespread negative attitudes towards homosexuality both inside and outside the school context, it would take a very brave young man to stand up and be counted by expressing tolerant attitudes toward homosexuals (Harrison 2000). It is perhaps easier to remain silent or to join the rest of the boys in expressing negative attitudes. Once again the dominance of heterosexuality and the fear of being suspected of being homosexual led to performances of hegemonic masculine identities. According to Connell (1995), in Western societies, hegemonic masculinities are heterosexual, aggressive and competitive. The connections between hegemonic masculinities and homophobia become lucid when we look at the number of characteristics that are ascribed to gay men are also applied to women.

Boys who performed well in school and were seen as being popular with teachers were suspected of being homosexual. Boys also attached labels to other boys who spoke in a high-pitched voice, sat with their legs crossed, or walked in a certain way. For example:

> *You can see from the way certain boys sit like girls, that they are gay. I stay very far from them (b#45)*

It seems that boys who are seen to be "weak" are labelled as being gay so that the power and status of other boys are emphasised. Boys appear to perceive being gay as being "unnatural" or "abnormal" as it conflicts with their ideas of hegemonic masculinity. Their homophobic performances are attempts to achieve and display normative heterosexuality. Mac an Ghaill (1996:199) has noted that to be a "real boy" you need to publicly distance yourself from the feminine and "feminised versions of masculinity". In another expression of this labelling and distancing, during a boys' group discussion, one of the boys mentioned the name of another boy and got up and started walking in an exaggerated feminine way that is often associated with an effeminate gay stereotype, and was rewarded with laughter and approval in the form of a "high five" (a raised clap with one hand each).

The following boy displays more acceptance of homosexuality among girls.

Makosi (b)   *I know girls. I saw a girl with another girl and they are in love. You can see this one is serious.*

5.8.3. Girls and boys: responses to homosexuality

Figure 5.4. shows that both girls and boys were largely unaware of homosexual relationships in school. Of those who responded that they were aware of homosexual relationships in school, there were more boys than girls.

In a mixed-sex group, the boys' discussion about homosexuality is markedly different from those in boys-only groups. For example:

Shakila   *Do you know of any same-sex relationships in your school?*
Jay (b)   *Yes. I know girls.*
(Girls giggle and look at each other)
Anitha   *Gays in our school?*
Raj (b)   *They kiss each other.*
Jay (b)   *Why are girls lesbians?*
Simmi (g)   *Why are boys gay?*
Jay (b)   *It's like this. Say a boy goes out with a girl and he breaks her heart, she thinks every other boy is like that and a girl can give her more comfort, which means a girl turns into a lesbian.*
Simmi (g)   *What about boys? Why are they gay?*
Jay (b)   *The same thing happens.*

In the above citation, both the girls and the boys discuss homosexuality with more openness and sensitivity, although the girls' initial giggles show some embarrassment. It is clear that these young adults do not have a clear understanding of homosexuality, but they do attempt to explain it. There was a general willingness on the part of the boys to engage with these issues in the mixed-sex setting, but they mainly talked about girls and construed homosexuality as failed heterosexuality.

My findings concur with those of Nayak and Kehily (1996), who found that girls were less likely to express extreme forms of anti-homosexual feeling than boys in mixed-sex schools. This can be seen in the boy's assertion of dominant notions of masculinity so as not to be seen as being homosexual.

These dominant notions of femininity and masculinity are collectively held and policed by the peer group and wider society. In order to challenge this, these young people have to bravely risk being labelled homosexual or "fags". When questioned about this young girls and boys indicated that it was much easier to conform than to resist dominant notions. Some girls and boys, in individual accounts, displayed more sensitively and awareness of the asymmetry of heterosexuality. There was a confusion and contradictions in their privately held views and their public performances, both verbal and actions. It is clear that learner homophobia is closely linked to their boundary maintenance of compulsory heterosexuality and that silences about homosexuality continues across generations.

5.9. Disciplining of pleasure

HIV/AIDS discourses has had an impact on the ways in which young people experience their sexuality. One of the open ended questions in the questionnaire was 'Why do young people engage in unsafe sexual practices?" I grouped the responses into categories, and these are represented in figure 5.5. below.

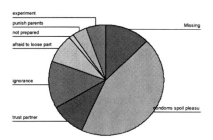

Figure 5.5. : Graphical representation of why young people engage in unsafe sexual practices

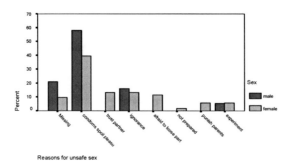

Reasons for unsafe sex

Figure 5.6. Graphical representation of why girls and boys think that young people engage in unsafe sexual practices

5.9.1. Girls: ideas of disciplined pleasure

"Condomise" is one of the key messages in the widely used "ABC" model of HIV/AIDS education. Girls often mentioned that condoms spoil sexual pleasure. Their responses were based largely in terms of what they had heard others say. For example:

> *Rumours go around and people say sex without a condom is better so they want to experience it (g#10)*
>
> *They feel more pleasure without a condom (g#12)*
>
> *Some feel unprotected sex is better sex. There is also the mentality of men that if they have unprotected sex they feel more "manly" (g#15)*
>
> *To experience the satisfaction or to get the real pleasure of having sex. (g#17)*

Some of the girls showed an awareness of unprotected sex as a HIV/AIDS risk in their responses. For example:

> *They probably feel it's better but what they don't want to realise is the risk they are taking especially in this generation when the AIDS epidemic is prevalent (g# 19)*

> *AIDS is a very risky thing. If young people want to have sex they should use*
> *protection. They stand the risk of having HIV/AIDS and also falling pregnant*
> *(g#40)*

Although the majority of the girls felt that it was the boys who should take the
responsibility of carrying condoms, there were a few girls who said that they share in
this responsibility.

> *I think about it whenever I think about doing sex, because I don't really trust*
> *condoms. But to reduce the risk I do use a condom even though I don't trust it.*
> *I make sure it is on. I even carry one myself just in case he is short. (g#72)*

In the citation above, the girl demonstrates an attempt at asserting herself as a
responsible agent, in terms of her sexual safety ("I even carry one myself"). However,
she also suggest an acceptance of the idea that boys are expected to be relatively more
sexually active than girls are, hence, "in case he is short", and not, "in case he is
without". This is a further example of girls challenging and maintaining traditional
gender roles.

Many girls felt that it was more important that the partner did not see you as being
sexually knowing and experienced, than to take control of your sexual health. In a
girls group discussion it was unanimously agreed that it was inappropriate for girls to
initiate condom use. It would be seen as "cheap" behaviour.

Ayesha (g)	*I think that's a problem. Sometimes people are not prepared and it just happens.*
Shlo (g)	*So what do you expect? That girls must carry condoms around?*
Shakila	*If they do, will it be easy to use it?*
Zubi (g)	*No. How do you ask a boy to use a condom? He will think you always do this and that you are cheap.*
Thami (g)	*He will also think that you don't trust him.*

5.9.2. Boys: ideas of disciplined pleasure

The majority of the boys (see figure 5.6.) felt that condoms reduced sexual pleasure.
They were more explicit in their reference to sexual acts and genitalia.

132

Because the sex is better and the feel of the vagina rubbing against my penis is very nice. (b#45)

They want to feel the penis in the bare skin. (b#46)

They think using a condom is different from doing unprotected sex. They say you don't feel the goodies. (b#54)

They believe in "flesh to flesh". Some girl I know told me that condomising is boring, they'd rather not. (b#57)

Some boys talked about sex without condoms as being "natural".

They feel it is much better without a condom and they can do it free flow. (b#44)

It's a best part of life and you have a natural feeling. (b#50)

Some of the boys mentioned that knowledge about HIV/AIDS have ruined their experience of sex. This is an indication of some the ways in which HIV/AIDS knowledge impacts on sexual identity constructions. For example:

I do not enjoy sex now because I know about HIV/AIDS. If I have to make love, I feel like I am not because of the condom I use (b#53)

In the following input, the boy feels that HIV/AIDS knowledge prevents him from achieving his masculine identity. He sees having many partners, as being a normal part of "boyhood" and being faithful is a reluctant response to HIV/AIDS knowledge. He also indicates that HIV/AIDS knowledge creates suspicion within relationships.

It keeps me faithful to the one I am with and makes you not a trusting person. It practically limits my desires of fulfilling my boyhood (b#57)

The following is an excerpt from a boys' group discussion. This group of boys were identified as the popular boys (with girls) in school. Here they clearly display dominant versions of masculinity, such as being knowledgeable about girls, about sex and being irresistible to girls.

Shane (b)   Hey, I don't take chances, with AIDS and stuff.

133

Alan (b)	*Well you got to play it safe. You don't want to get her pregnant and at the same time get diseases and stuff.*
Shane (b)	*Anyway some girls, you can check. I won't take even if she gave for free.*
Alan (b)	*If I know a girl and if I ask her to have sex, then I am always prepared.*
Shakila	*What if she says "no" to sex?*
Alan (b)	*She won't say "no". Besides you got to know who to ask.*
Shakila	*How do you know?*
Alan (b)	*Other boys. They don't keep quiet after they had it with a girl. All the other boys get to know.*

5.9.3. Girls and boys: ideas of disciplined pleasure

In mixed-sex settings, girls and boys talked openly about what they expected in a relationship.

Simphiwe (g)	*I think I believe in different things. Most of the girls believe that they should just have sex anyhow. I believe that sex is something special, something that you have to enjoy with the one you really love.*
Mduso (b)	*How can you enjoy something you don't know?*
Smanga (b)	*Ya, people say that practice makes perfect.*
Simphiwe (g)	*Not in all cases. There are some things you have to wait for until the time is right.*

Simphiwe believes that sex is something to enjoy, but one needs to wait until the time is right. Elsewhere, in the course of this discussion, she makes it quite clear that the right time is after marriage.

In the following citation, the boys dominate the discussion by displaying their knowledge about sexual matters.

Raj (b)	*What I got to say is that we ous[22], we smaak[23] women and we like having sex and we know about AIDS and all that but anyway we always use a condom. I sometimes use two condoms, double protection.*
Jay (b)	*You use two? There's no feeling.*
Vukani (b)	*You must condomise, ya.*
Shakila:	*How do boys feel about condoms?*

---

[22] meaning: boys

[23] meaning: like

134

Jay (b)	*My point of view? I feel I like using condoms.*
Vukani (b)	*I don't like condoms. I feel like I am eating a sweet with the wrapper on.*
(Laughter)	
Shakila	*What do girls do when boys refuse to wear a condom?*
Girls	*Don't sleep with them.*
Shakila	*What do boys do when girls ask for condoms?*
Jay (b)	*They use it.*
Simmi (g)	*But not all boys.*
Vukani (b)	*Ya, but you can see a girl with which you have to use a condom and you can see...*

In the above except from a mixed-sex group discussion, it is clear that boys have differing views on condom-use. Vukani displays contradictory ideas, first advocacy for condom-use, then a view that condoms reduce sexual pleasure. He also voices a common view held by girls and boys that it is possible to know whether someone is infected by HIV by looking at them. In the following excerpt from the same discussion, the boys and the girls point out to him that his sexual practices may put him at risk to HIV/AIDS infection, and he answers in a way that shows he thinks he is invincible.

Vukani (b)	*Before you get married, you must first have sex so that you will know what you taking. Taste it then take it.*
(Laughter)	
Simmi (g)	*Ten years down the line you will definitely have to go for an AIDS test, maybe sooner.*
Jay (b)	*Maybe you already got AIDS.*
Vukani (b)	*Me? I'm as strong as a bull.*

Sexual double standards for girls and boys are evidenced again in the next citation. The sampling of potential partners that Vukani referred to was not applicable to girls. A commonly held view by girls and boys was that it was acceptable, even preferable that boys had many sexual partners, while girls would acquire a bad reputation for the same.

Shakila:	*You were saying that boys who have many girls are called "players". What are girls who have many boys called?*
Vukani (b)	*B.I.T.C.H.*
Raj (b)	*Can I say it? She's called a bitch.*
Shakila:	*Why do you think girls have a bad name and boys have a very stylish name?*

135

Jay (b)	*We are not spoiling anything on our bodies.*
Shakila:	*What are they spoiling on their bodies?*
Jay (b)	*You want me to say it? It's no more tight.*

This is a frequently voiced idea, by girls and boys, that sex is something that "spoils" the "bodies" of girls.

5.10. Intergenerational dynamics

Communication with adults, especially about relationship and sexual issues was voiced as a common problem. This was not surprising since teenage sexuality continues to lack social acceptability.

5.10.1. Girls: experiences of intergenerational dynamics

Many of the girls mentioned that parents were not understanding of their experiences, and that the opportunities to talk to adults were very limited.

> *They don't get attention at home so they tend to seek it from boys at school (g #12)*

In their ranked matrix of their jointly experienced problems, all of the groups mentioned communication with parents as a problem. One of the girls' groups specifically mentioned "mothers" as being a source of difficulty at this stage in their lives.

Parents were seen by many of the girls as people to be opposed. This girl offers defying parents as a reason for unprotected sex:

> *Maybe because they want to get back at their parents in a way (g#23)*

The dynamics of power and resistance between young people and their parents is evident in the excerpt below.

Reena (g):   *... some of my friends say that they have that they have boyfriends just to get back at their parents.*

Shakila: *That's interesting. I have heard that before. Can you tell me more about that?*

Reena (g):   *You see parents, especially Indian parents – they make it hard for us. They don't understand that times have changed and always tell us "when we were young..." and things. My parents say that if I have a boyfriend then I won't concentrate on my schoolwork.*

Some girls mentioned that if parents did not approve of a certain relationship then the girl would deliberately attempt to become pregnant because then the parents would be forced to agree to a marriage. It was clear that marriage was an important goal for the girls and their parents.

> *Maybe they have unprotected sex just to fall pregnant, that's if the parents don't agree for either the girl or the boy. Then they would have to agree because then you would have to get married. (g#12)*

> *I think that young people have girlfriends or boyfriends because they want someone to share problems with. Because some of us cannot share problems with our parents and we also need someone to talk to when we are experiencing problems at home. (g#66)*

In my informal discussions with the learners, it became clear that the relationships between adults (especially parents and teachers) and the teenagers were dominated by dynamics of control and resistance. Parents were often seen as the people to be opposed, and a display of power over them was valued in the peer group.

In individual interviews, girls often suggested the lack of social acceptance of youth sexuality. Especially for girls, it was seen necessary to perform the identity of a sexually unknowing, "good girl". The girls, not only felt that they could not talk to adults about personal and intimate issue, but they also could not trust them to respect the confidentiality of personal issues. For example:

Shakila: *Whom can you talk to about relationship and sexual matters?*

Reena (g):   *Actually no one. Definitely not my parents, and other girls – they will think that you are loose or that you are interested in sex.*

Shakila: *What about your teachers?*

Reena (g):   *I don't think so. I am sure that they will discuss it with other teachers and when you do bad in class, they will pick on you and stuff.*

Reena demonstrates an understanding that youth sexuality lacks social acceptance by adults, which is what makes communication with them about sexual matters impossible. The message from the adult world was clearly that "sex is dangerous". Furthermore, she demonstrates a lack of trust in adults.

5.10.2. Boys: experiences of intergenerational dynamics

In the matrix ranking exercise of problems boys experienced at this age, each of the groups mentioned parents as being a problem. Unlike the girls, none of the boys expressed a need to talk about relationships and sexuality issues. The problem with parents was mainly associated with lack of money from their parents to be able to date girls. In an individual interview, one boy mentioned that boys of his age had to compete with older men who had more financial power, hence a better chance with the girls.

Shakila:	*What kind of boys do girls like?*
Siven (b):	*Rich. They like boys with money and designer brand clothes and can give them presents and stuff. And expensive cars-that's what they like. That's why they go for older guys who are working. If you have no money, you can't get girls.*
Shakila:	*Do many of the girls in this school have older boyfriends?*
Siven (b):	*You can just see after school, some boyfriends come with cars to pick them up. And girls are always showing off with presents and things that their boyfriends give them.*

Siven talked about girls, like many other boys did, as commodities, something to "get". The commodification of girls by boys was also evident in the girls' accounts of interpersonal relationships. In many cases this was not problematised, but accepted as being "normal".

5.10.3. Girls and boys: experiences of intergenerational dynamics

Young adults' understanding of themselves as being of a separate generation from their parents, with a different set of expectations, was one that came up often in the group discussions as well as informal discussions.

In a mixed-sex group interview:

Themba (b):   *Mam, you probably believe in sex after marriage. Do you think that it is possible these days?*
Precious (g):   *It is possible.*
Lucky (b):   *I don't think it is possible.*
Themba (b):   *There are 10% of the men who don't sleep with the girls when they are young who isn't cheating on their wives. Most of the men who didn't have sex in the early stages are cheating on their wives now.*

In the extract above, Themba recognises my identity as an adult researcher, of a different generation from him, and points out to me that there are different expectations of the present generation. Both Precious and Lucky suggests that perhaps it is unreasonable to expect that the rules for behaviour from the previous generation would be applicable to the present generation. While Anne expressed a similar view to many other girls, of virginity until marriage, the boys in this group thought that this was not possible. I have mentioned before that boys saw their teenage years as period of preparation for adulthood. Here, Themba explains that lack of early sexual experiences results in men cheating on their wives later on by estimating a small percentage (10%) of the cases where this does not happen. This was an often-used justification for the compelling need for early sexual experience by boys, and came up often in mixed-sex group discussions.

In addition to older adults being a source of struggle rather than guidance, Themba suggests the lack of good adult examples in everyday life. In his view, since priests are generally considered to be models for society:

You will find that most of the priests are cheating on their wives.

He also uses this as support for his argument (in the excerpt above) that sexually abstinent men make unfaithful husbands, hence the need for as much sexual experience as possible, before marriage.

5.11. Conclusion

In this chapter, I discussed the findings relating to the performance of sexualities/sexual identities within the context of HIV/AIDS. My analysis relies on an understanding that sexual identity (and/or sexuality) is profoundly shaped by social factors. At the same time individuals actively construct and reconstruct their sexual identities over time and in different contexts, dependent partly on their experiences.

The next chapter presents a synthesis of the findings from this study in dialogue with the literature reviewed, the theoretical framework employed in this study, and methodology, with a view to understanding young adults' sexual identity constructions within the context of HIV/AIDS.

CHAPTER SIX

SYNTHESIS: UNDERSTANDING YOUNG ADULTS' SEXUALITIES WITHIN THE CONTEXT OF HIV/AIDS

6.1. Introduction

In this chapter I attempt to synthesise the data generated from the (empirical) study, with the methodology employed in this research and the existing literature/research in this field, in an attempt to interrogate current theoretical conceptions of teenage sexual identities, especially in the context of a HIV/AIDS pandemic.

I have structured this chapter into different sections, which are in many ways linked, and I specifically discuss the themes in the context of the HIV/AIDS pandemic. I start with a discussion on *Generation as an identity dimension* (section 6.2) where I discuss the perceptions of the participants of age as a social dynamic. I then discuss *The discourse of romantic love* (section 6.3.), which was an overwhelmingly prevalent theme, especially among girls. *Marriage and the nuclear family* (section 6.4.), is the next theme, since much of the data points to an understanding of marriage being a solution to unsafe sexual practices. In section 6.5., *Power and resistance*, I discuss the issues of power among and between young adults, and adults and young adults. In *Hetero/sexual performances* (section 6.6.), I problematise the participants' performances of normative heterosexuality and in the final section, *Private/public performances* (section 6.7.), I discuss the dissonances between young adults' public and private sexual identity performances.

6.2. Generation as an identity dimension

Studies of generation as a dimension of identity are rare. As West (1999) has pointed out, studies of youth sexuality have focused mainly on issues of gender. Sexuality research that focus on power relations that define male and female roles and positions in intimate relations and society in general, are certainly crucial, but focusing on gender relations alone, omits other important aspects. I think that generation as a dimension as identity needs specific attention. As West (1999) argues, while age is often mentioned in the description of the sample, there is little systematic or theorised examination of age or generation as a social dynamic. Much has been written about the psychological and physiological development of young adults (usually referred to as adolescents) in psychology textbooks. These theories of development (predominantly cognitive development) are usually based on notions of ages and stages, loosely connected to social and cultural aspects. Concentrating on the voices of the participants, I focus, here, on the social construction and expectations of teenage years as an identity dynamic. *Generational identity* is understood in terms of the participants' performances and expectations of themselves and each other, as well as those of the adult generation.

Epstein and Johnson (1998: 151) note that it is considered a truism that young people find their teenage/ adolescent years a period of confusion and experimentation around sexuality, that they (especially boys/young men) have racing hormones, changing bodies and developing, but intense, interest in the opposite sex. Maart (2000) agrees with this commonly held view that "adolescence" is the growth spurt between childhood and social maturity and financial independence. These views of a fixed age range that define specific characteristics assume a homogenous society. However in a society as diverse as South Africa, delimiting the age range of adolescence is extremely difficult, since, for example, there are huge disparities between the rich and the poor; a large number of teenagers are not in school; many have had to seek employment from an early age; and teenage pregnancy rates are high.

Considerable power has been invested in conceptualising teenage years as a *stage* or *phase* in order to define what is socially and culturally acceptable as age appropriate behaviour (see for example Erikson 1968, Paul and White 1990). My approach is to challenge the construction of *generation* as a *phase* and propose *generation* as a dimension of *identity*. As I have discussed in section 3.6., identity is not fixed, but a fluid construction that changes in each spatial, temporal and social context, which implies that as a social construction, generation as identity can be reconstituted.

My sample consisted of participants aged 15-19. I did not look at the various ages within this group, but looked at the age range as being the group of "young adults"[23] in my study. In the following subsection (section 6.2.1.), I problematise the commonly held biological conception of "adolescence" and then propose a reconfiguring of generation as a dimension of identity (6.2.2.)

6.2.1. Troubling biology

There is no doubt that the physical changes that take place during this period clearly are an important part of young people's lived experiences, but I argue that the social and cultural expectations of people within a certain age group, in this case teenagers who are in school, shape their understanding of their generational identity. For example, a sixteen-year-old "girl" who is a mother will certainly have very different ideas about her identity (sexual, or otherwise) from a sixteen-year-old secondary school learner who is not a mother. In the case of the 'school girl', her sexual identity will be influenced by her understanding of what it means to be a sixteen year old teenager, by her peers (who are also in school), and a social structure that she will most likely rebel against. In the case of the young mother, her sexual identity will be influenced by her understanding of motherhood, her peers (other mothers, who are most likely older woman), and a social structure she most likely has no choice but to conform to. This illustrates the point that we make sense of the biological through discursive practices, which are deeply embedded in our culture. These discursive constructions include the discourses of the adult world and the peer world, which are often in conflict with each other (see section 7.5.1.).

---

[23] I discuss my preference for the term "young adults" to represent the participants of this study in section 4.8

My findings confirm the commonly held idea that that during these years interest in forming relationships with the 'opposite sex" moves to the forefront of consciousness. The participants understand this stage of their lives to be necessarily experimental, and the idea of 'just passing through' makes the teenage years, an even more confusing identity dynamic. The teenage years are understood by many of the participants to be transitional, hormonal and necessarily experimental. Their transitional status, as interpreted by adults as well as themselves, is likely to diminish their sense of agency with regard to sexual safety. For many of the girls this was a time to foster romantic relationships. For many of the boys it was a time to gain sexual experience, in preparation for later marriage.

Male sexuality is unproblematised in the accounts of the boys as well as of those of the girls and is understood to be naturally aggressive because of hormonal development during teenage years. For instance, risk taking and acting in accordance with presumed biological urges are seen to be a male prerogative. However, this does seem to be the same for girls. Dominance and aggressiveness seem to be the fabric of young men's lives, hence their sexual risk-taking is seen as normal, or as an unquestioned rite of passage.

Girls, on the other hand, display confusions and contradictions in their sexual identity performances. They feel that they are required to be sexually alluring and struggle to attain norms of physical attractiveness, and at the same time be devoted to chastity (see section 6.4).

6.2.2. Reconfiguring generational identity

Young adults often find that they have to negotiate two competing worlds: that of the adults (such as parents, teachers), and that of their peers. To adults, they are positioned more as children and hence their sexuality is forbidden rather than affirmed. Within the peer culture, especially in the case of boys, sexuality is celebrated. Young adults feel that they are constantly under scrutiny. Others are always assessing them, and the different expectations in different contexts results in much confusion.

Much of the stereotypically teenage behaviour is seen as "normal" and/or "natural" for someone of this age (15-19, in this case). Lesko (1996: 141) argues for the deconstruction of the concept of "natural" adolescence, noting:

> *Youth is not an immutable stage of life. Free from the influence of historical change. Rather adolescence can be seen as the effects of certain sets of social practices, across numerous domains of contemporary legal, educational, family, and medical domains. This conceptualisation highlights the constructedness and mutability of what are to be assumed to be natural and naturally occurring teenagers.*

Perhaps I could add HIV/AIDS to Lesko's list of domains that influence the construction of teenage characteristics. How does HIV/AIDS influence generational identity constructions? It appears from the data generated in this study that the young adults feel that the HIV/AIDS discourse have made an impact on their constructions of sexual identity. For example, they understand that their knowledge about HIV/AIDS contributes to a reduction of sexual pleasure, by the advocacy of condom-use and monogamous relationships. There is clearly an awareness of the risks of contacting HIV/AIDS, and its connection to sexual behaviour. While in some cases this encourages young adults to act reckless and invincible, in other cases it leads them to think that the appearance of HIV/AIDS has unfairly ruined their chances of a "normal" (sexually promiscuous) teenage life. These are also indications of the contextual nature of sexual identity constructions, and some of the ways in which identity construction can be wilfully or circumstantially manipulated. This opens up the possibility for accepting and fostering agency, as opposed to a strict adherence to biological determinism for an understanding of generational identity.

Accepting particular aspects of teenage sexuality as being "natural" and immutable can lead to powerlessness to act against the dominant and expected notions. This can result in falling into a trap of performing expected behaviour which is risky, or even adopting a fatalistic attitude towards disease and death. Alternative messages, such as "Boys *can* control sexual urges" need to be postured. Reformulating generational identity as being productive in nature enables us to negotiate its constituents, rather than accept them as "given". In educating teenagers about sexuality, emphasis should be placed on the degree to which teenagers can subvert and transform structural underpinnings (what is expected from them by adults and peers) of teenage years as a component of identity, through exercising their individual choice and self-expression.

6.3. The discourse of romantic love

The findings from this study suggest that there is a powerful discourse of romantic love together with the promises that accompany it, presented by girls. Relationships with the "opposite sex" are also seen as being important to boys, for different reasons (as shown in the discussions in Chapter Five). The desire to love and be loved is one of the principle reasons why young women begin sexual relations and unsafe sexual practices. The findings from this study add to the existing research, which suggests that teenage girls link sexual activity with love, and love is a legitimate reason for sex. According to Lees (1993), the "legitimacy" of love is precisely its role in steering female sexuality into the only "safe" place for its expression. In the following section I discuss the implications of these dominant discourses of love for safer sex practices.

6.3.1. Safe sex or safe love?

The need to love and be loved is a powerful determinant of the extent to which girls are prepared to assert or compromise their agency in a relationship. Girls often focus on the need to satisfy their loved ones, rather than on their own needs or desires, or what they know to be unsafe. Boys, on the other hand, regard satisfaction (sexual and otherwise) as being their right.

The participants' (especially girls') understanding of *love* further complicates their notions of sexuality in that "love", which is closely tied to "trust", in itself sanitises sexual practice. Risk, then is assessed in terms of love for and trust in a partner, therefore demanding condom-use, for example, undermines that love and trust. The discourse of love is clearly contradictory to the discourse of safe sex. Girls' accounts suggest that their locating themselves within romantic love discourses regulates them in a variety of ways. The accounts of the girls suggest that their experiences of sexuality are closely tied in within the competing discourses of romantic love and sexual safety. Some girls and boys manipulated the knowledge they had about safe sex to rationalise their risk behaviour and explain why safer sex was not necessary for them.

Given teenagers' increased interest in relationships with the "opposite" sex and in sexual relationships, for girls, adopting safer sex practices may hinder the achievement of other perceived important outcomes like excitement and intimacy. Girls indicate that they understand the risks of giving in to demands for sex, but they often feel compelled to choose submission for fear of being dumped or cheated upon. In their search for what they understand as ideal relationships and love, young women encounter fear, anxiety, confusion and inner conflict.

A consistent stance of many sex education programmes is one which encourages abstinence or delaying of sexual activity. While the reasoning behind this stance is to protect one against potential negative consequences of sexual activity (such as unwanted pregnancy and sexually transmitted diseases, including HIV/AIDS), it does not take into account that this stance increases the likelihood of other negative consequences (such as loss of a partner and love). My findings illustrate that many young women construct casual sex as a strategy for the possibility of "love" and a long-term relationship. In this sense, for many of the girls "unprotected sex" is seen as "safe sex", and "protected sex" is seen as "unsafe sex". Introducing condom-use, for example, may put trust into suspicion, and risk compromising the important goal of perfect "love".

For many of the girls there was a close connection between love and sex, and "sex" was "making love". While "love" was not part of the boys' discussions about sex, except when they talked about promising love to gain access to sex. They understood "love" to be something that occupied the minds of girls, and admitted manipulating this knowledge for their own purposes. To position themselves as being interested in love, meant that they were "soft" and "weak" and they could be hurt and rejected by girls. This loss of power is inconsistent with the performances of hegemonic masculinity of majority of the boys. Falling in love makes boys vulnerable, and it seems that achieving successful masculinity puts them under pressure to mask the vulnerability associated with loving, caring or any characteristics usually associated with girls. Some of the boys, especially in private discussions, revealed their conflict between their emotions and masculine performances.

147

6.3.2. Love them enough to talk about "love"

The need for love and romance is understood by the participants as an essential part of teenage life. This being the case, it is important to situate sexuality education *within* relationships and not use an approach that discourages relationships. There is a definite silence on the topic of love in the literature on sexuality. Mcleod (1999) asks whether "love is not talked about in educational contexts because it is a taboo subject, because sex without love is more containable, or because love is relevant but not really mentionable". Despite the silences about love in sexuality education, it is clear that love is constituted as something powerful, and its messages are ever-present in popular culture in songs, films and novels.

It was interesting to note that the boys' were silent on the issues of love and talked about it as been something that girls focused on. McLeod (1999) explores the idea that because love is considered to belong in the private realm and is not to be spoken about, it is women's business, whereas men's business lies in the public realm. She contends that sexuality education must at least examine the constitutive effects of maintaining the silence about the discourse of love, and that ideally, students should be given the chance to examine the profound tensions between safer sex practices and the discourse of love.

While there is general agreement about the need to talk openly to children and young adults about sex, this has been largely a discourse of danger. The talk has been predominantly about the avoidance of pregnancy and disease. Many of the participants suggested that they were tired of hearing about HIV and AIDS. A few learners were initially reluctant to participate in the research until they were reassured that this was not an exercise focused on HIV/AIDS per se. Varga (1999) also found this to be the case when recruiting for urban focus group. It is possible that the young people do not engage with the current HIV/AIDS messages since these talk past their intended audience. It is necessary to find ways of how to avoid AIDS fatigue by listening to the voices of young adults and aiming education at their lived realities. Judging from the accounts of the young adults in this study, it is clear that the talk has to go further than the medicalisation of sex and disease to include issues of feelings, desire and pleasure.

6.4. Marriage and the nuclear family

The data from this study suggests that the cultural preoccupation of a "productive" marriage is strongly valued in this community. Both girls and boys understand marriage as being a natural development within heterosexuality, and that teenage years are preparation for marriage. Girls prepare themselves for marriage by endorsing and valuing virginity, while boys claim to prepare themselves for marriage by gaining sexual experience that is necessary for a successful marriage. While some of the girls, rebel against the prevalent sexual double standards, many others accept them as natural.

The findings from this study demonstrate that overwhelmingly, the young adults locate themselves within the dominant ideology, which includes the dominance of heterosexual norms and the sanctity of the nuclear family. However, Kraak (1998) argues that the HIV/AIDS epidemic testifies to the transience of monogamy, and is proof that most people have more than one sexual partner in their life-time. This means that the idealised notion of the nuclear family is an illusion, and positioning this as the ultimate goal within heterosexual morality may not be a useful strategy within this HIV/AIDS climate.

Over and against the subculture of promiscuity, there is a construction of a culture of monogamous relationships and faithful partners. Over and against the construction of "high risk" sexual behaviour there is the construction of the marriage and the family as the exemplar of sexual safety. According to Singer (1993), the notion of "safe sex", has been appropriated by culturally conservative critics to argue that the nuclear family is the safest sex around: "In the era of panic sexuality, the family is repackaged as a prophylactic social device".

The data from my study confirms Singer's idea of the move toward marriage and the nuclear family being an answer to the HIV/AIDS pandemic. However, this notion needs to be challenged. In the next section, I examine the young adults' construction of marriage as a safe haven (section 6.4.1), and then discuss the sexual double standards prevalent in participants' views about expectations in and off marriage (6.4.2.).

6.4.1. Marriage means sexual safety

The nuclear family continues to be presented as a safe haven from sexual risk.

According to Singer (1993: 68):

> *"One of the strategic utilities of the campaign for safe sex is the possibilities such a discursive framework offers for remarketing the nuclear family as a prophylactic social device. This strategy again takes on an ironic cast when viewed from the history of women's and children's position within the family. That history reveals that the family has never been a particularly safe place for women and children. Most violence against women occurs within the family, as does the sexual abuse of children. Whereas defence of the family was not an explicit element in the generation of safe sex practices, its disciplinary logic leaves such practices open to mobilization by discourses which offer differing and competing visions of what constitutes sexual health and safety, as well as competing senses of the utilities to be preserved and protected"*

An overwhelming majority of the girls positioned themselves as virginal future brides, and believed that their fears about sexual safety will be erased by marriage. However in many of the group discussions, there were a few girls who did not see marriage as the safe haven it was being made out to be. These girls expressed that as long as they were ignorant about their partner's sexual history, they would insist on condoms until both partners have been tested for HIV/AIDS.

Women's safety also depend on the social organisation of the family, which is another hegemonic concept that is currently being repackaged for a new sexual era. There is an advocacy of domesticated monogamous marital sexuality in this age that is concerned with the risks of multiple sexual contacts. As a consequence, the family has re-emerged as a prominent figure and as a sanctuary from disease. If the messages about safe sex are to stop at those advocating abstinence and delaying of sexual activity until marriage, it does nothing to prepare young women for sexual negotiation and sexual risk within a marriage.

6.4.2. Sexual double standards

The majority of the girls proudly announced that they were "saving themselves" for marriage. This was obviously the thing to say, and be heard saying in peer group discussions. Whether this is actually their experience is hard to tell. It was clear that virginity, is closely connected with respect, and is viewed as a gift and virtue in women, but as a stigma in men. In fact, it was desirable, to both boys and girls that boys are sexually experienced before marriage. Much has been written on the subject of sexual double standard: promiscuous boys are valued as studs; promiscuous girls are devalued as slags (Lees 1987; Varga 1997). The research data of this study shows that this sexual experience that boys necessarily had to gain, was to ensure their fidelity when they do marry, rather than only to promote their masculine 'stud'' image. Boys were very clear that if they did not gain enough sexual experience before marriage, it would force them to stray from the marital bed.

Girls' ideas about abstinence and virginity until marriage for themselves, but desirable sexual experience in their marriage partner, is a further indication of the confusions and contradictions in their understanding of safe sex discourses. The boys in this study also saw marriage as being an important (adult) goal and preparation for successful marriage necessarily included sufficient sexual experiences.

It is evident that the AIDS pandemic and the cultural discourses surrounding it has in many ways led to a change in the ways in which sexual identities are produced. For example, abstinence and monogamous domesticated sexuality has become fashionable, or at least respectable again (Singer 1993). While it can be easily seen in the ways in which girls present themselves, it is not so blatant in the boys' projections of their sexual identities.

6.5. Power and resistance

The data from this study demonstrate that interpersonal relationships are characterised by notions of power and resistance. Deveaux (1994) notes that Foucault's work on power and the notion that "where there is power, there is resistance", as well as assertion that individuals contest fixed identities and relations in ongoing and sometimes subtle ways, has been particularly helpful for feminists who want to show the diverse sources of women's subordination as well as to demonstrate that resistance is engaged in our everyday lives.

In this section I examine the issues of power and resistance, in the accounts of the participants that point to intergeneration (adults and teenagers) contexts as well as intragenerational (peers and partners) contexts.

6.5.1. Intergeneration power dynamics

The participants in this study suggest that there is much control in terms of the "family gaze". This family gaze, within which the young adults feel constantly under surveillance, is an important factor that contributes to the intergenerational interactions being characterised by dynamics of control and resistance. The control by parents and teachers, in their messages that sexuality is dangerous, and the resistance by the young people to forms of adult control, produces negative outcomes in the sexuality domain.

The powerful message from the "adult world" is that sexuality is dangerous. The promotion of abstinence is a key feature in AIDS campaigns where young people are taught to control their sexuality rather than affirm it. The ABC model of AIDS education where "A" is for abstinence, "B", for being faithful and "C" for condomise, has been widely used. At the same time there is no end to the commercialisation and commodification of sexuality in our media. For example music videos that are aimed mainly at young people portray overtly sexy images of provocative dress and erotic dances. Many of these show dominance of males over females and reproduce stereotypical notions of men possessing women. In spite of the silences about teenage sex and sexuality in communications with adults (such as parents and teachers), teenagers are able to talk frankly about traditional taboos, such as, masturbation. Their language about body, pleasure and desire is bold and uninhibited. It would be interesting to examine where and how young people acquire their sexual language and knowledge.

From their enthusiasm to share with me details of their private lives, it is evident that opportunities to talk to adults are limited. There are social constraints on young people in their opportunities to talk and discuss issues about sex and sexuality. This is the case because there is limited social acceptance of teenage sexuality. Talk seems to be a key element of identity and self-expression and the young adults in this study talk about the lack of opportunities to talk, especially to adults, especially about issues related to sexuality. According to Frith and Kitzinger (1998) when young people talk about "the need to talk" they construct themselves as silenced and as searching for self-discovery. West (1999) asserts that the need to talk expresses not just the absence of marginalised issues but the demand to be heard, for exchanges between equals, for dialogue. She adds that as important as the need to talk is the need for privacy and also respect. Participants often suggested that they did not trust their educators enough to discuss personal issues, but they opened up to me very easily. It is possible that this is because I was a relative stranger. Even though I spent an extended time in the school, and the less of a stranger I became, the more comfortable they were to talk to me. How was it different from the other adults with whom they interacted?

It became evident from their accounts that personal relationships with adults in the contexts of families and schools are more of an obstacle than a facilitating factor, especially where personal intimate matters are concerned. The participants' responses indicate ways in which youth sexuality still lack social acceptability. Adults (especially parents and educators) either discipline or avoid issues of sexuality and the young people themselves police themselves and each other. The proscription on talk across generations is connected to the general separation of 'children' and adults, and closely coupled with the greatly valued concept of "respect". Maintaining the boundaries between the generations meant maintaining respect for adults. Attempts by "children" to minimise the boundaries was tantamount to "disrespect". Being from a former generation to my participants, I was struck by the enduring nature of intergenerational struggles reminiscent of the difficulties and struggles of my own experiences and those of my peers during our teenage years.

Epstein and Johnson (1998) point out most adults are likely to have memories of sexuality playing a big part in their experiences of schooling from the earliest days at school and find it to be surprising that talking about sexuality and schooling in the same breath can seem disturbing. They suggest that this may be partly because schooling stands on the 'public' side of the public/private divide, while sexuality is definitely on the private side. The popularly held view that sex is today talked about more openly than in the past exerts some pressure on the private /public divide. The meanings of public and private may alter, and the border constituting them as such may shift, but they remain significant (Harding 1998).

The intergenerational border is certainly strongly policed by adults. Young adults are in effect positioned more as children than as young persons, and this contributes directly to the difficulties they face in articulating their concerns and in achieving their sexual identities. Central to this is the need for greater opportunity to talk about sex and relationships, yet these opportunities are limited by dominant models of heterosexuality and also by the status of youth (West 1998). This need to talk to young people about sex has been taken up by recent media campaigns, with many prominent personalities, including former South African president, Nelson Mandela voicing the slogan "love them enough to talk about sex". The assumption behind the popular slogan mentioned is that sex is a perilous thing and needs to addressed within a specific context of love. This is itself a mixed message. This stance of 'talk to them' is still a paternalistic approach, which implies talking down to them (young people) and that adults know and young people do not know. Talking *to* them is not a useful idea, rather we should think about talking *with* them. In this study, I have found that giving voice to young people has enormous potential for growth and empowerment (see section 4.2.2.).

Presently, talk about sex is increasing. Does this necessary mean that this is liberating? In addition to the content of the talk, we need to think about the contexts within which talk is possible and effective. Given the social relations between adults and young people, talk about sex can be as indicative of regulation and power as is repression. The nature of the talk needs considerable thought.

There clearly continues to be generational sanction on teenage sexuality, which denies it and reduces to silence. Foucault (1981) writes about the "repressive hypothesis" in relation to sex. This hypothesis proposes that power is principally exercised by means of prohibition and repression, for example through denial, censorship and injunction to silence. Sex is kept a secret, and Forbes (1996) notes that the history of sexuality, especially within modern discourses, has been a struggle against secrecy and constraints. Forbes (1996) adds that according to this view, if the past is one with

154

sexual repression, more recent history is of efforts towards increasing sexual choice, expression and freedom. In this study, it became evident that young adults' sexual expression was closely policed by adults, and they certainly did not experience sexual freedom. In terms of intergeneration communication about sex, it seems that Foucault's "repressive hypothesis" is not something of the past, it has either continued through the years (since the classical ages), or it has made a return. Within the peer group, however, the participants demonstrated the ability to talk openly and fairly informedly about sexual matters.

Foucault (1976) argued that power is not possessed, it is exercised, and that power produces corresponding resistance. Singer (1993) follows the Foucauldian position that pleasure can no longer be understood in opposition to power, for power is the discursive matrix by which pleasure is produced and circulated. Singer (1993) notes that the disciplinary apparatus that emerges with the purpose of limiting or even abolishing certain forms of sexuality, can work by becoming itself the site for the production of new sexualities. The power exercised by parents in their efforts to suppress youth sexuality is resisted by the young adult and this resistance is often acted out in extreme forms and in acts of defiance. For example, many of the girls indicated that they engage in unsafe sexual practices in an attempt to defy their parents for being so restrictive.

It appears that the adult-child context is currently an inappropriate one to manage an effective dialogue about sex. The issues of control and resistance that characterises intergenerational relationships and discourses, particularly, sexuality, need to be addressed for any messages about safe sex to be effectively embraced by the young adults. We can perhaps learn from the interactions between peers. In the next section I discuss issues of power and resistance that was evident within the peer context.

6.5.2. Intragenerational power and resistance

The discussion above focused on intergenerational issues of power and resistance, I would now like to turn my attention to power and resistance *within* relationships. In most societies, gender relations are characterised by an unequal balance of power

(Weiss et al. 2000). The construction of male and female sexual identities reflects the inequalities of the social spheres of life. This is evident in the ways in which young men are more likely to initiate and control sexual interaction.

Some girls demonstrated that they understand the sex/gender structuring within heterosexual relationships and that they are not always victims. This is important since embracing a "victim" status is likely to lead to helplessness and lack of agency on the part of girls to take responsibility of their sexual health. Many of the girls, however, do not question the unequal power within relationships and accept sexual double standards as being "normal". Equity does not appear to be the cornerstone of young adults' relationships. It seems that it remains largely the responsibility of the young women to avoid pregnancy and STD's, and this is not surprising in a society where when pregnancy does result, the blame and responsibility is placed on the woman.

In gender relations it is not just the relations of power between men and women that is a problem; it is also the way in which masculinities and femininities are constructed as separate categories that describe and circumscribe individual persons (Johnson 1997). It is evident from the data that the boys and girls sometimes challenge the dominant notions of masculinities and femininities. It is also evident that girls are aware of their position as legitimators of masculinity, and although not consistently, attempt to exercise power by withdrawing consent, and/or positioning themselves in terms of "equality of sex".

Although it is not possible to ignore the continuing dominance of men's power at the structural and personal level, the data from this study shows that girls are not always passive victims. They do not lack the capacity to act in these situations and can operate powerfully against boys on occasions. In the cases where girls continue to perform conventional feminine identities, they relinquish their control and power.

Some of the girls and boys seem to be reconstructing sex as an "equal rights" issue, in terms of initiating sexual activity and experiencing desire and pleasure. The boys who mention sexually desiring girls, do so either to judge them as being promiscuous, or as being objects to increase their (boys') own sexual pleasure. According to Forbes

(1996), with sex reconstructed as an "equal rights" issue, women are encouraged to think that they want what men have had, and to claim what they have been denied. With such a model of "equal rights", all practices within heterosexuality are constructed as equally desirable, acceptable and accessible to both men and women. Forbes (1996) cautions however, that within such gender equivalence is the normalisation and legitimation of male sexuality. Accepting male sexuality as the norm and modelling a new female sexuality against that norm has the potential of multiplying existing problems. For any real attempts at gender equity, it is clear that both male and female sexuality must be problematised. Furthermore, the differences between equality and equity must be made clear, since it is evident that some girls and boys are posturing an "equal rights" approach, which serves to legitimate and reproduce existing the gender hierarchy. For any positive political change, it is necessary to understand the social justice agenda associated with "equity".

It appears that the patriarchal control of young women, their bodies, and their sexuality are not limited to previous generations. From the accounts of the young adults in this study, it seems that power and control of men over women remain part of the lived reality of young women. It appears that patriarchal control, traditional double standards, and gender-based cultural stereotypes are still very much at the core of developing youth sexuality and conceptions of gendered relationships.

Some of the girls and boys seemed to challenge traditional versions of femininities and masculinities, suggesting that changes may be underway. Butler's (1990) concept of *performativity* is useful for what it can tell us about how we are produced as subjects within prevailing power relations. Her arguments about the instabilities within performative processes suggest the possibilities of transgressing, destabilising and "resignifying" the identities one is called upon to perform. There are, for Butler (1990), constraints on what can be "performed", and she contends that the terms within which it can be performed are set by the normalising, regulatory effects of prevailing power relations.

In this study, it is evident that the different gazes: of self, peers and family, are important factors in production of sexual identities, and resignifying these demands that prevailing power relations be directly challenged. In the next section, I discuss the dominance of heterosexuality and its implications for young adults' sexual identity constructions within the context of HIV/AIDS.

6.6. Hetero/sexual performances

The emergence of HIV has significantly altered discourses about sexuality and presents a particular challenge to hegemonic masculinity and normative heterosexuality. The ways in which young men and young women attempt to achieve a normative heterosexual identity, a process which relies on a rejection or othering of difference, are therefore made particularly transparent in the context of HIV/AIDS education (Harrison 2000).

> *Man is the Hunter, women is his game:*
> *The sleek and shiny creatures of the case,*
> *We hunt them for the beauty of their shins;*
> *They love us for it, and we ride them down*

Alfred, Lord Tennyson *The Princess* (1847) (cited in Siann 1994)

This view that females and males are essentially different in nature has deep historical roots in most cultures and permeates mythology, folklore, literature and philosophy in most cultures. The enduring nature of these 'essentialist' views is evident in the ways in which the participants positioned themselves as "opposites' in terms of gender. This construction was never questioned by any of the girls and boys in the study. This emphasises their understanding of heterosexuality as been natural, and as Steward et al. (2000) notes, one key truth in which heterosexuality has been socially constructed remains the masculine–feminine dichotomy whereby women are defined in opposition to the masculine, and to a particular type of man. The boys define themselves by what the girls are not, and vice versa. These ideas emerge frequently in the data, especially in the participants' explanations for coupling.

Cornwall and Lindisfarne (1994: 18) contend that masculinity and femininity have been portrayed as polar opposites, which only change in relation to each other. They quote Kimmel (1987: 12) who asserts:

> *Masculinity and femininity are relational constructs.... One cannot understand the social construction of either masculinity or femininity without reference to each other.*

Cornwall and Lindisfarne (1994) question some of the assumptions behind this popular idea, for instance the idea that these qualities cannot be ascribed to a single individual at any time. In many of the hegemonic discourses, the focus is on an absolute, naturalised and typically hierarchicised male/female dichotomy whereby men and women are defined in terms of differences between them. As Cornwall and Lindisfarne (1994) reminds us, to adopt such a perspective to the exclusion of others is to ignore, first, how any hegemonic discourse produces subordinate and subversive variants and second, the existence of multiple and competing hegemonic masculinities within any particular setting.

Paulsen (1999) suggests that the construction of hegemonic masculinity inhibits school life for both girls and boys. He uses an interesting example, based on David Gilmore's (1990) work on *Manhood in the Making* to help deconstruct the sociobiological argument for gender and roles. Here the traditional cultures of the Tahitians and Semai (from central Malaysia) are examined and both societies are shown to be extremely non-violent and the behavioural roles of men and women are indistinguishable. Paulsen (1999) contends that programs created to achieve equity for girls in schools could more appropriately be directed at boys, who are often the case of the disadvantages faced by girls.

The findings from my research show that this is only partly true. It appears, from the findings in my study, that girls often construct themselves in terms of traditional notions of femininity, and are in some ways complicit in their domination by boys. They do not question the naturalness of heterosexuality and position themselves largely in terms of the male gaze. It is my contention that in order for any real changes towards gender reform to occur, both dominant versions and femininity and of masculinity must be challenged. It is not useful to continue to position girls as helpless victims of male domination and violence. For both girls and boys to become active agents of change, hegemonic masculinities and femininities must be problematised. It is important to understand these versions of masculinity and femininity that inhibit positive behaviour change and to modify these in relation to sexuality and HIV risk.

6.6.1. Troubling femininities

To be conventionally feminine was to appear sexually unknowing, to aspire always to an ideal relationship, to trust and to love and to make men happy. In addition, according to Harrison (2000), the gendered/sexual social positioning of young women in relation to their boyfriends include: not to be assertive, not to initiate sexual activity, not to say "no", and not to say "yes" too quickly. This is because of the hierarchical sexuality, which presents itself as the truth of femininity and the truth of sex. For example, girls would be reluctant to suggest condom-use, since this would imply an active sexual life, and is not in keeping with the passive, innocent image of a "good" girl.

In girls' accounts, "normal" sex is largely defined by an act which is seen as meeting male need and desire. The satisfaction in the act for girls is that they succeed in pleasing the boy, and the chance of it leading to intimacy and love. While girls often articulated these views in speaking about other girls, when is comes to talking about themselves, the majority of the girls articulate their sexuality in terms of "virginity and respect", which they see as being interdependent. They learn about sexuality through a discourse of "danger" to their bodies, which result in "loss" of virginity and possible pregnancy. The discourse of desire and pleasure is largely absent and becomes subsumed by a discourse of danger and disease.

It was clear that the dynamic within the relationship is usually guided by the preferences of the male partners. Girls have to take a decision, either to insist on condom-use and risk rejection, or to remain silent and risk HIV/AIDS infection. It was apparent that different sexual standards exist for boys and girls regarding sexual practices, and these differences encourage high-risk sexual behaviour. There was awareness among the girls about the inequality in sexual decision-making and dyadic negotiation. While a few of the girls challenged this, many others accepted it as being "normal".

The accounts of the girls suggest that young woman face tremendous social pressure to maintain an image of innocence, regardless of the true extent of their knowledge and sexual experience. This was also found to be the case by Weiss et al. (2000). This poses difficulties to girls taking precautions against pregnancy, sexually transmitted diseases and safe sex negotiation, because raising the issue of safe sex (such as condom-use) would imply a degree of sexual knowledge, which is inappropriate. Many girls suggested that it was easier to submit to unsafe sex, than to be labelled "cheap" or "loose", yet in the very action of submission, they are branded as "cheap" and "loose" by their peers. This is a further indication of the contradictions in girls' sexual lives, and their self-fulfilling sexual disempowerment.

The dominant discourse of femininity through which these young women made sense of their sexual selves, stood in direct contraction to their sexual safety (Holland et al. 2000). The conclusion that femininity constituted an unsafe sexual identity, and that conventionally feminine behaviour was putting young women at risk, was an observation also made by Holland et al. (2000). There are obvious tensions between the girls' sexual identity constructions and safe sex discourses. However, despite the power and privilege that accompany compulsory heterosexuality, the payoff for young women who conform to heterosexual norms of femininity in terms of attention and acceptance from young men and their female peers, teachers and society at large cannot be underestimated (Holland et al. 1992). The girls in this study, who unquestioningly conformed to traditional notions of femininity, are implicated in their own disempowerment. It is necessary to destabilise their notions of normative heterosexual femininities, in order for them to take charge of their own sexual health.

There were contradictions in the young women's accounts, in particular between expectations and experience; between intention and practice; and between different discourses of femininity (Holland et al. 2000). Girls learn to look sexy, but say "no"; to attract boys' desire, but not to respond to their own. Girls had to walk a narrow line between being sexually desirable and sexually active. Their socialisation is fraught with discontinuity and conflict. Lees (1993) notes that girls' identities are fractured by the widespread depiction as sex objects, yet indications of sexual desire on their part can render them as "whores", "good-time girls", or "slags".

Some of the girls described experiencing sexual desire. This is important because girls' sexual feelings are often neither recognised nor acknowledged. Through constructing themselves as desiring subjects, instead of objects of desire, girls are beginning to claim their rights of bodily pleasure that they have often been denied. Conceptualising female subjectivity and female desire as diverse, shifting, mediated by individual agency and choice, Vance (1984) argues that women can effectively transform their experience of and position within an institutionalised heterosexuality through a conscious self-stylisation in relation to erotic desire and bodily pleasure.

Although young women are beginning to construct their own definitions and assumptions of sexuality and gendered relationships, they often continue to do so in terms of a "male gaze" (van Roosmalen 2000). This performance of traditional femininity in relation to traditional masculinity is conforming to compulsory heterosexuality (see Butler 1990). By understanding gendered identities as tied together in an unequal yet dynamic relationship, the suggestion is that the achievement of conventional masculinity and femininity are mutually dependent. By performing feminine identities, young women are actively involved in reproducing dominant masculine identities that are contrary to their own sexual safety. We live in a society where girls are not supposed to talk about sex. Sexual silence is detrimental within sexual encounters and must be overcome in order for girls to actively engage their agency within sexual relationships.

Young women have to be active agents in reconstructing the dominant discourse of femininity through which they understand themselves in relation to young men. In accepting the dominant discourse of masculinity as being "natural" they contribute to their dominance and oppression. It appears from my findings that boys assess their masculinity in terms of their ability to exercise power against girls. This is easy enough where girls position themselves within dominant versions of femininity. Where girls resist subordination, express themselves as desiring (not just objects of desire), they are seen as a threat to hegemonic masculinity. In many cases they are seen to be "more like boys". The assumption is no longer that girls' sexuality is fundamentally different from boys but that they now want to act as boys always have.

6.6.2. Troubling masculinities

Traditionally boys were encouraged to have a string of girlfriends, so that when they marry they would have had enough experience with women. Their ideas of what it means to be a man is constructed through interaction within the family, and peer group. Masculinities are policed by other boys as well as by girls. Men who do not adopt these dominant versions of masculinity are often seen to be outside the heterosexist structuring and rendered "other". This suggests that living up to the image of what a real man should be like may be a more salient factor in determining one's social and sexual practices than even the fear of disease and death. In many cases death is not fearful. The construction of masculinity in the form of being invincible and being able to stare death in the face is a further contributing factor.

It is necessary to deconstruct normative heterosexuality and question its naturalness. Given that young adults' have strong cultural and psychological investments in policing the boundaries of heterosexuality, any challenges are likely to be met with resistance. Butler (1993: 238) argues:

> *Precisely because homophobia often operates through the attribution of a damaged, failed or otherwise abject gender to homosexuals, that is, calling gay men "feminine" or calling lesbians "masculine", and because the homophobic terror of performing homosexual acts, where it exists, is often also a terror over losing proper gender ('no longer being a real or proper man' or 'no longer being a real or proper woman'), it seems crucial to retain a theoretical apparatus that will account for how sexuality is regulated through the policing and shaming of gender.*

Such arguments suggest that, as historically specific constructions, contemporary heterosexual masculinities presuppose an opposition to homosexuality, and that, at least in part, they derive their coherence as identities from this opposition (Redman 1996)

Boys use gendered language that takes as given the representation of men as having uncontrollable sexual desires. They do not see any need to apologise for their voracious sexual behaviour towards girls since they see this as a natural state of things.

As a result of family, social, and peer influences, sexual experience is seen as a desired goal for boys and linked to their developing concept of masculinity (Weiss et al. 2000). Coercive sex related to boys' inability to control themselves in a sexual situation was seen to be acceptable to boys and girls. Such an interpretation of coercion, that it was natural male reaction, provided forced sex with considerable social legitimacy (Varga 1999). The extent to which sexual coercion is minimised by both the girls and the boys is particularly disturbing. This is possibly because as pervasive as it is, it is often hidden and even in some case not recognised. In many cases it was not even seen as coercion, but as a natural state of things. For example, subtle forms of coercion, which accompanied a promise of love and intimacy, or threats to break off the relationship, were not seen by girls to be coercion at all. Some forms of coercion were understood as unavoidable given that boys naturally had uncontrollable sexual urges. Of course, coercion was not a feature of all boys' sexual practices, since boys demonstrate sensitivity and self-reflection, particularly in mixed-sex groupings and individual accounts.

It became clear from much of girls' and boys' accounts that they attempt to both challenge as well as leave dominant gender relations in place. For women to negotiate safer sex practices with their male partner, questions the traditional basis of sexual activity, where men usually determined when and how sexual activity took place. The growing awareness of HIV and its transmission has importantly put the naturalness and universality of heterosexuality into question.

Many of the boys assumed a powerful position of being knowledgeable about sex and about STD's including HIV/AIDS. According to Holland at al. (1993) the assumption that men have knowledge can be disempowering for the individual young man who may, in fact, not know, but cannot reveal that lack because he is expected to know.

Butler (1990) argues for a concept of politics as the constant undoing of the categories of gender and norms that derive from and are perpetuated by " sexual performances". This is possible by constructing a coherent narrative of themselves as different from traditional versions of masculinity, and finding a coherent identity by having the skill and competency to disconnect from traditional versions of masculinity.

6.7. Private verses public performances

People may oppose and resist dominant versions of heterosexuality, or they may conform directly to them, or they may occupy contradictory positions simultaneously by positioning and repositioning themselves in different contexts. How did different groupings shape the interactions and reflections between the participants? The ways in which grouping were organised, was to allow the participants to articulate to themselves and their peers who they were and the kind of persons they want to be.

There were dissonances between public and private sexual identity performances of the participants and these were more resounding in the accounts of the boys than that of the girls. There were marked differences in dominant constructions of heterosexual masculinity and individual experiences when I spoke to boys individually, and in the presence of other boys. This was also a significant finding by Blackmore et al. (1996) in their study of power and sexual harassment in school.

The different group settings saw performances of different sexual identities. The mixed-sex group was useful in that it allowed for girls to challenge hegemonic notions of masculinities and femininities and assert themselves as agents. The boys, in single-sex groups conformed to more traditional versions of masculinity and displayed more aggressive attitudes toward homosexuality. Boys' public discussions about sex subordinate female and certain male identities and only allow certain kinds of heterosexual masculinities to be displayed.

For girls and boys, it seems that "fitting-in", and being seen as "normal" was a powerful determinant of what the participants said in public. In private, girls and boys often admitted that what was expected from them was in conflict with their own views about what they should be doing. What does this mean for actual sexual practices? What is the relationship between the internal policing that goes on with regard to sexuality issues and the peer policing? Sexual activity, even though a private matter, usually involves another person. Since the young adults in this study seem more concerned about the social costs of adopting safer sexual practices than the health consequences of not doing so, they are likely to compromise their judgement in favour of expected norms within sexual relationships, and this can clearly lead to risky practices.

The articulation of the boys in mixed-sex focus groups was markedly different from those in boys' only groups. While they often displayed bravado in boys-only discussions, they displayed a lot more sensitivity in mixed-sex discussions. There is the possibility that it is an attempt to appear "politically correct", but another interesting feature of the mixed-sex interviews is that there was always at least one girl who challenged the traditional and stereotypical versions of dominance within heterosexual relationships. Another possible reason for a more sensitive performance within mixed-sex discussions is that the boys have some investment with regard to the friendships and intimate relationships with girls. Given the importance of such interaction, it is critical that interventions include opportunities for men and women to discuss issues of sexuality and sexual risk and responsibility. Morrell et al. (2001) suggest that unless policies and programmes take seriously the diverse responses of learners, they will talk past the realities and will themselves become disarticulated from engagement with the epidemic (HIV/AIDS) and efforts to ameliorate its tragic effects.

Findings by Nahom et al. (2001) on youth in the US suggests intentions to engage in sexual behaviour and use condoms, feelings of pressure to have sex, and perceptions of the number of friends engaging in sexual intercourse differ by gender and sexual experience status. Also those perceptions of peer's sexual behaviour influence adolescents' decisions to engage in sexual behaviour more strongly than peers' actual behaviour. Extent and impact of peer pressure seems to vary by gender and age. Often practices are not just a result of intention between partners since reward and sanction are in the hands of the wider peer group.

Haywood (1996) argues that in both style and content 'talk' is a material relation of power and a technique to police and regulate normative assumptions about gendered relations. For example, young men's public talk about sex problematises female and subordinates male identities, allowing only certain kinds of heterosexual masculinities to show their identities. My study shows that division between public and private is not always clearly defined, but that the composition of the audience has an influence of the kind of public performance. This has implications for planning and delivery of intervention programs, for example, we need to consider who delivers sexuality education messages and in what kinds of group settings.

The performative nature of sexual identity is evidenced in the public/private sexuality discourses in this sense because public practices are used to convey the desired identity one wished to project. This also means that there may not be a direct correspondence with what one says and what one does, if what one says is different in different settings. It is very likely that ones' practices, like ones' talk, is contextually determined as well.

6.8. Conclusion

It is clear that HIV/AIDS education, and sexuality education, presents a particular challenge to dominant forms of masculinities and femininities and that programs need to address gender, power and the compulsory nature of heterosexuality. Furthermore, intergenerational relationships that are characterised by dynamics of power and control, act as mechanisms to constrain rather than affirm young adults' sexuality. An understanding of the dynamic and contextual nature of sexual identity construction and reconstruction are critical for any effective response to the HIV/AIDS pandemic.

In the next Chapter, I conclude this research report with a discussion of the emerging insights from this study of young adults' sexual identity constructions in the context of HIV/AIDS, and propose a reconstitution of identity as a negotiated *process*. I then discuss the implications of this study for HIV/AIDS and sexuality education and future research.

CHAPTER SEVEN

TROUBLING SEXUALITIES WITHIN THE CONTEXT OF HIV/AIDS

7.1. Introduction

In this thesis I have attempted to map out some of the troubled areas of young adults' sexual identity constructions within the context of HIV/AIDS. The two fundamental propositions that guided this study are that:

➢ identity constructions are dynamic and profoundly shaped by other social factors, and

➢ in order to plan any effective response to the HIV/AIDS pandemic, understanding the constructions of sexuality and sexual identity are crucial.

The following critical question was addressed in this study:

> *How do young adults construct their sexual identities within the discourse of HIV/AIDS?*

In the previous chapter, I have presented a discussion of the synthesis of the findings of this study with the existing literature in this field, the theoretical framework and the methodological considerations of this study. In this concluding chapter, I reflect on the processes and products of this study. This chapter is organised into three parts in the following way:

PART ONE

In Part One, I summarise some of the key theoretical, contextual and methodological insights that emerge from this study.

PART TWO

In Part Two, I propose a conceptualisation of *identity* as a negotiated *process* between often competing forces. I further discuss the interrelatedness of HIV/AIDS, sexual identity and sexual practices and develop the notion of a *mutating trilogy*.

PART THREE

In Part Three, I discuss the pragmatic insights generated through this research in terms of its implications for HIV/AIDS and sexuality education (section 7.5.), and suggest ways in which this research can be usefully extended in section 7.6.

PART ONE

SUMMARY OF KEY INSIGHTS EMERGING FROM THIS STUDY

7.2. Troubling sexualities

The feminist perspective, which informs much of this research, has the effect of problematising 'normal' heterosexual behaviour (see for example, Holland et al. 2000). In this study I have troubled gender relations, and extended the feminist position, which examines power relations within gender relations to include an attempt to understand age relations as well, by challenging the notion of generation as a fixed phase (see section 6.2.).

7.2.1. Troubling age relations

The findings from this study confirm the popular view that teenage years are understood, by teenagers to be a natural phase, which is characterised by biological changes and necessary sexual experimentation. Taken together with the dominance of heterosexual morality and the transitional status of teenagers, these ideas work to erode young adults' power to act as responsible agents. Reconstituting generation as *identity* rather than a *phase* diminishes the notions of biological determinism and opens up the possibility for actively creating and recreating identities based on individual choices. While the changes due to physiological development during these years cannot be ignored, generational identity reconstructs teenage years not just as a "natural state" based on biology, but a socially constructed notion, which means that we interpret our biology through our cultural and social experiences. Conceptualising generational identity in this way, as being constructed, opens up the possibilities of aspects being deconstructed and reconstructed to include individual expressions. This is important within this HIV/AIDS climate as it helps to diminish ideas of helplessness and fatalism that are prevalent among young adults.

Many young adults find themselves caught between the discursive complexities of sexual liberation and sexual regulation, and what seems to be the insurmountable boundary between the sexual identities and practices associated with each. There continues to be a proliferation of erotic and sexual messages via media and popular culture, often depicting young adults. On the other hand, young adults' sexuality is condemned and reduced to silence, particularly if they are at school.

The attempts by parents at desexualising young adults, and positioning them more as children, is a key source of their resistance to the messages about sex and disease that come from the adult world. The ways in which sexuality features in most interactions between teenagers and adults involve strategies of control and resistance. This results in an obstructive mutual "lock out". Clearly these intergenerational struggles detract from the important educational value of sexuality education, particularly in the context of HIV/AIDS, while energies are directed toward intergenerational power struggles.

The cultural discourses surrounding HIV/AIDS has advocated open communication between adults and young people about sexual activity, and parents are attempting to discuss the long taboo topic of sexuality. In fact the HIV/AIDS pandemic has forced communities to directly confront *three* taboos of society: youth sexuality, sex and death. However, the communication has been largely one-way: from adults to "children". The powerful messages from the adult world are that sex is dangerous, male desire is natural, and girls are victims of male desire. The talk, then, is far from liberating, but is as indicative of regulation and power, as is repression and silence.

The challenge is to be able to broach these crucial issues in a less forced and threatening manner. Some of the difficulties in intergenerational talk about sex are due to a lack of vocabulary in traditional discourses on sex. The vocabulary consisted mainly of medical terms or colloquialisms and euphemisms, which makes direct talk about sex difficult. The participants in this study displayed a sophisticated sexual vocabulary, which allowed them to talk about desire and eroticism in a very open way to each other.

7.2.2. Troubling gender relations

Understanding the ways in which sexual identities are constructed within gender relations is crucial for the achievement of gender equity. This is especially significant in developing strategies for protection against HIV/AIDS. Heterosexuality is predominantly socially constructed along the masculine/feminine dichotomy, where women are defined in opposition to men. Both girls and boys often define femininity and all things feminine as the counterpart of masculinity. This means that girls are all things that boys are not; that boys are dominating and girls are submissive; boys are aggressive and girls are sensitive. The messages that young adults get through learning to be the "opposite sex", include that which accepts that girls and boys live in two different worlds, in terms of sexuality. As a result, relationships between young men and women are characterised by curiosity, mistrust, fear and vulnerability. It is clear that the conventional sexual scripting that young adults receive in our society needs to be challenged directly.

The participants in this study have demonstrated the flux, fluidity and uncertainty in the constructions of contemporary sexual identities. The shifting extent to which the practices of people are determined by structural influences, and the extent to which they are free and responsible agents, are evident in their different performances to different audiences. Femininities and masculinities are constantly created, adapted and contested in everyday interactions among men and women, among men, and among women. The findings from this study suggest that the reproduction of hegemonic sexualities is predominantly a masculine agenda; girls are defined in relation to masculinities. These constructions offer both young women and young men limiting masculine and feminine identities. Relinquishment of power and control is a key defining feature of conventional femininity, as exercising power and control is of conventional masculinity. It is important to recognise diversity among girls and among boys and what needs to be changed is not just individual boys and individual girls, but the relations between them.

The findings from this study confirm that sexual negotiation is clearly not an issue of free choice between equals but one of negotiation between structurally unequal power relationships. Sexual encounters may therefore, become sites of strife between the exercise of male power and the male definitions of sexuality, and of women's ambivalence and resistance. Woman insisting on safe-sex or expressing sexual desire and need for sexual satisfaction challenges male sexual power, and the privileging of men's sexual pleasure. Many of the girls who did attempt to assert themselves as responsible agents, admitted that because of the fear of rejection or "othering", they were not able to practice safe sex consistently. Sexual encounters may be potential sites for both pleasure and danger, but it seems that not too many young adults are prepared for the dangers, or any of the pleasures.

The language and practices used by these young men and women in constructing their sexual identities affords some insight into the processes of policing and regulation involved in maintaining the gender/sexual order. It appears that the main protagonists are young men, although young women too, are engaged in these processes in perhaps more subtle ways. It is apparent that girls and boys conspire together to reproduce the notions of femininity that keep female sexuality under strict control, and the notions of masculinities that allow male sexuality a free reign.

The difficulty of deconstructing normative heterosexuality at school level need not be underestimated. As Harrison (2000) points out, many young men and women have a considerable investment in continuing the privileges that normative heterosexuality brings. Young people are likely to resist partly because traditional discourses are still more convincing to them. Young men have to be prepared to give up the pleasure that exercising power over women bring. Likewise, young women have to be prepared to give up the pleasure they experience in gaining and maintaining conventional heterosexual relationships. The choice to conform to hegemonic notions or to depart from convention is not easy. In order to challenge the imbalances of gender power relations, young adults have to transgress collectively held and policed boundaries and risk becoming "abnormal" or "other". The tightly policed boundaries force young adults to seek private solutions, while keeping public values intact. There is, however, some evidence of change being underway. It is evident that girls and boys both comply with and resist existing gender regimes. Furthermore, not all boys or girls take up the same kinds of sexual identities, or experience maleness or femaleness in the same way. In Butler's (1990) terms, masculinity and femininity might be seen as "imitative text". There are ways in which boys tend to live up to expected identities as "studs" that are after " one thing" from girls. Of course not all boys are comfortable with such positioning and show signs of resistance, but it would take a very brave boy, who would stand up to his peers at the risk of being labelled "gay" (since anything other than hegemonic masculinity was rendered *other*). Similarly, girls are beginning to challenge the double sexual standards that have been for a long time taken as given, for example the incidence of boys demanding multiple sexual partners as their right while insisting on virginity in their partners.

7.2.3. Making "private" matters "public"

The HIV/AIDS pandemic has compelled societies and individuals to engage with sexuality, which has been traditionally regarded as a private issue, as a public issue in ways that were inconceivable in previous decades. Public and private domains are often seen to be necessarily discreet. The very idea of dichotomising 'private' and 'public' appears to be central to understandings of sexuality, and in addition, sexuality helps to distinguish the public and private as opposite and discreet domains. In an HIV/AIDS climate, it is important to deconstruct this private/public binary and to address issues within and across generations, in as public a manner as possible.

Harding (1998) contends that the private and public are interdependent, that neither has meaning without the other. Furthermore, many meanings of sexuality are constituted in relation to changing definitions of public and private, and a shifting border between them. Transgressions of the border help to constitute categories of sexual experience and perform a normative function, because, according to Harding (1998) representations of private sex made public are accompanied by an indication of whether they should be tolerated.

Just as the discourses and practices mobilised under the rubric of 'sexual revolution' recast the relationship between the personal and the political (Singer 1993), the HIV/AIDS pandemic gives good reason for a reconsideration of the politics of the personal, and in particular the politics of pleasure that is associated with it. The discourse of pleasure is largely absent in HIV/AIDS discourses; instead, there have been widespread efforts to control sexual practices through old and new forms of sexual discipline.

Young people in South Africa have historically been part of a socio-cultural context which has not fostered sexual negotiation skills, and in which segregated gender roles that are culturally sanctioned exists. There have, over the years, been many changes in the political and social climate, and while some socio-cultural traditions are enduring (such as the valuing of marriage and the nuclear family), many others (such as girls being taught to be submissive and boys being taught to be assertive) are in the process of undergoing serious transformations. Culturally sanctioned differences in gender roles and expectations have been important factors in the production of limiting sexual identities, that add to sexual risk. Such ideas are evident in girls and boys emphasis on girls' virginity or sex as an expression of love and trust, in contrast to the compulsory multiple sexual partners for boys. While earlier western ideas have cast HIV/AIDS as a homosexual disease, in South Africa, with predominantly heterosexual transmission of HIV, it has not been sexual orientation which is at issue, but promiscuity. In most cases, the intervention has been in terms of moralising against women and sex workers. Male desire was and still is seen as an unquestionable right.

Love is seen as an important factor through which the girls understand their sexuality, while for boys, talking about *love* is embarrassing. This is not surprising in a society that associates "soft" emotions with girls and "aggressive" emotions with boys. However, in private, some boys admit that love and emotional pain is a feature of their lives as well, but in conforming to hegemonic masculinities, they neither acknowledge, nor display these "feminine" characteristics. Girls, in their construction of ideal partners, indicated that they value sensitivity and some of those "feminine" characteristics that boys often mask. This is one of the possible reasons why boys appeared more sensitive and less macho in mixed-sex group interactions than in boys-only groups (see section 6.7).

The internal policing of sexuality, together with the "peer gaze" (see section 5.7.) and the "family gaze" (see section 5.10.), form a dynamic complexity within which sexual identities come to be negotiated. There is generally a greater policing of girls: by each other, the boys, as well as by adults. Mirembe and Davies (2001) also found this to be the case in their study in a coeducational school in Uganda, and note that as the girls experience greater domination and policing, there is a subsequent cycle of lack of self-direction and increased dependency. Girls are generally positioned as being in danger of boys' sexual desires, and have to be protected from them. Paradoxically this "victim" role and protectionism actually does not protect girls, but works to reinforce female helplessness. It is clear that we need to move away from this understanding of gender relations that accentuates domination and victimisation, to broader notions of the role of power in women's lives. This facilitates a productive view of power, which assists us to understand the interweaving nature of our social, political and personal relations.

7.3. Methodological reflections

The seriousness of HIV/AIDS necessitates the obligation from social science and public health researchers to seek innovative approaches, and to be critical in both their epistemological (how do we know what we know? and what is the relationship of the knower to the known?) and methodological (how do we get to know?) undertakings.

7.3.1. Privileging young adults' voices

Privileging the voices of the participants has facilitated an understanding of young adults' sexual identities through their perspectives. Furthermore, it gave research participants an opportunity to take responsibility to do their own thinking in this area. The gendered approach employed in this study allowed not only for differences and similarities between girls and boys to be examined, but for differences within each category to be demonstrated. The assumption, to begin with, was that neither the male experience nor the female experience is homogeneous. This research provides evidence for the blurring of these traditional male/female boundaries.

While much of the sexuality research focuses on single-sex groups, I worked with single-sex as well as mixed sex groups. Working with mixed-sex groups allowed for stereotypes and assumptions about the "other" to be challenged. This provided the opportunity for girls and boys to test their ideas against each other. Thinking together in different group settings provided interesting data on the ways in which identities are produced and interact with each other in different contexts.

In single sex groups, boys tend to display hyper-heterosexual performances. It is a place where uncertainties and fears are masked by display of bravado and predatory behaviour. Sex education has largely been organised around single-sex groupings and Epstein and Johnson (1998) argue that this has the potential to exacerbate the generally competitive macho performances of many of the boys. The mixed–sex groups saw markedly different performances by boys. This demonstrated the potential usefulness of mixed-sex education, since it probably disrupts and subverts the hegemonic discourses of masculinity. Within single-sex groups there was much blaming directed from one sex to another, and this had the effect of reflecting responsibility from themselves to the *other*, while in the mixed-sex grouping these ideas were openly discussed and challenged.

7.3.2. Knowledge-building in teams

A further methodological innovation in this study was the *collaborative-grounded analysis* approach that I developed in the course of this study. This entailed using a grounded analysis approach (allowing for themes to emerge from the data) and two parallel processes of collaboration: negotiation with participants, and negotiation with research colleagues. This has the potential for strengthening analysis themes (categories). Taking preliminary themes to participants had the effect of testing some of them and introducing new themes. As I discussed in Chapter Four, because of the anonymity of the responses, it was not possible to go back to specific respondents, to test themes. Instead, I took preliminary themes to other participants for discussion. This led to a snowballing of themes until I had plateaued with the generation of themes.

An important outcome of such a collaborative approach is the positive effects of building knowledge in teams. One of the guiding principles of this study was to privilege the voices of the participants, and this meant throughout the research process, including generation of data and analysis of data. Reflexivity and collaboration are tied up with the same feminist goals of meaning making. Both are central to the process of representation, which is involved in generating knowledge about the world. It is generally accepted that researchers can no longer stand apart from their research setting, and that their relationships with their participants must be acknowledged as part of a wider social and political engagement than simply that of researcher/researched. In addition, theory building, while a necessary part of any knowledge production activity of should not be seen as end in itself, but the course taken should be empowering to all those involved in the process. This means that the emphasis should not just be on the outcomes, but on research processes as well.

PART TWO

IDENTITY AND HIV/AIDS

7.4.   Identity as a Process

Throughout this research I have been especially concerned with the ways in which sex/gender differences are entangled with the relations of power that characterise teenager/adult relations. What are the influences of general social institutions such as marriage, family, and peers as well as wider media portrayal of identity on young adults' sexual identity constructions?

Butler's (1990) ideas of the *performative* nature of gender have been a useful analytical tool for understanding young adults' sexual identities. Furthermore, this research has provided evidence for the mutable nature of sexual identities. Acknowledging and using the concept of mutation recasts sexual identity as a *process*, rather than as a fixed set of characteristics. This, then means that as a process, there are possibilities and space for negotiation. The process of negotiation is often between competing forces, such as peers, adults, the wider society and the media.

The reconceptualisation of identity as a negotiated process opens up possibilities for "agency" that are insidiously blocked by positions that take identity categories as foundational or fixed. For identity to be a process means that it is neither fatalistically determined, nor fully artificial and arbitrary. That the constituted status of identity is misconstrued along these two conflicting lines, suggests the ways in which the discourse on cultural construction remained trapped within the unnecessary binary of free will and determinism. Moving away from this dichotomy, identity as a process is not opposed to agency; it is the necessary site for agency.

Identity construction is an active process on the part of those involved and struggling to acquire a means to represent oneself to self and others is part of ones development. However, this active process always occurs under socially given conditions, which include structures of power and social relations, institutional constraints and possibilities as well as the available cultural codes.

7.4.1. *A mutating trilogy: HIV/AIDS, sexual identity, and sexual practices*

The conjunction between HIV/AIDS discourses and young adults' sexualities, provides insights for gender theories and sexuality theories into how young adults experience their developing sexuality, and the meanings that they have made of HIV/AIDS.

The bi-directionality of the relationship between sexual identities and sexual practices is evidenced in the data from this study. Different contexts (both within and across) societies interpret different practices as *sexual*, and connect different sexual practices with different meanings (such as what is permissible and what is taboo) in constructing sexual identities. Simultaneously, individuals actively interpret and reinterpret their sexual experiences, creating their identities as sexual beings. Furthermore, my analysis suggests that sexual identities are fashioned and regulated through the creation of new demands, as well as old and new forms of sexual regulation and control, in the HIV/AIDS environment. This is not a linear process. It is evident that the AIDS pandemic and the cultural discourses surrounding it has in many ways led to a change in the ways in which sexual identities are produced and experienced. As sexual identities and sexual practices mutually shape each other, they form a backdrop against which HIV/AIDS is experienced. HIV/AIDS in turn impacts on the construction and reconstruction of sexual identities and practices. This relationship between, and mutual shaping of the three domains: HIV/AIDS, sexual identity and sexual practices, which I refer to as a *mutating trilogy* is shown in figure 7.1.

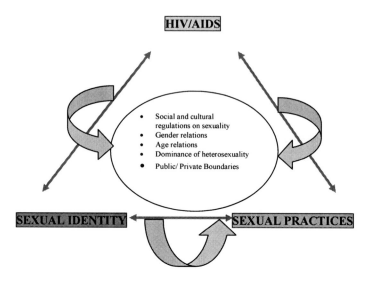

Figure 7.1. Interrelatedness of HIV/AIDS, sexual identities and sexual practices.

We require a response to the pandemic that includes changes in policy and practice to accommodate identities and diversity within these experiences and knowledges. It is evident that there are multiple ways in which people respond. This study offers the perspectives of young adults, their conflicts and contradictions. We need to take these varied responses into account and plan interventions which acknowledge this diversity. It is necessary that interventions articulate with the realities of the youth, taking into account their confusions and contradictions.

PART THREE

PRAGMATIC INSIGHTS EMERGING FROM THIS STUDY

7.5. Implications of this study for sexuality and HIV/AIDS education

Past initiatives have been largely a top-down approach; usually adults addressing young adults as children, with the consequence that key messages did not reach their intended audience. Currently, peer education is being increasing used and its rewards are becoming clear. There is a definite need to give voice to young people and to use their voices. We cannot plan effective programs without foregrounding young adults' voices and understanding how relationships are explored and identities negotiated, and it is their lived experiences that HIV/AIDS education must address. Where and how should their voices be included? It is not enough to get young people to deliver programmes designed by "experts" (usually adults). It is vital to include young people at all levels of development and implementation of all aspects of policies and programmes.

In addition to the content of sexuality education, we need to carefully consider contextual factors such as: who is speaking, and who is listening, and what is the composition audience? My research has shown that these are important considerations, and the different performances of sexual identities in different group settings (single-sex, mixed-sex and individual) is an indication of this.

The conventional critique of HIV/AIDS and sexuality education – that it offers "too little, too late" – misleadingly suggests that information deficit alone is the problem. It is clear from this study that young adults need opportunities for discussions on matters that concern them most, namely feelings and relationships. The present education programmes for example the "ABC[24]" model, and the "just say no" (to sex) campaigns are inadequate. They do not articulate with the experiences of the young people. For instance, there is a powerful discourse of love and romance, especially amongst the girls, which competes with the discourse of safe sex. Educators need to consider that while advocacy for abstinence, may be an attempt to prevent disease, it does not take into account that this stance increases the likelihood of resulting negative consequences such as loss of partner and love. Given the preoccupation with young adults with forming and maintaining relationships with the "opposite sex", it is important to situate sexuality education *within* relationships rather than to employ an approach that discourages teenage relationships.

It is clear that talk about sex and sexuality has to go beyond the biological and medicalisation of sex and disease to include important aspects related to feelings, desire and pleasure, and to be aware of social, biological, emotional embeddedness of sexual identity constructions. Sex education should begin with relationships, desire and respect, taking up issues of biology and medicine along the way, instead of privileging it from the start (Epstein and Johnson 1998).

The findings from this study indicate that sexual identity constructions are not fixed, but are mutable. This opens up a space in which sexual identities can be deconstructed and reconstructed toward positive change at the individual and collective level. Designers of teenage sexuality education programs should place emphasis on the degree to which the teenagers are able to subvert and transform structural underpinning of teenage years as a component of identity, by enabling them to value and exercise their individual choice and self-expression. It is necessary to provide connections to spaces where young men and women can learn new relational identities, since it has become clear in this study that many have limited access to alternate identities.

---

[24] A-abstinence
B-be faithful
C-condoms

7.6. Implications of this study for future research

The school is no doubt a significant arena where sexual identities are negotiated and acted out. This study importantly foregrounds learner voices in the production of data. An important area for further research is that of the structural components of schooling, educators' conceptions of teenage sexuality and their influence on teenage sexual identity constructions.

Curriculum issues are certainly deserving of ongoing attention. Given the intergeneration struggles that the findings of this study demonstrate, teacher education programmes focussing on HIV/AIDS education is an important research area. How are teachers being prepared for open dialogue with learners about issues of sexuality?

Young adults as a generation emerged as a salient identity construction. In this study I worked with a shifting sample of 15-19 year olds. It is not my intention to homogenise this age range and I do explore differences in responses. It would be important for further research to examine the differences in sexual identity constructions within, and across this age range.

The dominant culture is heterosexual and it was clearly not possible to deliberately seek out gay/lesbian learners, due to the closely policed boundaries of heterosexuality within schools. Although I have attempted to allow for alternative positions to emerge, I did not pursue the silences I encountered when I asked questions about homosexuality among the learners. This is a very under researched area, especially in the South African context.

There was a great degree of commonality of experiences from diverse racial and cultural settings. However, it became evident that even in a mixed race school in a mixed race area, there is also evidence of a separate and unifying African and Indian culture, and some ethnic differences within the different race groups. In a country as diverse as South Africa, especially noting its apartheid history, racial and cultural differences influencing sexual identity production is another interesting area that deserves further research.

7.7. In closing

Questions of homogeneity and diversity are at the core of many of the traditional philosophical metaphysical explorations into the question of identity. Current poststructural theorising on identity emphasises the contingent and tentative nature of identities. My analysis suggests that sexual identities are negotiated processes and are produced in many different contexts, often with competing intentions and representations which include all aspects of everyday life as well as all the discourses and interactions. It is evident from the data in this study that sexual identities are accomplished as individuals interact in local situations that are powerfully influenced by broader social patterns of expectation and restriction. As the boundaries between that which is legitimate and taboo, between proper and shameful, are becoming blurred, it is apparent that constructions of sexual identity are negotiated endeavours in the context of competing, contradictory and complex influencing factors, including biological, social and cultural conceptions of sexual relations.

The HIV/AIDS pandemic has created worldwide panic – yet in this crisis there is a liberatory facet. While HIV/AIDS has undoubtedly had a devastating impact on societies worldwide, it has had the positive effect of opening up new ways of thinking and talking identities and relationships, both at individual and structural levels. My research has demonstrated that change, even though not on a large scale, is underway as both girls and boys begin to challenge existing gender regimes. The HIV/AIDS pandemic has importantly brought many long-standing detrimental, toxic aspects of gender/sexual identities that were regarded as normal, into question, and these can importantly be linked to the broader social and political struggles for equity and justice. It is grudgingly accepted that there is no present cure for HIV/AIDS. If a vaccine or a cure for HIV/AIDS had been discovered, would we have been so vehement in our struggles to understand and intervene at every level? Paradoxically, it has taken a pandemic of colossal proportions to bring into focus many long-standing fundamental ills of society, such as domination, subordination and violence.

TABLE OF CONTENTS OF APPENDICES

APPENDIX 1

Lesson plan for Self identity responses

Grade: 12

Expected outcomes:
- Learners would think about the different aspects of their identity
- Learners will be able to write a list of the important things that identify themselves

Educator activity

Since I am not an educator in the school, I explained my role as a researcher and briefly explained my area of research.

I wrote the word IDENTITY on the chalkboard and discussed this word with the whole class.

Learner activity

The learners had to write down a list of aspects of their identity that they thought was important. They had to think about:

Who am I?

How do I think of myself?

APPENDIX 2

Learner questionnaire for use in focus-group discussions

Please complete the following questionnaire. All information will be kept strictly confidential.

Male	Femal e	Race		15-17 years	17- 20years

1. What do you think are the reasons that young people (of your age) have girlfriends/boyfriends?

    _____
    _____
    _____
    _____
    _____

2. Do you have a girlfriend/boyfriend?   Y / N_____

3. Is he/she in school?   Y / N _____

4. Is having sex part of your relationship?   Y / N_____

5. How does knowing about the risks of HIV/AIDS affect the choices you make in a relationship?

    _____
    _____
    _____
    _____
    _____

6. Why do you think young people have unprotected sex?

    _____
    _____
    _____
    _____
    _____

7.   Do you know of any of your school friends who are sexually active? Y / N___
8.   If yes, how do you know this?

_____
_____
_____
_____
_____

   9.   Do you know of any same-sex relationships in your school? Y / N_____

10.   If yes, Are these mostly girls or boys? How do you know this?

_____
_____
_____
_____
_____

___

Thank you for your time and cooperation.

APPENDIX 3

Frequency tables of questionnaire data

Statistics

		Sex	Race	Age	Have a partner?	Partner in school?	Sexually active?	Influence of AIDS knowledge	Reasons f unsafe se
N	Valid	72	72	72	72	58	71	68	
	Missing	0	0	0	0	14	1	4	

Frequency Table

Sex

		Frequency	Percent	Valid Percent	Cumulative Percent
Valid	male	19	26.4	26.4	26.4
	female	53	73.6	73.6	100.0
	Total	72	100.0	100.0	

Race

		Frequency	Percent	Valid Percent	Cumulative Percent
Valid	Indian	48	66.7	66.7	66.7
	African	24	33.3	33.3	100.0
	Total	72	100.0	100.0	

Age

		Frequency	Percent	Valid Percent	Cumulative Percent
Valid	15-17	40	55.6	55.6	55.6
	17-19	32	44.4	44.4	100.0
	Total	72	100.0	100.0	

Have a partner?

		Frequency	Percent	Valid Percent	Cumulative Percent
Valid	yes	55	76.4	76.4	76.4
	no	17	23.6	23.6	100.0
	Total	72	100.0	100.0	

Partner in school?

		Frequency	Percent	Valid Percent	Cumulative Percent
Valid	yes	20	27.8	34.5	34.5
	no	38	52.8	65.5	100.0
	Total	58	80.6	100.0	
Missing	System	14	19.4		
Total		72	100.0		

Sexually active?

		Frequency	Percent	Valid Percent	Cumulative Percent
Valid	yes	16	22.2	22.5	22.5
	no	55	76.4	77.5	100.0
	Total	71	98.6	100.0	
Missing	System	1	1.4		
Total		72	100.0		

Influence of AIDS knowledge

		Frequency	Percent	Valid Percent	Cumulative Percent
Valid	use condoms	10	13.9	14.7	14.7
	abstain	14	19.4	20.6	35.3
	no difference	3	4.2	4.4	39.7
	faithful	4	5.6	5.9	45.6
	faithful+condoms	7	9.7	10.3	55.9
	checkout partner	8	11.1	11.8	67.6
	is aware	15	20.8	22.1	89.7
	spoil relationship/pleasure	7	9.7	10.3	100.0
	Total	68	94.4	100.0	
Missing	System	4	5.6		
Total		72	100.0		

Reasons for unsafe sex

		Frequency	Percent	Valid Percent	Cumulative Percent
Valid	condoms spoil pleasure	32	44.4	50.8	50.8
	trust partner	7	9.7	11.1	61.9
	ignorance	10	13.9	15.9	77.8
	afraid to loose partner	6	8.3	9.5	87.3
	not prepared	1	1.4	1.6	88.9
	punish parents	3	4.2	4.8	93.7
	experiment	4	5.6	6.3	100.0
	Total	63	87.5	100.0	
Missing	System	9	12.5		
Total		72	100.0		

Do u know friends sexually active?

		Frequency	Percent	Valid Percent	Cumulative Percent
Valid	yes	43	59.7	61.4	61.4
	no	27	37.5	38.6	100.0
	Total	70	97.2	100.0	
Missing	System	2	2.8		
Total		72	100.0		

How do you know about others?

		Frequency	Percent	Valid Percent	Cumulative Percent
Valid	friends confide	18	25.0	39.1	39.1
	gossip	2	2.8	4.3	43.5
	boys talk	9	12.5	19.6	63.0
	girls talk	17	23.6	37.0	100.0
	Total	46	63.9	100.0	
Missing	System	26	36.1		
Total		72	100.0		

knowledge of same-sex relationship

		Frequency	Percent	Valid Percent	Cumulative Percent
Valid	yes	11	15.3	15.9	15.9
	no	58	80.6	84.1	100.0
	Total	69	95.8	100.0	
Missing	System	3	4.2		
Total		72	100.0		

gay boys, girls

		Frequency	Percent	Valid Percent	Cumulative Percent
Valid	girls	7	9.7	53.8	53.8
	boys	3	4.2	23.1	76.9
	both	3	4.2	23.1	100.0
	Total	13	18.1	100.0	
Missing	System	59	81.9		
Total		72	100.0		

why have partners

		Frequency	Percent	Valid Percent	Cumulative Percent
Valid	peer pressure	20	27.8	28.2	28.2
	phase of life	23	31.9	32.4	60.6
	companionship	16	22.2	22.5	83.1
	sex	12	16.7	16.9	100.0
	Total	71	98.6	100.0	
Missing	System	1	1.4		
Total		72	100.0		

8

APPENDIX 4

Information about Boss Secondary and photographs

1. Name: Boss Secondary school
2. Location: Durban, KwaZulu Natal

The following information was obtained from the EMIS (Education Management Information Services) records.

3. Number of Educators:

FULL/PART TIME	NO.OF MALES	NO. OF FEMALES
Full time	14	16
Part time	2	5

4. Boss secondary has 5 support staff

5. School fees R500 p.a.

6. Number of learners per race:

RACE	NO. OF MALES	NO. OF FEMALES
African	276	309
Indian	226	263
Coloured	15	9
TOTAL	517	580

7. Home language of the learners

LANGUAGE	NO. OF LEARNERS
English	521
IsiZulu	546
isiXhosa	15
SeSotho	6
XiTsonga	8

8. The total number of learners in Boss Secondary: 1097

   The number of learners in grade 11:   155
   The number of learners in grade 12:   101

The area
The school
typical houses
school grounds

Sample scenarios

Scenario 1 – written by a girl (16years)

Topic: A boy pressurising his girlfriend to have sex

A boy said to a girl, "my girlfriend, I want to say something to you today. I know that you are going to say 'no', but I love you. You are my girlfriend. You are my only girlfriend, sweetheart. Darling, please for only today I want to show you how much I love you and how much I care about you. Please sweet come and lets kiss. Please girl, I feel like we can have sex". The girl says "no". "Why not? Please sweet I love you. See girl, there is nothing that can happen because I love you. Lets have sex." The boy romance the girl until the girl becomes very on. The boy said " I cant do it, honey". The girl said, " but…what but, because you love me and I love you". After the girl said "yes" they have sex. The boy feels very nice. The girl feels the same thing, terrible.

Scenario 2 written by a girl (15years)
Topic: A boy pressurising a girl to have sex

Kim does want to wait until she's married to lose her virginity, but on the other hand, Kim's boyfriend, Joe wants to have sex with her. I have'nt been in this situation before but if I was in Kim's predicament, no matter how much I love him, I would never lose my virginity to someone I am not sure I would be would forever. Things about boys is that you never know when they are lying or telling the truth. But in this case I believe that its not hard to make a decision because I believe that virginity is something that cannot be regained once it is lost. And no matter how much you know this person and how much you love this person, you'll never know if you'll regret it. Joe may be a boy who might or might not be there for his girlfriend when he has sex or gets her pregnant because they want to take a chance and then when it comes to responsibility, they run. And then what stops him from getting another girlfriend because he thinks "I've had her and I have had sex with her, so it will be boring to stay with her. So I'll get another girl"

13

Girl gets pregnant, where is the boy? That's a whole new life. And then the girl feels used and abused because she believed him. She believed he loved her and she thought they'd stay together. So life is something you'll have to think hard about what decisions make what mistakes to learn from and so-on. To have sex for the first time is something you'd really have to think about. You will have sex with? When you will have sex?

If I was her, I wouldn't think twice no matter how much you love this person. I'd wait. And if he says he love me then he must wait until marriage. To lose your viginity is to someone you must really love and spend the rest of your life with. I'd dump him if he does not want to wait. He's not the one.

Scenario 3 written by a girl (15 years)
Topic: A girl who is finally getting attention from a boy she has always fancied.

For about years she has always wanted this guy. She's been madly in love with him for years and years and she even tried to tell him face-to-face but it was not easy because it is just not right to tell a boy that you love him without him telling you first. She tried contolling her feelings for him but it did not help because she is in love at first sight and she thinks that she has met her dream guy. But the problem is that her loverboy looks like he is not interested in her because everytime when she tries to make some moves he ignores them as if he cannot see that she love him. She had tried different ways of showing him that how much she cares about him but he pretends as if he cannot see that. She even lost her self respect because she cant even concentrate on anything not even her schoolwork because she is always dreaming and thinking about him and everytime that she thinks about him she even cries because she thinks that this guy will never love her or even like her as a friend.

But finally she has found the way to get to his heart and she found that he is also madly in love with her. She is so happy that she cannot believe that it is happening to her. She's in love.

Scenario 4 written by a boy (16 years)
Topic: A boy pressurising his girlfriend to have sex

Boys should not pressurise their girlfriends to have sex. Be must be patient and not end
the relationship if the girl is not ready to have sex with him.
So to let the relationship carry on she will have to say yes although she does not want or
not ready to have sex.

The girl will be in a situation that is big because if she says 'no' she will lose the boy of
her dreams and if she says yes she will either end up pregnant or HIV positive which
would ruin her life.

If the guy leaves her when she says 'no' she would be hurt and terrified that she would
commit suicide. Which is sad because there are lots of boys who are caring, loving and
patient. If the girl says 'no' the boy will start calling her names like' sluts tarts pigeons
bats etc" which are not good because a boy who wants sex demands it from his girlfriend
and if she says 'no' will beat her up and say she is a no good woman.

There is no such thing as a no-good woman because every no good woman was made by
a no-good man.

Scenario 5 written by a girl (15 years)
Topic: A boy pressurising his girlfriend to have sex

This girl, a very close friend of mine told me of how this had happened to her. On day she invited me and some of her friends and her boyfriend to her house . We were having a lot of fun playing games and watching TV. The next thing I know my friends boyfriend ask her to go with him to the room. So she went . the door was locked. They talked a little and then he kissed her and then she kissed him back. But then he started touching her all over her body and she didn't like it. She told him to stop but he didn't listen. She did not want to scream because we were outside of the room. so he touched her and she tried to get way but he grabbed he and pushed her on the bed and said "have sex with me" and she said 'no' but he did not listen and he kept touching her and he ripped her blouse open. But at that time I walked in and saw she was in tears. She ran away as fast as she could. She was so frightened and scared. On the next day I talked to her she was so distant. She did not listen to what I said. She looked terrible and angry and scared. Later that day he came over to talk to her and said that he was sorry but she knew that he did not mean it and he tried to kiss her again. She pushed him and she ran away. She told her mother after that and they did something about it. He was arrested a short while after that

APPENDIX 6

Sample single-sex interview (boys)

B1   Shane

B2   Alan

B3   Anil

B4   Colin

R   Shakila

R   Do you consider yourself to be the popular boys in the school? Others think so.
B1   I think everyone knows us.
B2   I don't know about popular, but the girls are always after us
R   Is that what makes you popular, you think?
B3   If you think you are popular then you are popular. There are many boys and girls
      in the school that everyone gets to know. It's a small world here.
R   What makes people get to know others?
B1   Maybe we look hot.
B2   Sometimes girls like you when they think that other girls are after you. Once you
      are seen with one girl then the other girls just come after you.
B1   maybe they think that if you don't have girls then you are a fag or something.
R   Do girls come after boys?
B4   Oh, yes mam. Some girls are like boys. They just come up to you and ask you out.
R   How do you feel about such girls?
B2   It's cool. They have equal rights. They always say they are equal to us. Then they
      must prove it.
B4   I don't really feel comfortable with that. I think that I like a girl then I must go up
      to her. I don't like a girl who has been with every boy in the school.
R   Do you have girlfriends?
B2   Yes girlfriends. We cant be tied to one girl and she wants to be with you 24 7.
      You cant be with the guys and
B1   sometimes girls like to show other girls that they like own you and stuff. You
      have to be with her and hang around at lunchtime and after school.
R   So when should you be with your girlfriend?
B1   Maybe after school and go out to clubs and things.
R   when do you think is the right time to have sex?
B2   Anytime is the right time. It just depends. If you are in a place where you can do
      it, then why not?
B1   Hey I don't take chances, with AIDS and stuff.
B2   well you got to play it safe. You don't want to get her pregnant and at the same
      time get diseases and stuff.
B1   anyway some girls – you can check. I won't take it even if she gave for free.
B2   If I know a girl, and if I ask her to have sex, then I am always prepared.
R   What if she says "no' to sex.
B2   She won't say "no". besides you got to know who to ask.
R   How do you know?

17

B2	Other boys. They don't keep quiet after they had it with a girl. All the other boys get to know.
R	Even if she is a steady girlfriend?
B3	Sometimes after they break up with the girl then they say stories about her.
R	Do boys even lie?
B3	Ya, maybe. They can't say the girl gave her a duck. So they say they did this and that. And that they gave her a duck.
B2	Guys like to think that they are so hot and that the girls cant say "no"
R	Many girls say that they would only have sex after they are married.
B2	that's what they say. They can't say that they like it. Girls can't say "yes" the first time you ask them. They say "no' for their pride.
B4	Its funny because some boys like girls that are easy and go for them but then they call them names and tell everyone she is easy.
R	Do you think that girls talk about what they do?
B1	Sometimes they tell their best friends but others always get to know about it because when they have a fight, their friends talk.
R	do you think that boys should wait to be married before they have sex.
B1,b3,b4. No	
B2	No because then you wont know what to do and the girl will think that you are not experienced.
B1	Girls like you to be the only one but they will be happy if you know what you are doing, you know what I mean.
R	What kind of boys do girls like?
B2	They like guys with money and that wear name brand clothes.
B3	They like guys who they can have their own way with. And tell them not to talk to other girls and things.
R	Does that work?
B3	that's what they think. But the guys are always checking if they get other girls too.
B1	Some girls like to treated rough.
R	How do you know this?
B1	You see the girls-how they go for guys who treat them like dirt.
B2	not all girls. Some girls like to be loved and you have to tell them you love them and things.

APPENDIX 7

Sample single-sex interview (girls)

A scenario written by another learner was used to stimulate discussion in this focus group

Topic: A boy pressurising his girlfriend to have sex

A boy said to a girl, "my girlfriend, I want to say something to you today. I know that you are going to say 'no', but I love you. You are my girlfriend. You are my only girlfriend, sweetheart. Darling, please for only today I want to show you how much I love you and how much I care about you. Please sweet come and lets kiss. Please girl, I feel like we can have sex". The girl says "no". "Why not? Please sweet I love you. See girl, there is nothing that can happen because I love you. Lets have sex." The boy romance the girl until the girl becomes very on. The boy said " I cant do it, honey". The girl said, " but... what but, because you love me and I love you". After the girl said "yes" they have sex. The boy feels very nice. The girl feels the same thing, terrible.

Interview with 4 girls (Indian and African)

G1	Thami
G2	Zubi
G3	Ayesha
G4	Shlo
R	Shakila

R	Is this a likely scenario?
G1	yes, it does happen. Boys think that if they tell you that they love you then you have to do anything to please him.
G2	And some girls are scared that if they refuse him then they will get dumped.
G3	Some boys are only interested in one thing.
G1	Not all boys mam, some boys, not all, know how to teat a girl.
R	How do girls like to be treated?

G1	To be made special. To except me for what I am.
G2	To be faithful to you. Not to dump you for someone else as soon as you say you don't want to go further than kissing.
G4	Some girls like rough boys. These boys that act like gangsters and other boys are scared of them.
R	What do you think about the end of the story?
G1	The girl was sorry that she gave in.
G2	She didn't give in –she wanted to as well
G1	she didnt. She was forced.
G2	she wasn't forced, because when the boy said "no" she wanted to go on.
G4	some girls also are interested in sex
G1	its true that boys are more interested in sex than girls.
G2	ya, I think so
R	What do you think she should have done?
G1	I don't think she was thinking clearly, she was taken in by the moment. She didn't think about the risks, she just wanted to please her partner.
G2	actually I think she also wanted to please herself too. She should have stopped, why didn't she stop-the boy was not going to rape her or something.
G4	I think that she was foolish that's why boys don't take it seriously when girls say "no". I think some girls like sex.
G2	Yes maybe they do-did she think of pregnancy or AIDS?
G3	I think that's the problem – sometimes people are not prepared and it just happens.
G4	So, what do you expect? That girls must carry condoms around?
R	If they do, will it be easy to use it?G2 No, how do you ask a boy to use a

condom? He will think that you always do this and that you are cheap.

G1	He will also think that you don't trust him.
G2	I think that if you decide that you will not have sex until you are married and stick

to it.

R	Is that difficult to do?
G2	no
G3	but maybe you wont have a boyfriend
G2	Look I have a boyfriend and he knows how I feel.
G1	Theres a lot you can do with your boyfrind. It does not mean that you have to

sleep with him to prove your love for him.

G2	Yes, I think he will have more respect for you if you are a virgin.
G1	It is important to keep your self respect until you are married. Besides you don't

know if he is only after one thing and says that he loves you and all that but after you
sleep with him, he might dump you for someone else.

R	To g2. Are you afraid that your boyfriend may leave you for someone else?
G2	Mam. If he really loves me, he will wait until I am ready. If he cant wait then I

don't care if he leaves me. It is more important to me to save myself until after I am
married.

G1	Trust is the most important thing in a relationship.

Sample mixed-sex interview

Started off with a group of girls and then joined by boys

G1   Anita
G2   Riat
G3   Simmi
B1
B2   Raj
B3   Vukani

...

G1   It works both ways. From everyone elses experience, they always say that there's one way you can prove your love for someone if you sleep with them or something.
G2   I don't believe you can prove your love by sleeping with the person, honestly. I believe in sex after marriage. Maybe the guy is unfaithful but I believe a girl should never sleep with a guy before marriage?
G1   Mam what do you think about sex before marriage?
R   ..
G2   Guys can easily fool you and dsay that they will marry you. Every guy wants a girl that has their virginity when they marry. I mean no guy wants a girl who has slept with every other guy- you know when they finally marry then he picks on and stuff.
R   What about girls? Do you want to marry a boy that's a virgin?
G3   Its better if the guy is experienced and the girl is not.(double standards by girls)
R   Who is he going to experience with?
G2   By him experiencing he can pick up HIV and stuff
G3   Let's face it right-guys are generally non-virgins. You can't find one that's not
G2   It's true
G3   If a guy likes you right-he probably liked someone before you and slept with the person.
G2   And after when you find out he lies about it.
G3   No you know the guys that I went out with-they were always honest
G2   How do you know?
G3   See I don't only ask them, I also ask the friends around me.
G2   Sex is a natural thing. Every guy and every girl wants sex,
Laughter as the girls are joined by a group of boys
G2   (To boy 1) What do you thing about sex?
B1   Sex is a wonderful thing but girls find it unattractive
B2   Sex is pleasure, I love it.
G3   Would you like girls to be a virgin or a non-virgin
B2   I don't care but as long as my wife is a virgin if my wife is a virgin, I don't care about girls being virgins-Ill do it with anyone.
R   Girls or boys?

21

B2   (visibly annoyed) I'm talking about girls of course
G3   So he just wants sexual pleasures
B2   Exactly. True true true. Sex is true sex is fun. Its true what they say about a dog and a master.
R   What do the say?
B2   We the masters and they the dogs.
Girls protest loudly
G1   They are pigs
G2   You're a dog
G3   (to boys)Why do you cheat on girls?
B2   Well Playa ZN Playa ZN.
B3   Just say when you going out with a girl right- just say you not going out with anyone at the moment, nobody wants you, the moment you get someone, everyone wants that boy.
R   Why does that make a boy attractive?
B2   Its more of a challenge. If you not single, it's more of a challenge.
B3   Like I was saying when a boy has a girl then everyone wants him and whats the use of him hanging- then he must go ahead and do anything.

(I leave the tape on while they continue the conversation and I leave for a few minutes)

B2   What I got to say is that we ous we smack women and we like having sex and we know about AIDS and all that but anyway we always use a condom I sometimes use 2 condoms- double protection
B   You use 2-theres no feeling
B4   (African) Hey let me say something
G3   (Takes over interviewing) We are in a discussion. What do you think about sex?
B4   Sex is good sex is nice
G3   Have you had sex?
B4   Yep
G3   What do you think of teenage relationships?
B4   I think its cool because they get to know each other for a long time
G3   Do you think teenagers go out with each other just because they want to have sex?
G2   OK majority but not all
B4   Especially Boys
G2   Exactly-the males especially the males
B2   All I want to say is, if your'll are having sex your'll must use a condom
B4   You must condomise, ya
R   How do boys feel about condoms?
B2   My point of view, I feel I like using condoms
B4   I don't like condoms I feel like Im eating a sweet with the wrapper on.
Laughter
R   What do girls do when boys refuse to wear a condom?
Girls Don't sleep with them
R   What do boys do when girls ask for condoms?
B2   They use it

G3   But not all boys

B4   Ya. But it depend on a girl. You can see a girl with which you have to use a condom and you can see ...

R   How do you see?

B4   Ay

B1   A condom is good to use but it takes the feeling away

B3   For now a condom is good because of pregnancy

R   What is a bigger problem-pregnancy or AIDS

Girls & Boys : Both

B3   You might get AIDS when you are married too

B1   Ya before you get married you must make the girl go for an AIDS test

B3   Before you get married you must wear acondom

B1   Both of us must o for an AIDS test

B4   Before you get married you must first have sex so that you will know what you taking. Taste it then take it.

Laughter

G3   Ten years down the line you will definitely have to go for an AIDS test – maybe sooner

B2   Maybe you already got AIDS

B4   Me-I'm as strong as a bull

R   Do you think boys your age are sexually active

Boys   Yes

R   How do you know

Boys   (Laughter) we are

R   Do boys talk about it? Do you think boys even lie?

B1   Ya most of them exaggerate. If they just kiss a girl they say-no, we done this, we done that.

R   Do you think girls lie?

Girls   No

Boys   Yes

G2   Probably some of them

R   What do they lie about?

G3   No girl will want to tell her friend that this is how far she went with her boyfriend

R   You were saying that boys who have many girls are called "playas" what are girls who have many boys called?

B4   B.I.T.C.H

B1   Can I say it? Shes called a bitch

R   Why do you think girls have a bad name and boys have a very stylish name?

B2   We are not spoiling anything on our bodies

R   What are they spoiling on their bodies?

B2   You want me to say it?

R   Why is it spoiling?

B2   Its no more tight?

R   Is this embarrassing stuff?

Boys   no

G3   Its nice to be open

23

B4   To get the answer (about players and bitches) you have to look at the dog. Why do female dog called bitch and why do a male dog called a male dog? You have to start on that

R   Why? Because we are not dogs

B4   Girls are compared to dogs of course

R   Why

B1   You see like like for dogs the male is a bastard and the female is a bitch and a bastard is a playa

B3   A playa is when you play with your thing all over

R   Do you know any gay relationships in your school?

B1   Yes. I know girls

G1,2 (Giggle) gays in our school?

B2   They kiss each other

B1   Why are girls lesbians?

G3   Why are boys gay?

B1   Its like this. Say a girl goes out with a boy and he brakes her heart, she thinks every boy is like that and a girl can give a girl more comfort which means a girl turns into a lesbian

G3   What about boys why they are gay?

B1   The same thing happens

G2   Why don't boys express their feelings? Its so simple for a girl to cry why is it so hard for a boy to cry in front of their girlfriends?

B1   I don't know. You see what happens in a house-say theres 3 girls and theres 1 boy and he's the smallest-obviously he will become like a girl because…that's why the girls in the house must make him tough

G3   Are you the smallest in your house?

B1   No.

Sample individual interview (girl: 17 years)

G   Reena
R   Shakila

R   Many of the learners say that girls and boys in this school are sexually active. Do you know anything about this?

G   Yes. There have been cases where girls had to leave school because they were pregnant-so it is true. Besides the girls and boys always talk about other people.

R   Do you think that knowing about HIV/AIDS makes any difference to the way school kids behave?

G   I wonder- because some people don't care. Me-I will wait until I am married. Because you cant really trust guys. They say they love you and stuff – but it doesn't mean that if you love someone then you have to go to bed with them. Theres a time and place for everything.

R   Why do girls have boyfriends?

G   Depends- there are many reasons. Some think that it is cool and that others will laugh at you if you don't. Sometimes it's just nice to have someone to share your problems and to go out with and stuff. Some of my friends say that they have boyfriends just to get back at their parents.

R   That's interesting. I have heard that before. Can you tell me more about that.

G   You see parents, especially Indian parents – they make it very hard for us. They don't understand that times have changed and always tell us "when we were young" and things. My parents say that if I have a boyfriend I wont concentrate on my schoolwork and …

R   What about your friends? Are any of them sexually active?

G   You see, girls wont really say about these things. Sometimes they say that their boyfriends are forcing them and stuff, but the wont say if they did it or not. But boys always say they did this and this with someone even if they did'nt.

R   Who can you talk to about relationship and sexual matters?

G   Actually no one. Definitely not my parents, and other girls-they will think you are loose or that you are interested in sex.

R   What about your teachers?

G   I don't think so. I am sure they will discuss it with other teachers and when you do bad in class they will pick on you and stuff.

R   What about the boys in this school. How are they towards girls?

G   Mam, some of the boys are fine. But when they are with other boys, they tease you and pick on you.

R   What kind of girls do boys like?

G   They like girls that are easy-from who they can get what they want. They like girls who wear mini skirts and belly tops and go to clubs.

R   Do you want to be like that?

G   Never. I am proud of who I am and I wont change for anyone.

R   What kind of boys do you like?

G   I don't like anyone in this school. I don't have a boyfriend at the moment but I like guys who know how to treat a girl. Who can talk about things and problems and not just want a good time.

R   Are there many like that?

G   Not in this school. These boys are very silly. They are not serious about relationships. I am sure the right guy will come along someday.

R   Do you feel pressured to have a boyfriend?

G   Yes mam, these boys when they know that you done have a boyfriend and if you say "no" when they ask you out- they say you are gay and spread rumours.

R   Do you know of anyone who is gay in this school?

G   Not personally. Some say that some girls are-I'm not sure because it is normal for girls to hold hands in the playground. I think that if they are gay, they would not show it.

R   Would you like to ask me any questions?

G   Can you get pregnant or get AIDS the first time you have sex?

R   Yes it is very likely.

G   Even if you are half a virgin. Some girls say that they are half-virgins?

R   Explain what half a virgin is?

G   I am not sure.

R   As long as semen comes into contact with a virgina, its possible to get pregnant or AIDS.

G   Thanks mam. Its not easy to ask anyone.

R   What do you do if you have questions?

G   We talk about it between girls, but like I say other girls will think that you have a problem or you are interested in sex.

Sample individual interview (boy 16 years)

B   Sibusiso
R   Shakila

R   Some of the girls say that boys pressurise them to have sex.
B   A boy who pressurises his girl to have sex is not a patient person. He wants to rush the relationship just to have sex and if the girl says "no" then the relationship will end. So to let the relationship carry on she will have to say "yes" although she does not want or not ready to have sex.
R   What do you think about that?
B   The girl will be in a situation because if she says 'no" she will lose the boy of her dreams and if she says "yes" she will either end up pregnant or HIV positive.
R   Do you think knowledge about HIV/AIDS makes any difference to the way people behave?
B   Me, I'm scared. Some people don't care and it can ruin their lives. Some boys think that they are so strong and that it can't affect them.
R   What should people do?
B   OK. Young girls and boys like to experiment and want to try it and stuff but they must be careful and maybe use condoms.
R   some boys say that they don't like condoms.
B   Ya, they say it's like eating a sweet with the wrapper on – that's a famous one. But what is better- getting someone pregnant or worse even getting AIDS?
R   What kind of girls do you like?
B   Good looking. Must dress nice but not too sexy- maybe only when she is with me.
R   Do you have a girlfriend?
B   (hestitates) Ya- but not in this school.
R   What kind of boys do girls like?
B   Rich. They like guys with money and designer brand clothes and can give them presents and stuff.
R   What about having boyfriends for companionship?
B   OK. Some. And there are some boys who are caring and patient.
R   What about your friends, do they talk about what they do when they are with there girlfriends?
B   Ya, they do but you can talk what they say and divide it by five.
R   What do you mean?
B   They lie of course. You think they will say that they went with a girl and nothing happened? Sometimes they go with a girl and then start calling her names like "slut", "tart" "pigeon" "bats". I think that it is maybe because she said "no".
R   The girls I have spoken to say that boys sometimes beat them up?
B   I have heard that. But I don't know anyone.
R   Who do you talk to if you have questions about girls and sex?
B   Mainly my friends. I think I can talk to my mum because she tries to talk to me about things ,like when we are watching TV. But it would be embarrassing.
R   Are the questions I am asking you embarrassing?

B No, not really. Its natural and everyone is interested in AIDS.
R Would you like to ask me any questions?
B What are you going to do with this tape?
R I am going to write down the conversation, without using any names, so no one will be able to know who I interviewed and then I will put it together will all the other interviews and try to understand what school kids are saying.

APPENDIX 11

Sample mindmaps

APPENDIX 12

Matrix ranking: Individual girls ranked lists of an ideal partner

Girls
1

Honesty
Trustworthy
Handsome
Sebsitive
Big chest
Nice hair
Humorous
Personality
Nice Butt
Romantic
Good dress
Rich
Discipline
Good morals
Good goals
• 2

honest
glooking
respect
dimples
intelligent
cute smile
sensitive
nice bum
outgoing
humour
nice dress
nice car
• 3

Faithful
Honesty
Christian
Love me as is
Decent
Respect
Intelligent
Kind
Personalit
Humour
outgoing
Nice dress
• 4

good ooks
rich
honest

faithful
humour
put me first
decent
understanding
outgoing
good dress• 5

honesty
goodlooks
personalit
humour
friendly
sensitive
style
rich
height
clean
famous
sexyeyes
nosmoke
good kisser• 6

good ooks
kind
respect
discipline
innocent• 7

kind
goodlooks
tall
friendly
respect
• 8

Tall
Good looks
Intelligemt
Sixpack
Kind
Rich
Respect
Style
faithful• 9

personaliy
rich
cute
honest
faithful
decent
soulmate
nice bum
love me as is
body

good kisser
good car
outgoing● 10

loving
good kisser
humour
taller
goodlooks
sexysmile
sixpac
cellfone● ●

11
goodlooks
tall
thin
goodkisser
thinlips
sexyeyes● **12**
caring
committed
respect
understan
goodjob
humour
ownhouse
faithful
goodsmile
taller
● **13**
sweet
nodominate
respect
thin
unselfish
gooddress
goodeyes
goodlooks
nice bum
maketime

● **14**
goodlooks
rich
independ
humour
decent
responsib
loveme
Christian
Bighouse
Personali

36

Cutebum
Muscles
Goodjob
Cleanteeth
sexy● 15
goodlips
goodlooks
goodkisser
tall
gooddress
goodlegs
friendly
shorthair
bigeyes
● 16
rich
style
goodlooks
personali
tough
respect
taller
● 17
trust
personali
kind
gentlman
honest
goodlooks

● 18
personali
respect
goodlooks
money
sexy
taller

● 19
loving
friendly
money
kind
humour
personali
short
goodlips● 20
goodlooks
tall
personali
style
goodkisser
goodlips
cut
gooddress● ●

APPENDIX 13

Matrix ranking : Individual boys ranked lists of an ideal partner

1
funloving
beauty
wild
sexybod
humour
intelligent
• **2**
goodlegs
goodlooks
sexy
faithful• **3**
goodlooks
sexy
notrich
good behave• **4**
sexylegs
goodtits
goodlooks
tightcloth
strip
faithful
longhair
horny
g-string
personali• **5**
beauty
kind
goodbum
bigtits
pinklips
intelligent
thicthighs
enjoysex
faithful
money
funlovi
• **6**
sexy
goodlooks
money
goodlegs
goodbody
tall• **7**
goodlooks
personali
humour
goodtits
sexyleg
fairskin
goodlips
blonde

blueyes
shorter
job• **8**
loveme
humour
goodlooks
personali
honest
sexybod
shorter• 9
Beauty
Sexyleg
Bigtits
Bigbum
Shorter
Pinklips
Hairlegs
Money
Car
Job
Longhair
Biglips
browneyes• •

10
trusted
personality
humour
love and care
goodlooks
sexylegs
sexybod
noattitude• **11**
goodlooks
longhair
sexy• **12**
goodlooks
smoothface
beautiful
goodlegs
• **13**
nicebum
hairy
beauti• •

Self identity data

BOYS

1   I am in school
Parents want me to be decent
Good in relationship
Like good girls
Wish to be intelligent father
Like swimming

2   sportsman-karate
don't like girls as much as other boys do
that's why not afraid of AIDS
girlfriend is fat, but beautiful
have long hair

3   passionate to people who are close
kind
fair and just
natural and simple
love expensive things
not very friendly to all
except who I am

4   myself
had many trials in life
these trails are a result of my actions
not easy to identify myself

5   sexy
care about myself
love women
like having sex

41

like nightclubs
hate school
hate English teacher
like to be rich

6   character changes depends where I am
honest
trustworthy
kind
like working with others
friendly
trust no-one
keep people happy and laughing

like to be rich
kind
loving
            treat girls with respect
            like respectable girls
            well dressed and neat
            hard working

African
Sexy
Strong
Like sexy girls
Like to be free
Enjoy clubbing

I am the man
Girls love me
Sexy
Sexed
Love money
Don't wait around for nobody
Take me as I am

GIRLS

Indian female
Friendly, outgoing
Enjoy socialising
Have mood swings
Quick talker-sometimes gets me into trouble, know how to get out

understanding

simple
faithful
enjoy the company of opp. Sex
flirt to a certain extent

sometimes demanding
friendly and talkative
high integrity
understanding
down to earth
learn from other peoples mistakes
faithful partner
ambitious
enjoy the company of opp sex
excellent friend and listener

loving
give good advice
friendly but no-nonsense
like to be in discussions
faithful and trustworthy
love yself
short tempered

friendly
trustworthy, honest
ambitious
googlooking
simple, caring
good personality
sense of humour
respectable
fight for whats right
love my parents
very mature
give good advice
bad temper

Ambitious
Honest
Caring
Determined
Interesting
Strong believer
Faithful
Attractive

Unique
Exciting. Kind
Challenging, lovable

positive attitude to life
take full advantage of situations
love tackling challenges
hate not being in control
hate surprises
either trust wholeheartedly or not at all
play hard and work hard

extrovert
well-spoken
intelligent
charismatic
religious
beautiful
fun loving
dominant
childish
like to have my own way
yearn for status

single
goodlooking
charming
irresistible
tempting
faithful

friendly and charming
forgiving
loving
honest

Indian
Single, no children
Trustworthy, honest
Love someone for personality, not looks
Not racist
Depressed
Very friendly
Love fun
Big mouth
single

Indian
Like to socialise
Friendly
Good personality
Straight forward
Big mouth
Sweet
Honest, trustworthy
Love having fun and living on the edge
Believe in equal treatment for all

single but have a boyfriend
straight forward
very honest
friendly
Indian
Love my boyfriend
Love to live life to the fullest
Love going out

South African female
16 years
same interests as most of my friends
good sense of humour
happy to give advice
enjoy spending time with friends
honest and truastworthy
like school-often stressed by too much work

sweet, care about how I treat others
Proud to be Indian
Understanding
More popular with boys than girls
Dislike some gils because how the act towards me
I bottle up my anger most of the time

16
love socializing
always a pleasure to talk to
conscious of how I look
hate to be embarrassed
very curios
love attention esp from boys
very friendly
sexy
outskoken

love clothes and perfume

similar to other girls
very conscious
hate to be embarrassed
very friendly
easy to socialise
enjoy entertaining
love boys

loyal to friens
outspoken
appreciate who I am and where from
simple but can be demanding
learn from my mistakes
honest

caring
sweet
outspoken
friendly
not demanding
liketo communicate with others
like meeting new people

simple
not demanding
outspoken
enjoy making friends
hard working
love life
enjoy the opposite sex

REFERENCES

Abbott, S. (1988). *AIDS and Young Women*. The Bulletin of National Clearinghouse for Youth Studies, 7: 38-41.

Abrahamsen, B. (2001). *The Construction of Masculinity among Male Nurses*. Paper presented at the Gender, Work and Organisation Conference, Keele University, Staffordshire, U.K. June 26-29.

Ajzen, I. and Fishbein. (1977). Attitude-behaviour relations: A Theoretical analysis and review of empirical research. *Psychological Bulletin.* 84: 888-918.

Akande, A. (2001). Risky Business: South African youths and HIV/AIDS prevention. *Educational Studies, Vol.* 27 (3): 237-256.

Alcoff, L. (1992). The Problem of Speaking for Others. *Cultural Critique.* No. 20. Winter:5-32.

Armstrong, D.M. (1973). *Belief, Truth and Knowledge*. London: Cambridge University Press.

Auerbach, J.D., Wypijewska, C., Brodie, H.K.H. (eds.) (1994). *AIDS and Behaviour. An Integrated Ap*proach. Washington, D.C.: National Academy Press.

Bandura, A. (1992*).* A Social Cognitive Approach to the Exercise of Control over AIDS Infection, in, R. J. DiClemente (ed.) *Adolescents and AIDS. A Generation in Jeopardy.* J. Newbury Park, London, New Dehli: Sage Publications.

Bartky, S. (1988). Foucault, Femininity, and the Modernization of Patriarchal Power, in , I. Diamond and L. Quinby (eds.) *Feminism and Foucault: Reflections on Resistance*, Northeastern, Boston: University Press.

Baylies, C. (2000). Perspectives on Gender and AIDS in Africa, in, C. Baylies and J. Bujra (eds.) *AIDS Sexuality and Gender in Africa*. London and New York: Routledge.

Baylies, C. and Bujra, J. (1995). The Fight against HIV/AIDS in Africa. *AIDS*, in, P. Aggleton, P. Davis and G. Hart (eds.) *Safety, Sexuality and Risk*. Great Britain: SRP Ltd., Exeter.

Becker, M. (1994). The Heath Belief Model and sick role behaviour. *Health Education Monographs*. 2:409-419.

Bennell, P; Hyde, K. and Swainson, N. (2002). The impact of the HIV/AIDS epidemic on the education sector in Sub-Saharan Africa. Centre for International Education. University of Sussex Institute of Education.

Blackmore, J., Kenway, J., Willis, S. and Rennie, L. (1992). What's working for girls? The reception of gender equity policy in two Australian schools, in, C.Marshall (ed.) *The New Politics of Race and Gender*. London: Falmer Press.

Blaikie, N. (1993). *Approaches to Social Enquiry*. UK: Polity Press.

Bok, L. (1997). *Adolescents in Death-Defying Sex-Search. Integrating the Role of Constructions of Masculinity in a HIV/AIDS/STD Education Programme Designed for an Urban Tanzanian Context. A Gender assessment Study*. Occasional paper 69. Nijmegen: Third World Centre/ Development Studies Catholic University.

Breakwell, G. M. (1992). (ed.) *Social Psychology of Identity and the Self Concept*. London: Surrey University Press.

Brunskell, H. (1998). Feminist Methodology, in, C. Seale (ed) *Researching Society and Culture*. London, California, new Dehli: Sage Publications.

Burke, P.J. and Franzoi S.L. (1988). Studying Situations and Identities using Experiential Sampling Methodology. *American Sociological Review,* Vol. 53: 559-568.

Burke, P.J. and Reitzes, D.C. (1981). The Link between Identity and Role Performance. *Social Psychology Quarterly*. Vol. 44 (2): 83-92.

Butler, J. (1990). *Gender Trouble*. New York. London: Routledge.

Butler, J. (1993). *Bodies that Matter*. London: Routledge.

Cape Times (1991). January 24.

Carpenter, L.M. (2001). The ambiguity of "having sex": The subjective experience of virginity loss in the United States. *Journal of Sex Research*. Vol.38 (2): 127-140.

Castells, M. (1997). *The Power of Identity*. London: Routledge.

Cohen, L., Manion, L. and Morrison, K. (2000). *Research Methods in Education*. London and New York: Routledge Falmer.

Connell, R. (1995). *Masculinities*. Sydney: Allen & Unwin.

Connelly, F. M. and Clandinin, D.J. (1990). Stories of Experience and Narrative Inquiry. *Educational Researcher*, Vol.2 (5): 2-14.

Coole, D. (1995). The Gendered Self, in, D. Bakhurst and C. Sypnowich (eds.) *The Social Self*. London, Thousand Oaks and New Delhi: Sage Publications.

Coombe, C. (2000). Keeping the Education system Healthy: Managing Impact of HIV/AIDS on Education in South Africa. *Current Issues in Comparative Education, e-journal of Teachers' College Columbia*.

Coombe, C. (2002). Editorial: HIV/AIDS and education. *Perspectives in Education*, Vol. 20 (2), July 2002.

Cornwall, A. and Jewkes, R. (1995). What is Participatory Research? *Social Science and Medicine*. Vol. 41 (12): 1667-1676.

Cornwall, A. and Lindisfarne, N. (1994). *Dislocating masculinity. Comparative Ethnographies*. London and New York: Routledge.

Crewe, M. (1997). Reflections on the introduction of a comprehensive HIV/AIDS and life skills programme for South African youth. *AIDS Bulletin*, Vol.6 (4).

Denzin, N.K. (1978). *The Research Act: A Theoretical Introduction to Sociological Methods*. New York: McGraw Hill.

Denzin, N.K. (1989). *The Research Act*. Englewood Cliffs, NJ: Prentice Hall.

Deveaux, M. (1994). Feminism and empowerment: A critical reading of Foucault. *Feminist Studies*, Summer 94, Vol. 20 (2): 223-247.

Diclemente, R.J. (ed.) (1992). *Adolescents and AIDS. A generation in Jeopardy*. Newbury Park London New Delhi: Sage Publications.

DiClemente, R.J., Forrest, K. A., Mickler, S., and Principal Site Investigators (1990). College Students' knowledge and attitudes about AIDS and changes in HIV-preventive behaviors. *AIDS Education and Prevention*, 2: 201-212.

Dunne, M. (1996). The Power of Numbers: Quantitative Data and Equal Opportunities Research, in, Walsh and Morley (eds.) *Breaking the Boundaries: Women in Higher Education*. London: Taylor and Francis.

Epstein, D. (1996). Keeping them in their place: hetero/sexist harassment, gender and the enforcement of heterosexuality, in, L. Adkins and J. Holland (eds.) *Sexualising the Social*. Basingstoke: Macmillan.

Epstein, D. and Johnson, R. (1998). *Schooling Sexualities*. Buckingham. Philadelphia: Oxford University Press.

Erikson, E. (1968). *Identity: Youth and Crisis*. New York: W.W.Norton & Company.

Erni, J. N. (1998). Ambiguous Elements. Rethinking the Gender/Sexuality Matrix in an Epidemic, in, L. Roth and K. Hogan (eds.) *Gendered Epidemic: Representations of Women in the Age of AIDS*. New York and London: Routledge.

Fisher, J. D.; Miscovich, S. J., Fisher, W. A. (1994). Impact of Perceived Social Norms on Adolescents' AIDS-Risk Behavior and Prevention, in, R. J. DiClemente (ed.) ,*Adolescents and AIDS.A Generation in Jeopardy*. R. J. Newbury Park. London. New Delhi: Sage Publications.

Fawole, O.I., Asuzu, M.C. and Oduntan, S. O. (1999). Survey of Knowledge, Attitudes and Sexual Practices Relating to HIV Infection/AIDS among Nigerian Secondary School Students. *African Journal of Reproductive Health*. Vol. 3 (2): 15-24.

Fielding, M. (2001). Students as Radical Agents of Change. *Journal of Educational Change*. Vol. 2 (1).

Flischer, A.J., Cruz, C., Eaton, L., Mukoma, W. and Pillay, Y. (1999). *Review of South African Research Involving Adolescent Health. Report submitted to Youth Development Trust*. Cape Town: Department of Psychiatry, University of Cape Town.

Forbes, J. S. (1996). Disciplining women in contemporary discourses on sexuality. *Journal of Gender Studies*. Vol. 5 (2): 177-190.

Foucault, M. (1980). *Power/Knowledge: selected Interviews and Other Writings*, 1972-1977. Colin Gordan (ed.) New York: Pantheon Books

Foucault, M. (1981). *The History of Sexuality*. London: Pelican.

Friedman, S. (1993). AIDS as a Sociohistorical phenomenon, in, G. Albrect and R. Zimmerman (eds.) *The Social and Behavioural Aspects of AIDS, Advances in Medical Sociology*. Vol. 3. Greenwich, CT: JAI press

Frith, H and Kitzinger, C. (1998). Emotional wealth as a participant resource: a feminist analysis of young women's talk-interaction. *Sociology*. Vol. 32 (2): 299-320

Gauntlet. www.theory.org.uk resources: Queer Theory.

Grumet, M.R. (1990). Voice: the search for a feminist rhetoric for educational studies, *Cambridge Journal of Education.* Vol.20: 277-282.

Hadfield, M. and Haw, K. (undated). *The 'Voice' of Young People: Hearing, Listening, Responding.* Nottingham.

Haig, B.D. (1999). Feminist research methodology. In J.P. Keeves and G. Lakomski (Eds.). *Issues in Educational research.* Oxford: Elsevier Science Ltd, 222-231.

Haldenwang, B.B. (1993*). AIDS in South Africa: its impact on society: a literature review.* Stellenbosch. Institute for Future Research. Occasional Paper no 21.

Hall, S. (1990). Introduction: who needs identity?, in, S. Hall and P. Du Gay (eds) *Questions of culture and identity.* London: Sage.

Harding, J. (1998). *Sex Acts: Practices of Femininity and Masculinity.* Thousand Oaks, CA: Sage.

Harrison, A., Smith, J.A. and Myer, L. (2000). Prevention of HIV/AIDS in South Africa: A Review of behaviour change interventions, evidence and options for the future. *South African Journal of Science, 96,* June.

Harrison, L. (2000). Gender Relations and the Production of Difference in School-based Sexuality and HIV/AIDS Education in Australia. *Gender and Education, Mar 2000,* Vol. 12 (1): 5-20.

Haywood, C. (1996). Out of the curriculum: sex talking, talking sex. *Curriculum Studies,* 4: 229-250.

Holland, J.; Ramazanoglu, C.; Sharpe, S. and Thomson, R. (2000). Deconstructing virginity-young people's accounts of first sex. *Sexual and Relationship Therapy,* Vol.15 (3): 221-232.

Holland, J., Ramazanoglu, C. and Sharpe, S. (1993). *Wimp or gladiator: Contradictions in acquiring masculine sexuality.* London: The Tufnell Press.

Holland, J., Ramazanoglu, C., Scott, S., Sharpe, S., and Thomson, R. (1991). Between embarrassment and trust: Young women and the diversity of condom use, in, P.Aggleton, G.Hart, and P. Davis (eds.) *AIDS: Responses, interventions and care.* London: Falmer.

Holland, J., Ramazanoglu, C., Scott, S., Sharpe, S., and Thomson, R. (1992). *Pressure, resistance, Empowerment: Young Women and the Negotiations of Safer Sex. AIDS: Rights, Risk and Reason.* P. Aggleton, P, Davies, and G. Hart (eds.) London. Washington, D.C.: The Falmer Press.

Hollander, G. (2000). Questioning Youths: Challenges to working with Youths forming Identities. *School Psychology Review.* Vol.29 (2): 173-179.

Ingham, R. (1995). AIDS: Knowledge, Awareness and Attitudes, in, J. Cleland and B. Ferry (eds.) *Sexual Behavior and AIDS in the Developing World.* London: Taylor & Francis.

Jayaratne and Steward (1991). Qualitative and Quantitative Methods in the Social Sciences. Current Feminist Issues and Practical Strategies, in, M. M. Fonow and J. A. Cook (eds.) *Beyond Methodology.* Bloomington and Indianapolis: Indiana University Press.

Jayaratne, T.E. (1993). The value of quantitative methodology for feminist research. In M. Hammersley (ed). *Social Research: Philosophy, Politics and Practice.* London: Sage Publication, in association with the Open University Press: 109-123.

Johnson, R. (1997). Contested Borders, Contingent Lives: An Introduction,in, D. L. Steinberg, D. Epstein and R. Johnson (eds.) *Border Patrols: Policing the Boundaries of Heterosexuality.* London: Cassells.

Kaim, B., Chingwena, P. Gwata, S. (1997). *Adolescent Reproductive Health Education Project. Light on Learning: Using PRA to Explore School-Going Adolescents' Views on their Sexual and Reproductive Health.* Training and Research Support Centre.

Kayal, P. (1993). The Sociological Imagination in AIDS Prevention Education Among Gay Men, in, G. Albrect and R. Zimmerman (eds.) *The Social and Behavioural Aspects of AIDS, Advances in Medical Sociology.* Vol. 3. Greenwich, CT: JAI press.

Kimmel, M. S. (2000). *The Gendered Society.* New York, Oxford: Oxford University Press.

Kraak, G. (1998). Class, race, nationalism and the politics of identity: a perspective from the South. *Development Update. Quarterly Journal of the South African National NGO Coalition and INTERFUND.* Vol. 2(2): Editorial.

Lamptey, P., Wigley, M., Carr, D. and Collymore Y. (2002). Facing the HIV/AIDS Pandemic. *Population Bulletin.* Vol.57 (3).

Lather, P. and Smithies, C. (1997). *Troubling the Angels. Women Living with HIV/AIDS.* USA: Westview Press.

Lather, P. (1986). Research as Praxis. *Harvard Education Review.* Vol. 65 (3): 257-277.

Lather, P. (2001). Postpositivist New Paradigm Inquiry. Educational Policy and Leadership – *Cultural Studies Notes.* August 2001.

Paulsen, M. (1999). Deconstructing hegemonic masculinity. *Youth Studies Australia*, September 99, Vol.18 (3): 1-34.

Pitcher, G. P. and Bowley, D.M.G. (2002). Infant rape in South Africa. *Lancet, 00995355*, 1/26/2002, Vol. 359 (9303).

Race Relations Survey (Johannesburg: South African institute of Race Relations). 1994.1993/9.

Ramsay, S. (2001). "Shocking" AIDS data released in South Africa. *Lancet, 10/20/2001, vol.358 (9290) p 1345*

Ranson, G. (2001). *Under construction: A study of masculinities and careers in changing social and economic times.* Paper presented at the Gender, Work and Organisation Conference, Keele University, Staffordshire, U.K. June 26-29, 2001.

Reddy, S. (1999*). Student Beliefs on the Origins of Life.* Masters Dissertation. University of Durban Westville.

Redman, P. (1996). 'Empowering men to disempower themselves': heterosexual masculinities, HIV and the contradictions of anti-oppressive education, in, M. Mac an Ghaill (ed.) *Understanding Masculinities*. M. Buckingham. Philadelphia: Open University Press.

Reinharz, S. (1992*). Feminist Methods in Social Research.* New York. Oxford: Oxford University Press.

Richter, L. 1996. *A Survey of Reproductive Health Issues among Urban Black Youth in South Africa.* Final Grant Report for Society for Family Health. Pretoria: South African Medical Research Council.

Samet, N., and Kelly, E.W. (1987). The relationship of steady dating to self-esteem and sex role identity among adolescents. *Adolescence*. Vol. 22: 231-245.

Samuel, M.A. (2002). *Developing Rigour in Qualitative Research*. Workshop/Lecture at Spencer Consortium Summer School, University of Durban Westville, 03-09 February.

Santrock, J.W. (2001). *Adolescence.* Boston Burr Ridge, IL Dubuque, IA Madison, WI New York, San Francisco, St. Louis, Bangkok, Bogota, Caracas, Lisbon, London, Madrid, Mexico City, Milan, New Delhi, Seoul, Singapore, Sydney, Taipei and Toronto: Mc Graw Hill.

Schoub, B.D. (1994). *AIDS & HIV in Perspective: A guide to Understanding the Virus and its Consequences.* Great Britain: Cambridge University Press.

Seale, C. (1998). (ed.) *Researching Society and Culture*. London, New Delhi: Sage Publications Ltd.

Sears, J.T. (1992). (ed.) *Sexuality and the Curriculum. The Politics and Practices of Sexuality Education*. New York: Teachers College Press.

Shell, R., and Zeitlin, R. (2000). *Positive Outcomes: The chances of acquiring HIV/AIDS during the school-going years in the Eastern Cape* 1990-2000. Working paper no: 26. Presented at the South African Epidemiological Conference.

Shell. R., Quattek, K., Schonteich, M. and Mills, G. (2000*). HIV/AIDS: A Threat to the African Renaissance?* Occasional Papers. RSA: Konrad-Adrenauer-Stiftung.

Siann, G. (1994). *Gender, Sex and Sexuality. Contemporary Psychological Perspectives*. United Kingdom: Taylor & Francis.

Singer, L. (1993). *Erotic Welfare. Sexual Theory and Politics in the Age of Epidemic*. New York: Routledge.

Skeggs, B. (1994a). The Constraints of Neutrality: The 1988 Education Reform Act and feminist research, in, D.Halpin and B. Troyna (eds.) *Researching Education Policy: Ethical and Methodological Issues*. London: The Falmer Press.

Skeggs, B. (1994b). Situating the Production of Feminist Ethnography, in, M. Maynard and J. Purvis (eds.) *Researching Women's Lives from a Feminist Perspective*. London: Taylor and Francis.

Steward, F.J.; Mischewski, A. and Smith, A.M.A. (2000). ' I want to do what I want to do': young adults resisting sexual identities. *Critical Public Health*, Vol. 10 (4): 409-422.

Stryker, S. and Burke, P. J. (2000). The Past, Present and Future of Identity Theory. *Social Psychology Quarterly*. Vol. 63(4): 284-297.

Sunday Tribune (2000). March 19

Swain, J. (2000). " The Money's Good, The Fame's Good, The Girls are Good": the role of playground football in the construction of young boys' masculinity in a junior school. *British Journal of Sociology of Education,* Vol. 21(1): 5-109.

Szasz, I. (1998). Masculine Identity and the meanings of sexuality: a review of research in Mexico. *Reproductive Health Matters*, Vol.6 (12): 97-104.

Tajfel, H. (Ed) (1982*). Differentiation Between Social Groups*. London: Academic Press.

Terry, D. J., Gallois, C., & McCamish, M. (1993). *The Theory of Reasoned Action. Its Application to AIDS-Preventive Behavior.* Oxford, New York, Seoul and Tokyo: Pergamon Press.

Turtle, A. M., Ford, B., Habgood, R., Grant, M., Bekiaris, J., Constaninou, C., Mecek, M., Polyziodis, H. (1989). AIDS Related Beliefs and Behaviors of Australian University Students. *The Medical Journal of Australia.* Vol. 150, 371-376.

UNAIDS. (1998). Epidemiological Fact Sheet on HIV/AIDS and Sexually Transmitted Diseases. Geneva.

UNAIDS / WHO. (2000). Global AIDS Statistics, *AIDS Care.* April: 12.2.

UNAIDS/WHO. (2002). AIDS epidemic update: December.

Usher, P. (1996). Feminist approaches to research, in, D. Scott and R.Usher (eds.) *Understanding Educational Research.* London: Routledge.

Van der Vliet, V. (1994). Apartheid and the Politics of Aids, in, D. A. Feldman (ed) *Bergin and Garvey Global AIDS Policy:* Westport, Connecticut. London.

Van Roosmalen, E. (2000). *Youth and Society,* December 2000. Vol.32 (2): 202-228.

Vance, C. (ed) (1984). *Pleasure and Danger: exploring female sexuality.* London: Routledge and Kegan Paul.

Varga, C. A. (1997). Sexual decision-making and negotiation in the midst of AIDS: youth in KwaZulu/Natal. *South Africa. Supplement 3 Health Transition Review,* Vol. 7: 45-63.

Varga, C. A. and Makubalo, E.L. (1996). Sexual (non) negotiation. *Agenda.* 28: 31-38.

Varga, C.A.1999. South African young people's sexual dynamics: implications for behavioural responses to HIV/AIDS. Resistances to Behavioural Change to Reduce HIV/AIDS Infection in Predominantly Heterosexual Epidemics in Third World Countries. Health Transition Centre, Canberra.

Walker, M. (2001). Engineering Identities. *British Journal of Sociology of Education.* Vol. 22(1): 75-89.

Webb, D. (1997). *HIV and AIDS in Africa.* London, Chicago, Illinois: Pluto Press.

Weekly Mail (Johannesburg). 1991. March 28-April 4

Weiss, E., Whelan, D. and Gupta, G. R. (2000). Gender, sexuality and HIV: making a difference in the lives of young women in developing countries. *Sexual and Relationship Therapy.* Vol. 15, (3): 234-245.

West, J. (1999). (Not) talking about sex: youth, identity and sexuality. *The Editorial Board of the Sociological Review 1999*. USA: Blackwell publishers.

Whiteside, A. and Sunter, C. (2000). *AIDS: The Challenge for South Africa*. Cape Town: Human and Rousseau Tafelberg.

Wood, K, and Jewkes, R. (1988), *"Love is a dangerous thing": Microdynamics of Violence in Sexual Relationships of Young People in Umtata*. CERSA, Women's Health.

Woodward, K. (ed) (1997). *Identity and Difference*. London. Thousand Oaks. New Delhi: Sage Publications.

World Bank (1999). Intensifying the Action against HIV/AIDS in Africa. Responding to a Development Crisis. Washington, DC: The World Bank.

World Health Organisation (WHO). (1992). A study of sexual experience of young people in eleven African countries: The narrative research method. Geneva: Adolescent Health Programme, Division of Family Health (WHO/ADH/92.5)

Other readings

Ashmore, R.D. and Jussim, L. Eds. (1997). *Self and Identity. Fundamental Issues.* New York: Oxford University Press.

Barker, G. (2000). Gender equitable boys in a gender inequitable world: reflections from qualitative research and programme development in Rio de Janeiro. *Sexual and Relationship Therapy.* Vol. 15, No. 3: 263-282.

Barnett, T. and Blaikie, P. (1992). *AIDS in Africa. Its present and future impact.* Chichester, New York, Brisbane, Toronto, Singapore: John Wiley & Sons.

Bhavani, K-K and Phoenix, A. (1994). Eds. *Shifting Identities Shifting Racisms. A Feminism and Psychology Reader.* London, California and New Delhi: SAGE Publications Ltd.

Blackmore, J., Kenway, J., Willis, S. and Rennie, L (1996). Putting up with the put down? Girls, boys, power and sexual harassment, in: L. Laskey and C. Beavis (Eds.). *Schooling and Sexualities: teaching for a positive sexuality.* Geelong: Deaken University Press.

Boffin, T. and Gupta, S. (Eds.) (1990). *Ecstatic Antibodies: Resisting the AIDS Mythology.* London: Rivers Oram.

Boulden, K. (1996). Keeping a straight face: schools, students and homosexuality. Part 2, in L.Laskey and C. Beavis (eds).

Bujra, J. (2000). Target Practice: Gender and Generation struggles in Lushoto. In: *AIDS Sexuality and Gender in Africa.* (eds.). C. Baylies and J. Bujra. London and New York: Routledge.

Carasso, M. J. (1998). Renegotiating HIV/AIDS prevention for adolescents. *Issues in Comprehensive Pediatric Nursing, 21: 203-216*

Carrigan, T. Connell, R.W. and Lee, J. (1985). Towards a new sociology of masculinity. *Theory and Society.* 14 (5): 551-604.

Coleman, J.C. and Hendry, L. (1990). *The Nature of Adolescence.* London: Routledge.

Craig, A. and Richter-Strydom, L. (1983) Unplanned pregnancies among Zulu schoolgirls. *South African Medical Journal.*

Denzin, N.K. & Lincoln Y. S. (1998). *Collecting and Interpreting Qualitative Materials.* Newbury Park London New Delhi: Sage Publications.

Dunphy, R. (2000). *Sexual Politics. An Introduction.* Edinburgh: Edinburgh University Press.

Edley, N. and Wetherell, M. (1996). Masculinity, power and identity. p97-103.In Mac an Ghaill (ed) Understanding Masculinities. Buckingham. Philadelphia: Open University Press.

Eisner, E. (1991). *The Enlightened Eye: Qualitative Inquiry and the Enhancement of Educational Practice.* New York: Macmillan.

Fine, M. and Gordon, S.M. (1991). Effacing the Centre and the Margins, *Feminism and Psychology,* Vol. 1 (1): 19-25

Fonow, M.M. and Cook, J.A. (1991). Back to the Future. *A Look at the Second Wave of Feminist Epistemology and Methodology.* In Beyond Methodology. Feminist Scholarship as lived Research. P.1-15. Bloomington and Indianapolis. Indiana University Press.

Foucault, M. (1976). *The History of Sexuality. Vol. 1: The Will to Knowledge.* London: Penguin.

Foucault, M. (1984). *The Care of The Self: Volume 3. The History of Sexuality.* Great Britain: Allen Lane The Penguin Press.

Friedman, S. (1993). AIDS as a Sociohistorical phenomenon. p 19-36. In: *The Social and Behavioural Aspects of AIDS, Advances in Medical Sociology*. G. Albrect, and R. Zimmerman, R. (Eds.). Vol. 3. Greenwich, CT: JAI press

Gardenfors, P. (1992). The Dynamics of Belief Systems: Foundations verses Coherence Theories. *Knowledge, belief and strategic interaction*. Ed. Bicchieri, C. & Chiara, M. L. D. USA: Cambridge University Press.

Giddens, A. (1991). *Modern Identity and Self-Identity: Self and Society in the Late Modern Age*. United Kingdom: Polity Press.

Goleman, D. (1996). *Emotional Intelligence. Why it can matter more than IQ*. London: Bloomsbury.

Hargreaves, D.J. (1986). Psychological theories of sex-role stereotyping, in D. J. Hargreaves and A. Colley (eds). *The Psychology of Sex Roles*. London: Harper and Row.

Head, J. (1997). *Working with Adolescents. Constructing Identity*. London, Washington, D.C.: Falmer Press.

Hekeman, S. J. (1990). Gender and Knowledge. Elements of a Postmodern Feminism. Great Britain: Polity Press.

Hogg, M. A. and Abrams, D. (1988). *Social Identifications*. London: Routledge

Holness, K., Wong, K. and Gazi, D. (1987). *AIDS-An African Perspective. A Report*. London: Black Health Workers and Patients Group.

Josselson, R. (1994). The theory of Identity formation and the Question of Intervention. In: *Interventions for adolescent identity development*. (ed.). Archer, S. L. California. United Kingdom. New Delhi: Sage Publications.

Kelly, M. (2002). Preventing HIV transmission through education. *Perspectives in Education*, Vol. 20(2) July 2002: 1-12.

Lincoln, Y.S. and and Guba, E.G. (1985). *Naturalistic Inquiry*. Beverly Hills: Sage Publications.

Marotti, A.F., Wasserman, R.R.M., Dulan, J. & Mathur, S. (eds.) (1993). *Reading with a difference. Gender, Race, and Cultural Identity*. Detroit: Wayne State University Press.

McNay, L. (1992). *Foucault and Feminism: Power, Gender and the Self*. United Kingdom: Polity Press.

Nahom, D; Wells, E, Gillmore, Mary Rogers, Hoppe, M.; Morrison, D.M.; Archibald, M; Murowchick, E.; Wilsdon, A.; Graham, L. (2001). Differences by Gender and Experience in Adolescent Sexual Behaviour: Implications for Education and HIV Prevention. *Journal of School Health*, Apr2001, Vol.71 (4): 153-158.

Pilkington, C.J. (1994). Is safer sex necessary with a "safe" partner? Condom use and romantic feelings. *Journal of Sex Research*. Vol.31 (3): 203-211.

Pilkington, H. (1996). *Gender, Generation and Identity in Contemporary Russia*. London, New York: Routledge.

Prybylski, D.: Alto, W.A. (1999). Knowledge, Attitudes and Practices concerning HIV/AIDS among Sex workers. *AIDS care*. Vol. 11 (4): 459-473.

Pryor, J. P. & Reeder, G.D. (Ed.) (1993). *The Social Psychology of HIV infection*. New Jersey: Lawrence Erlbaum Associates. Inc., Publishers.

Rivers, K. & Aggleton, P. (1999). *Men and the HIV Epidemic, Gender and the HIV Epidemic*. New York: UNDP HIV and development Programme.

Shively, M. G.and DeCecco, C. J. (1977). Components of sexual identity. *Journal of Homosexuality*, 2, p 41-48.

Shongwe, B. and Varga, C.A. 1997. *A Situational Analysis of Sexuality and Life Skills Education in South African Schools*. Durban: Health systems Trust.

Skidmore, D. and Hayter, E. (2000). Risk and sex: ego – centricity and sexual behaviour in young adults. *Health, Risk & Society*. Vol. 2 (1): 23-32.

Strunin, L., Hingson, R. (1992). Alcohol, drugs and adolescent sexual behaviour. *International Journal of the Addictions* 27(2): 129-146.

Unger, R. K. and Crawford, M., (1992). *Women and Gender: A Feminist Psychology*. London: McGraw-Hill.

Lightning Source UK Ltd.
Milton Keynes UK
UKOW050119200412

191110UK00001B/56/P

9 783838 349343